Dedicated to the memory of all those
who didn't make it.

What are facts?
        — balls in a juggler's hand?
        — stepping stones to a truth?
        — lies in the service of truth?
        — a swarm of will-o'the wisps?
Take your pick!

Walking with Ghosts

Literature and the Sciences of Man

Peter Heller
General Editor

Vol. 17

PETER LANG
New York • Washington, D.C./Baltimore • Boston
Bern • Frankfurt am Main • Berlin • Vienna • Paris

Elizabeth Welt Trahan

Walking with Ghosts

A Jewish Childhood
in Wartime Vienna

To Joan?
with my best wishes —
Liza Trahan
July 1998

PETER LANG
New York • Washington, D.C./Baltimore • Boston
Bern • Frankfurt am Main • Berlin • Vienna • Paris

Library of Congress Cataloging-in-Publication Data

Trahan, Elizabeth Welt.
Walking with ghosts: a Jewish childhood
in wartime Vienna / by Elizabeth Welt Trahan.
    p.   cm. — (Literature and the sciences of man; vol. 17)
Includes bibliographical references.
1. Trahan, Elizabeth Welt. 2. Jews—Austria—Vienna—Biography.
3. Jewish children in the Holocaust—Austria—Vienna—Biography.
4. Vienna (Austria)—Biography. I. Title. II. Series.
DS135.A93T73   943.6'13004924—dc21   96-39252
ISBN 0-8204-3692-5
ISSN 1040-7928

Die Deutsche Bibliothek-CIP-Einheitsaufnahme

Trahan, Elizabeth Welt:
Walking with ghosts: a Jewish childhood in wartime Vienna / Elizabeth Welt
Trahan. –New York; Washington, D.C./Baltimore; Boston; Bern;
Frankfurt am Main; Berlin; Vienna; Paris: Lang.
(Literature and the sciences of man; Vol. 17)
ISBN 0-8204-3692-5
NE: GT

Permission for this edition was arranged by Picus Verlag.
Geisterbeschwörung: Eine jüdische Jugend im Wien der Kriegsjahre
by Elizabeth W. Trahan

The paper in this book meets the guidelines for permanence and durability
of the Committee on Production Guidelines for Book Longevity
of the Council of Library Resources.

∞

Printed in the United States of America.

Acknowledgements

Before thanking those who contributed directly to this memoir by encouraging, reading, critiquing or suggesting improvements, I would like to express my appreciation to those who willingly shared their memories of that time, even when they were painful or very personal.

My special appreciation goes to the following who most generously gave advice and assistance: Eva Schiffer who spent a great many hours with my manuscript, Alex Page whose constructive criticism was much appreciated, Edith Ehrlich, Leonard Ehrlich, Eva Seinfeld and Ernest Seinfeld, all of whom provided valuable information and caught many an inaccuracy, Mary Buskirk and Peter Heller whose enthusiasm for the account made me persevere. Without their encouragement and support the book might not have come about.

All persons appearing in my account are real but some names were changed.

Contents

PART ONE:

Faces and Voices

1.

Why was that day different from all other days, the walk so unlike any other? I wish I knew. Whenever I walk to town—and I do so quite frequently—it is always the same pleasant but dull scenery: first the dusty road flanked by farms, barns and pastures, then a sidewalk with lawns, driveways and those homey New England cottages that are white wood with dark green or black shutters and have gabled attics and open porches. Then, shortly after the railroad crossing, the first stores appear, and soon the traffic light in the center of town comes into view. Nothing special, nothing unpredictable on the entire walk. Except on that day.

To be sure, the air was unusually crisp and sparkling, a spring morning such as one encounters only rarely. But there must have been more to it, for the entire landscape seemed transformed, had sharper outlines, deeper colors, more pungent fragrances. And some of its objects, sounds and scents began to talk to me, opened doors which I had not noticed before and had no reason to suspect. And through those doors I was pulled into another landscape, one I had long thought dismissed, done with, forgotten.

My father would have attributed all of it to the planets and their alignment on that particular day, and though I never took father's astrological theories very seriously, I wasn't quite able to dismiss them either. If only because more often than not he would guess a person's birth sign correctly after just a few minutes' conversation. And to be quite honest—haven't we all at one time or another been confronted by so startling a string of coincidences that even the nonbelievers among us were tempted to look for patterns, for traces of an overall design? Which is perhaps all to the good: however artificial such patterning may be, it can provide a foothold in this unstable, unpredictable world of ours.

Were there any signs, clues, portents? As I rethink the day, rewalk the walk, it almost seems to me that there were. But when I try to recapture them, I find myself overwhelmed by a mass of separate snippets, disjointed pieces from a giant jigsaw puzzle. Some align themselves almost without my participation, but many are missing and others don't seem to belong. As if they were parts of different puzzles, and it would be futile to search for an overall design, for the picture on the cover. What I can do though and suddenly feel a need to do, is assemble the pieces that came to me on my walk, add to them those which I have been able to retrieve or discover later and, whether they belong together or not, let them compose whatever patterns they will.

It was after lunch. I had meant to take the car but when I stepped out into the magnificent sun, the day seemed too special to be wasted. All the more since a glance at my watch assured me that I would have plenty of time to get to the bank, even if I walked to town.

The condominium complex in which I live sits high above the road, halfway up a hill. It consists of three buildings, with twenty-five apartments altogether. The buildings form a reversed L. Building A—in which I live—makes up the short side. The level space inside the L is blacktopped into a parking lot, and at the lot's far end a driveway curves to the right, downhill and out of sight. If you follow it and turn right once more when you reach the road—the yellow sign there admonishes CAUTION HIDDEN DRIVE—you are headed toward town. Perhaps none of this is important for my account, but how can I be sure?

When I face the rectangular parking lot, its short side with building A behind me, a heavily wooded hillside rises steeply on my left. I scaled it once and found among the shrubs and brambles at the top a small clump of radiantly blooming daffodils. When I tried to reach them again the following spring, the vines clung to me so tenaciously that I had to retreat. Along the parking lot's opposite side buildings B and C form an almost uninterrupted line. Behind them, a wide, undulating lawn ends rather abruptly as the slope resumes its downward angle toward the road, though now in a fairly gradual if uneven descent.

A, B, C—what a strange way to identify apartment buildings!

As if they were cell blocks. And they do look a little like cell blocks, these long, low rectangles with their narrow, slitlike windows and their entryways hidden behind dense shrubbery. On the other hand, they are rather attractive. With their mix of red brick, dark wood and sparkling glass, they had immediately appealed to me when, new in town, I was looking for a place to live.

My eye caught sight of a small gray cloud behind the trees, at the far end of the parking lot. Should I take the car after all? But the sky all around was transparently blue, without the slightest trace of a breeze. At most I might go back upstairs and get my umbrella, to be quite safe. As I was turning, I remembered that I also had an umbrella in my car door. Just as well—backtracking brings bad luck, as we used to say in Europe. Oh well, Europe was far behind me. Though I still go back occasionally, that's quite different. Now I am just another American tourist, a disinterested bystander. Once a store keeper even complimented me on my good German, and I didn't know whether to be embarrassed or indignant. So I shrugged it off, and now the incident seems merely amusing, even reassuring.

Another decision had to be made—around or through, along the parking lot or across the lawn and straight down the hillside? The parking lot would be kinder to my toes, since I was wearing fairly high heels, but the shortcut down the hillside was much prettier and of course shorter. The weather had been dry all week, which meant that the slope ought to be manageable if I took it slowly. Let's live dangerously! I said to myself and chuckled at the incongruity between intention and reality. It must have been the balmy air, intoxicating like new wine, that had brought on this unusual exuberance.

The grass was soft and resilient like plush carpeting on a thick pad. As I was crossing it, the slope was still invisible because of the fringe of tall grasses which bordered the entire length of the lawn. I knew that somewhere just beyond that grassy wall there was a footpath or, rather, a narrow swath cut through the weeds by our handiman's lawnmower. As so often, I tried to guess the exact spot where the trail would emerge so that I could angle toward that point. But what if the handiman hasn't been around and it is completely overgrown? Or if I come upon the incline so suddenly that I lose my footing and tumble down the hillside, straight into the path of an oncoming car? I was toying with the thought, knowing well that the danger wasn't real, that the path would be there as always, and I would reach the road safely as always.

When, at the edge of the lawn, the landscape opened out before me, its splendor took my breath away. The immense sunlit expanse of meadows, pastures and fields below resembled a gigantic patchwork quilt, assembled diligently from a multitude of swatches in ever so many shades of green, and stitched neatly to the silvery dome above with the dark thread supplied by the distant hills. In a few spots the quilt was tacked down by tiny grayish-green clumps to keep it from soaring up into the sky. Except for the steady droning of as yet invisible cars, I might have been miles away from civilization.

I recalled reading a column by Herb Caën in the *San Francisco Chronicle*, a few years back when I was still living in California. He reported taking some visitors around the Monterey peninsula. "What do people do here?" he was asked, but his explanation was interrupted: "No, I mean, what do they do to deserve living here?" What had I done to deserve living here, in this serene paradise?

Before starting downhill, I turned once more toward that gray cloud which had hovered in the far corner of the parking lot. It was still there but had neither moved nor expanded. The trail at my feet meandered gracefully down the hillside, looking like a wide ribbon, a green brick road to adventure. Thick clusters of feathery blades were bending over it from both sides, as if to hem it in. To me, though, they yielded without protest, barely tickling my legs. Like flies that keep coming back until you outrun them or they find another target. Flies? An association flitted across my mind but was gone before I could hold on to it. The wide expanse before me was sprinkled with squatting cottages, some red, others white, and with taller gray or red barns. Those dark spots in the distance must be cows or horses. Here civilization was not at all intrusive. No fences separated the fields, no roads cut through them. Even the droning of the cars sounded like a humming of bees.

A wave of sweet scent washed over me. Clover? To be sure, it was everywhere—specks of white, tan and purple which dotted an intensely green carpet, as did a scattering of yellow dandelions and clusters of tall buttercups, shiny golden stars twinkling in the still air. But for the still blooming dandelions it would have been hard to believe that it was only May, despite this suddenly hot sun which seemed full of the brooding stillness of a midsummer day in the country, when even the droning of the bees becomes part of the stillness.

And they were all around us, the bees, buzzing above that hot, sunny farmhouse garden while we were eating our lunch, Walter, his mother and I. We had *Palatschinken*, those delicious thin, rolled pancakes with a well-disguised filling of apricot jam or, now and then, raspberry, and sometimes even fresh blueberries. Doubly disguised because aunt Paula would pour thick, sweet vanilla sauce over the pancakes so that not even a trace of color gave away the filling until the spoon cut right into it.

Once when we had invented a new game and were shooting toothpicks into the sauce pitcher, she became very angry:

"What do you think you are doing? Don't you have any common sense?"

"But we are finished!"

"Aren't you ashamed of yourselves? The kitchen help could have had the rest of the sauce, and now it's ruined."

We hang our heads in shame and promise never to waste food again.

The smell of vanilla draws the bees or yellow-jackets or wasps or whatever they are. We let them sample the sauce on our plates. When they have settled on the table cloth to clean their feelers from the sticky treat, Walter or I, depending on whose territory they have landed, trap them under a water glass. We spend as much time trapping bees as eating. At first I am quite fearful but soon I learn to choose the right moment for turning my glass over a bee.

There were always four water glasses on the table, even if only three of us were having lunch. Once all four glasses had occupants, it was quite a feat to add another bee to one already trapped. I managed it only rarely. It meant lifting the rims of two glasses just enough so that, with some luck, one bee would crawl into the other's glass. Walter was very good at it and I admired him enormously. But his mother would again get angry.

"Stop it this minute! You'll both get stung."

"No, we won't. We know how to do it." We feel as heroic as you only feel at age six.

The buzzing could of course also mean flies. Farmyards come with bees, farm houses with flies. They tickle and tease you mercilessly but they don't bite so you learn to ignore them.

Every room had a fly strip suspended from the ceiling fixture. Even in the outhouse there was one. There it hung from a nail. We kept a close eye on the fly strip in our room, counting the flies on it and trying to identify newcomers. We were too short to collide with the fly strip, but once aunt Paula's curly black hair brushed against it and was briefly caught. Walter and I were giggling for hours.

In the outhouse the flies were a real nuisance despite the fly strip. They would walk up and down your exposed bottom, and since I had to hold on to the seat because it was too high for my feet to touch the ground, I couldn't even shoo them away, only dangle, wiggle and hurry. Normally, the neatly torn-up newspaper impaled on a nail on the door would have invited exploration, but in addition to the fly problem there usually wasn't enough light to read by, even at daytime. But when you had to be conducted out at night, half asleep, with flashlight and a jacket thrown over your shoulders, you didn't notice the flies at all. Perhaps they were asleep then.

Our summer vacations consisted of reluctant hikes up hot, dusty mountains, rewarded by huge glasses of deliciously cold buttermilk in the hut or inn at the top, and by metal decals to be nailed on our walking sticks. Testimony to our endurance, they displayed the name of the mountain we had just scaled. Surreptitiously we counted the decals on other children's walking sticks. Some of the plaques were very beautiful. The name would be draped around a majestic stag or bear or waterfall, or it might sit in the middle of a wreath, with the mountain's height given below, in tiny meters. Seven hundred—our usual climb to the *Ostrauer Hütte*— didn't amount to much, but anything over a thousand, like the *Lysá Hora*, the Bald Mountain—somehow we always used the Czech name, even when speaking German—was a real accomplishment which it was all right to brag about.

I hadn't thought of Ostravice in years. It must have been the combination of hot sun, buzzing bees and sweet clover that conjured up the farmhouse garden where we would spend our summers, in bathing suits, Nivea dabs on noses, cheeks and shoulders, white cotton hats to ward off the sun, *Palatschinken* before us, surrounded by waves of heat and clover and bees.

After lunch we might walk down the dusty road to the Ostravica river which was dammed up by a low rocky dam. You could cross the river on the dam if your balance was good, or you could splash around below it, with the water spraying all over you. You could also step behind the sparkling water curtain and feel very heroic in that mysterious, muffled world where you were invisible and dry though surrounded by water. You could practice breast stroke, safely ensconced in an air ring, or float lazily in the pool below the dam. The water felt wonderfully shivery after the heat of the sun, and after you had been called out to have more Nivea dabbed on red shoulders and peeling noses. Aunt Paula would read a book and look bored until we splashed her. Then she came to life.

She came to life differently on weekends when uncle Robert arrived. I hated those weekends. Not that aunt Paula was less nice to me, but uncle Robert would call me "a little monkey" and say it without a smile, with icicles darting from his eye glasses, so that I knew he meant it. Then I would try hard to prove him wrong by contradicting Walter, even though he was a month older and a lot smarter than I. To show my independence, I refused to play whatever game Walter would suggest, and we had a fight.

On those weekends I felt unloved, left out and sorry for myself, because my mother was dead and my father far away in Vienna instead of being right here to protect me and call Walter a monkey in his turn. But when uncle Robert took the train back to Ostrau on Sunday night, the summer became enormous again, with bees, *Palatschinken* and the river for hot days, and card games, dominoes and *Schwarzer Peter* for rain.

I had my moment of revenge, though. It happened during the school year, on one of our traditional Sunday walks to the *Schießstätte*, the big city park. Fortunately, uncle Robert never came along on these walks while grandma did, and that made me feel doubly safe and sheltered. Walter and I were trailing behind the grown-ups, licking our ice cream cones.

"When we are grown up," Walter said, "I will marry you."

8

"And what if I don't want to?"

"Then I'll beat you black and blue."

I thought of how angry uncle Robert would be at our marrying, and I was very happy.

2.

When the road came into view behind a last gentle rise, I was startled. Blindingly white, it looked like a gash cut into the landscape with a wide, blunt knife and kept from closing by an unending stream of cars. I quickly crossed to the other side, just before one of those roaring steam rollers. It was impossible to defy them. All one could do was cling to the shoulder, make oneself very thin and as invisible and untouchable as possible.

I wanted my thoughts to return to the fragrant summer garden in Ostravice, but they wouldn't. There were too many of those foul-smelling vehicles, and the fragrance of the grass was gone. Dust lay on everything, the dust of broken sidewalks. A few blades of grass were struggling to soften the rim of a small crater in the middle of the street. But at least the cars were now gone and the scent had returned. Except that it wasn't the scent of clover. Much sweeter, cloyingly sweet. I breathed it in and didn't recognize it but something in me was afraid, even though I was nineteen years old.

"What is that strange smell?" I asked Grete.

"Probably a dead body," she mumbled almost apologetically.

"Aren't they going to get it out and bury it?"

"It's too dangerous to dig. The rest of the building might collapse. And they have to take care of the injured."

"But they can't just leave it here! The stench is awful."

Grete put her arm around me. "Never mind. Someone will get to it. And the war can't last much longer."

The year was 1944.

On March 12, 1945, over two hundred and seventy people died in the Jockey Club cellar during a devastating air raid. They too couldn't be reached, because of the fire. When I was in Vienna last summer, I went to look for the building. It had been razed and

replaced by a small public park, right across from the popular
Hotel Sacher and next to Alfred Hrdlicka's controversial
"Monument against War and Fascism," with its crouching Jew
who is forever cleaning the pavement with a toothbrush. He has
been turned into bronze, but what about those still down there
and in so many other spots—have they become part of the ground
Vienna stands on, part of its new buildings and gardens, does
their emanation continue to permeate Vienna's soil and water,
even though we can no longer detect it?

3.

I continue along the left shoulder, the only pedestrian far and
wide. With the sun appearing and disappearing behind the trees,
I can't help squinting. Therefore I can't tell if the sky has taken
on a grayish tinge or if it just seems that way. The cars have
returned. With renewed fury they throw gusts of hot, evil-
smelling fumes into my face, and every time a truck thunders by,
the displaced air attacks me physically. I no longer mind. The
smell is reassuring, as is the sight of the fields which sprawl
toward the wooded hills with the same joyous self-abandon as
before.

On my side of the road a white farmhouse now comes into view.
It stands so close to the shoulder that I can see its chalk-white
lace curtains, stiff with starch. Truly a place of law and order,
reassuringly solid and stable. The adjacent red cow barn is long
and low. It looks just as neat, with its eleven square, evenly
spaced little windows. They give it the appearance of a human
habitat. Through their openings, I can see eleven similar windows
on the other side, facing pastures and fields. Each window has
nine small glass squares, held in place by thin black bars. Do the
cows have a choice of view or is the decision made for them, and
they are directed to the right or left in accordance with someone
else's plan or whim? Anyway, right now the barn is empty. The
cows are outside. Some graze with preoccupied faces, others
lounge in the grass with cruising jaws and soulful eyes—epitome
of cow happiness.

Two black-and-white cows—Holsteins, I establish, proud of my relatively recent expertise—are standing by the open-slatted white fence which separates their domain from mine, their faces turned toward me. We are old friends and I often stop to talk to them, though I can't be sure it is always the same twosome. At any rate, they seem to be listening. The first time I dared pet one, she held quite still as if to tell me, the city child, that I was accepted.

Yes, I was a city child though Mährisch Ostrau or Moravská Ostrava, as it was called in Czech, was not a big city. The coal mines and steel mills made it seem much larger than it was. My grandparents' second floor apartment had a balcony facing the courtyard. The balcony was too small for anything except airing the bedding and beating the dust out of the rugs. That was allowed only on certain days, but even so people would forget to take their wash off the clothes lines in the courtyard, and altercations between wash and carpet owners or their maids were common. They were fun to listen to from the seclusion of the balcony. Except for the clothes lines the courtyard was bare, an irregularly shaped concrete square planted with a row of trash cans.

You could ride your tricycle but that was about it, and we had outgrown tricycles. Instead, I would walk over to Walter's house which was within a few blocks, ring the downstairs doorbell, then cross the street so that he could see me from their fourth floor apartment window. If he was allowed to join me, we would walk to the school yard together. No trees or grass there either, just a wide asphalted space, but you could jump rope, play hopscotch and ball, or toss a rubber ring.

Sometimes we were kidded for being inseparable but Walter didn't seem to mind, and I felt flattered because he was tall and handsome while I was short, had freckles and wore glasses. I don't remember when exactly we began to go our separate ways, but by the time Walter was trying to avoid me and blushed whenever I spoke to him, I had Hanna and several other girl friends and did not care.

4.

A wooden mail box catches my eye. It is mounted on a post right in front of a cottage. Both are red, but while the house looks freshly painted, much of the color on the mailbox has flaked off. Did they overlook the mailbox when they were repainting the cottage, or don't they care? For me, mail always has something festive, even if it consists of nothing but ads. But that's perhaps because of the contrast between then and now.

By late 1942, when grandma and the rest of the family were deported from Ostrau, I had been in Vienna for almost three years. Overseas countries were out of reach because of the war but, since the Germans were occupying much of Europe, mail from these countries did come through, even if it was slow and often mutilated by the censor. I kept hoping for a note from grandma to tell me that they had arrived safely in the resettlement camp, that they had enough food and were able to keep warm. But that note never came. All the mailman brought were proclamations, warnings and summonses, so that we would heave sighs of relief whenever he bypassed our door or left only an innocuous flyer.

I remember the happy moment, though, when father, grandmother Vera and I sat around the table trying to interpret aunt Olga's postcard. But that was much earlier, shortly after the beginning of the war and during my first months in Vienna.

"Greetings from beautiful Italy! We are very comfortable here."[1] It was a great relief to hear from her, even though we had been quite sure that Olga would manage things. She always did.

Uncle Max had run the wine cellar at the Hübner Park Hotel in Schönbrunn. I don't think he was ever politically active. Even so, he was arrested shortly after the Germans took over Austria, possibly because he was born in Poland. Or perhaps he was still a Polish citizen. He was among the lucky few to be released within a few weeks, and he and Olga left for Italy. In the nick of time, too: a few days later the Gestapo was back at the door, asking for him. Some of those arrested never returned. Instead, their families were notified to pick up their ashes at the *Israelitische Kultusgemeinde*, Vienna's Jewish Community. (3/10)[2]

Normally, you had to show emigration papers to get someone

---

1. All translations are mine unless indicated otherwise.
2. The first number refers to an entry on the *Works Cited* page, the second to the entry's pertinent page(s).

released, and the visa fees were high. But Olga apparently got Max out without a visa and without a bribe, just by charming the Gestapoman with her beautiful green eyes. At least that was her mother's version. Before they let him go, Max had to declare that he was voluntarily turning over his possessions to the German government, and that he would leave the country within two weeks. This was easier said than done. Even if you succeeded in securing the necessary visas and transit visas, the Germans imposed a real squirrel cage of requirements. You needed a *Sittenzeugnis* or certificate of conduct from the police, permission to leave from the Gestapo, and assorted documents from the tax authorities to confirm payment of the *Reichsfluchtsteuer*, a high departure tax, and various other fees. It happened frequently that by the time you obtained one document, another had expired. Olga must have somehow secured the necessary exit documents and, since Italy was still neutral, its border was open and you did not require a visa. They would be safe there and able to move on, perhaps to Palestine or America.

I didn't remember uncle Max well at all. There had been too many new faces during the summer I had spent in Vienna in 1937: grandmother Vera, aunts Olga and Jenny, and uncle Paul. And of course my father. Since he came to Ostrau at best once a year, he too was really a stranger.

"I take long walks," the postcard said. Did that mean that aunt Olga was exploring different ways of getting out of Italy? During those early days of the war you could buy visas for Shanghai, Cuba and some South American countries if you were unable to secure the needed "affidavit of support" from someone in the United States.

"Aunt Vera has been very helpful." There was no aunt Vera, but Olga's mother's name was Vera and she had handed over to Olga what little jewelry she owned. It must have been enough to buy one or two Shanghai visas, for when Anny, whom Max married long after the war, turned his papers over to me after his death, I found among them Olga's passport with an unused Shanghai visa.

"Our friends are joining me in sending best wishes." Did that mean that she had made useful contacts? Was she perhaps in touch with the underground? Or was she suggesting that the war would soon be over? "From her mouth in God's ear," grandmother Vera said.

We cannot be sure that we have deciphered Olga's code correctly, but we are relieved that she and Max are safe, and confident that Olga will find a way out of Italy. She will get to Palestine or Shanghai or America and then send us the necessary papers, so that we too can leave Vienna. With Jenny in England and Paul in Morocco, there's only the three of us left here, and grandmother Vera is in pretty good shape for sixty-two and can handle a bit of hardship if necessary.

We don't dare keep the postcard, but before it is burned I am allowed to cut off the stamp to add to my collection.

5.

My stamp collection: I smuggled it across the Moravian-Austrian border, with my heart in my mouth, on December 31, 1939, on the train to Vienna. The stamps were something very special because they had belonged to my mother. Shortly before that trip—I had just turned fifteen—grandma gave me the collection to take along, together with a set of four fish knives and forks, and a matching serving knife. I think they were the only silver items left from grandpa's jewelry store. Heavy and ornate, they seemed the ultimate in luxury to me at the time. I still own them.

For a long evening we sat under the darkened lamp. I removed the stamps from their books and put them into thin envelopes, and grandma arranged the envelopes between shell and lining of her black Persian lamb muff before sewing the lining back in. They made the muff look plump and overstuffed, but only a very thorough examination would have revealed the envelopes. Grandma promised to mail the empty stamp books to me within a few weeks. Stamps were considered currency and you were not allowed to take them across the border, but empty stamp books posed no problem.

I left Ostrau accompanied by aunt Irma who had come from Vienna for her father's funeral. I liked her very much even though she was uncle Robert's sister. Uncle Robert was gone by then, shipped off to Poland in a transport of a thousand 'able-bodied' men. Luckily, Walter had been rejected as too young and grandpa as too old. The men were going to build a resettlement camp somewhere in Poland, with the families to follow later. After several anxious weeks, aunt Paula received a telegram saying that Robert was with aunt Minna—grandma's sister—in Drohobycz. We were immensely relieved. He must have escaped from the camp and made his way across the border to the safety of the Russian-occupied part of Poland. But we never heard from either him or aunt Minna again.

During the summer that followed my walk, that missing puzzle piece surfaced, quite accidentally. I was in Vienna, browsing through the Jewish Community's library, when I noticed a reference to Mährisch Ostrau in a thin paperback, entitled *Nisko*. There I read of a proposal, made in the fall of 1939, "to solve the Jewish question" by herding all Jews into a *Judenreservat*, a Jewish reservation. Eichmann, in charge of resettlements, selected Nisko in the Lublin district of the *Generalgouvernement*, as German-occupied Poland was called, as the site for such a reservation (12/50). A report of November 20 by the governor of the Lublin district speaks of the area's "marshy environment...[as] especially suited for bringing about a strong decimation of the Jews." (3/83)

Four transports were dispatched in October 1939, two from Ostrau, with 1000 and 291 men respectively, and two from Vienna, with 1000 men each. Vienna's Jewish Community provided its group with tools and provisions for four weeks. Shortly after the men arrived in Nisko, all except 500 were stripped of their belongings, told to head toward the Russian border and be out of sight within two hours if they didn't want to be shot (12/51). That's when uncle Robert must have made it to Drohobycz, where he probably thought himself safe. But when the Germans launched their surprise attack on the Soviet Union in June 1941, they quickly overran the Russian-occupied Polish territories and caught up with those Jews who had not yet been deported by the Russians to Siberian work camps. In July 1941 the Germans carried out mass shootings in the Drohobycz ghetto (17/81).

The Nisko camp was dissolved—for strategic reasons—long

before then, on April 13, 1940, and the inmates were transported back, 198 to Vienna (12/51), the rest to Ostrau (9/204). Another 90 returned to Ostrava—by then only the Czech name was used—after the end of the war (9/203). Uncle Robert was not among them.

In Ostrau, the first months of the war were chaotic and nightmarish. Shops had to display large signs indicating their Jewish ownership, and non-Jews—now called "Aryans"—were admonished to boycott them. Most non-Jewish shops bore signs saying *Juden unerwünscht*—Jews not welcome—which was a euphemism for "keep out!" Listening to foreign radio stations was declared treason punishable by death. All Jews had to turn their radios in at the Gestapo. Everyone we knew did so. "They are protecting us from treason," was the standing joke. Again and again people—at first only men—were summoned to police headquarters, lined up in the courtyard for hours, sometimes all day. The lucky ones were eventually sent home.

Long before then grandma had turned the jewelry store into a delicatessen to make ends meet, with grandpa's watch repair table relegated to one corner. Even so, money was always scarce, and the monthly sum which father was supposed to send for my upkeep was usually late, if it arrived at all. Many friends and customers took off for England between March 15, 1939, when the Germans occupied Czechoslovakia, and the beginning of the war on September 1. Others couldn't bring themselves to abandon their houses, shops and factories, especially if they had no relatives or bank accounts abroad. However, once the war started and the subpoenas began to arrive, a frantic search for escape routes got under way. If you had money and connections, you could secure visas and transit visas for Santo Domingo, Chile or Shanghai via Russia and Siberia, or for Madagascar and Palestine either through Italy or via Hungary and Romania, or down the Danube and through Turkey. But Palestine was almost inaccessible: the British had reduced Jewish immigration to a mere trickle. One or the other ship owner offered to smuggle you in illegally, for a substantial bribe and without any guarantees. Procurers of phony visas were making fortunes.

After aunt Erna lost her job, she handed her savings over to a

Mr. Laufer who was the proud owner of an affidavit from the United States. In exchange, he was to marry her so that they could emigrate together and divorce later. He married her all right but then disappeared and wasn't heard from again. My grandparents had no money, and aunt Paula and her family had very little, so that they could do nothing but stay put and lie low. Even then there were still many who had the means yet couldn't wrench themselves away from their possessions, especially since almost everybody believed that the war couldn't last long and that, even if the men were to spend some time in German labor camps, the hardship would be temporary. Quite obviously, no one had read *Mein Kampf*.

On the other hand, almost from the moment the Germans marched in, a great effort was made to get the children out to safety. Children's transports left for Palestine, Sweden, Holland and England. My best friend Hanna and her brother left for England in May 1939. Hans settled there permanently, Hanna eventually made her way to America. I missed her terribly and was keenly aware of being left behind.

Grandma was very anxious that "the child," namely I, be sent to a safe place. I was especially vulnerable because I had no passport. For a while she considered shipping me off to her relatives in Krakau. Luckily, nothing came of it, because the war broke out and the Germans occupied that part of Poland. Then she wrote letter after letter to my father, urging him to send the necessary papers so that I could join him in Vienna. That, however, was easier said than done. Since my father was a Romanian citizen, I, as a minor, was likewise considered Romanian, despite my Berlin birth certificate. Normally, I would have been entered on his passport (which wouldn't have done me much good as long as he was in Vienna and I in Ostrau) but just then my father didn't have a valid passport either.

Our citizenship was a complicated affair. Father was born in 1895 in Czernowitz, in the Bukovina. For centuries the Bukovina had been coveted and fought over by everyone, Russians, Turks, Ruthenians—today's Ukrainians—and Romanians, until it became a Habsburg duchy in 1775 and eventually part of the Austro-Hungarian Empire. During the first world war

Czernowitz, its capital and a university town as of 1875, became frontline territory, and in 1916 the entire family fled to Vienna. Father, who was in the Austrian army at the time and eventually taken prisoner by the Russians, rejoined the family in Vienna after the war.

In 1920 the Bukovina was incorporated into Greater Romania. Though the country wouldn't grant citizens' rights to Jews until 1923, father either neglected or decided not to opt for Austrian citizenship. That decision or omission saved our lives.

Czernowitz was a very German-Jewish town when father grew up there, and he spoke no Romanian at all. However, during the war he began to teach himself the language, and by the time we were in hiding at the Romanian Consulate General in Vienna in the summer of 1943, he spoke Romanian quite well. I didn't because, at father's request, I was concentrating on learning Hungarian, in order to do the interpreting, should it become advisable for us to cross illegally into Hungary on our way to Romania.

In 1923, father married my mother. I don't know how or where they met, but after an Ostrau wedding they settled in Berlin. After her death in 1929 her parents took me with them to Ostrau, and that was where I grew up. In 1936 father moved back to Vienna. I assume he had a passport then, but by 1939 at any rate the question of our citizenship was still or again unresolved. A lawyer in Bucharest was supposed to straighten things out. Instead, the court hearing kept being postponed and he kept writing for money. He did, however, send periodic attestations to the fact that a hearing was pending, and that seemed to satisfy the Gestapo. Even in 1942, the nightmare year when stateless, German, Czech and Austrian Jews were deported by the tens of thousands, we were left unmolested.

6.

My father? A complex and still painful chapter. I have often wondered if heredity or upbringing—the children were raised by a succession of wet nurses, nannies and governesses—made of him the man he was, strong-willed and resourceful but also self-focussed and hard. He saved my life more than once, and yet for a long time I hated him with a passion. I have always considered my mother's family very normal, both in their shortcomings and good qualities. Simple, unassuming people, hard-working and family-oriented, loving and lovable. My father's family, by contrast, seemed anything but ordinary. They were almost without exception very handsome people and yet it was as if a curse lay on that entire family, turning them into villains or victims. At any rate, aunt Jenny always found it painful to talk about her parents, her childhood and some of her siblings, especially my father.

My paternal grandfather had been editor in chief of the *Czernowitzer Morgenzeitung*, the morning paper. Early in World War One he was taken to Russia as a hostage, together with other town notables. When he returned, his health was undermined, and he died in Vienna soon after the family arrived there.

There were seven children, of two mothers and one father. My father was the oldest, Bruno, the second-oldest, was killed in World War One. During Isidor's birth their mother Lisa died, at twenty-four. On her deathbed Lisa made her nineteen year old sister Vera promise that she would be a mother to her children. Vera kept her promise. She parted from the young officer she was deeply in love with and married my grandfather who was much older than she and, according to Jenny, a real autocrat. She never learned to love him, although he gave her four children, Paul, Otto, Olga and Jenny.

I adored aunt Jenny. Whenever she visited me in Ostrau, she devoted herself almost entirely to me. She was very pretty, had a lovely voice and infinite patience, when I would slide off key in the duets she kept trying to sing with me. I was very disappointed not to find her in Vienna when I arrived there shortly after the beginning of the war. She had emigrated to England in 1938 as a domestic—the only category under which England admitted Jewish refugees. Later she worked as a bookkeeper.

According to her friends, Jenny was the life of every party with her guitar and the many songs she knew. Even languages she did not speak she could mimic to perfection. The officer to whom she was engaged was killed in the war, and she never married. She loved children and always had a bag of candy on her, so that the neighborhood children tailed her like a pied piper. "I don't love you," she would say to me whenever I visited, "but I adore you!" then she hugged me till I gasped. Or: "You are my most beloved niece, but of course—" and here she would burst out laughing, "that's easy because I have only one niece!" Despite much illness, a series of operations and very little money, she lived—many years with cancer—to be 81, outliving all her siblings.

After the war, I visited her as often as I could, and we remained close to the end of her life. She would compose simple little birthday and anniversary ditties for her friends—"I don't have any money to buy presents with but I can always make a poem!"—and even wrote one on the Queen's sixtieth birthday. I sent it off without Jenny's knowledge, with a short explanatory note. Though Jenny claimed to be upset when I confessed, she had me make copies of the thank-you note sent to her by Her Majesty's Lady-in-Waiting—on Buckingham Palace stationery—and distributed them among all her friends and acquaintances. She always had a vast supply of jokes on hand, even toward the end when she was bedbound. "Look, if I talk about my ailments, nobody will want to visit me," she would say. At one point the university sent her a long questionnaire to help them figure out what was keeping her alive. "Not taking all those pills!" she wrote on it.

Shortly after Jenny's departure for England, Olga made her way to Italy. I had met her briefly during my Viennese summer. I remember her as very striking, with a round face, very white skin, black hair, a dazzling smile and large, almond-shaped green eyes. One of the photos I have of her shows her in gypsy garb, hand on hip—a truly seductive Carmen. She had a wicked temper, but Jenny adored her and was heartbroken when Olga didn't resurface after the war.

That same summer I also met uncle Paul. He was taller than the others, very handsome and conscious of his good looks. His girl friend was not much older than I, and whenever they took me along to one of the outdoor swimming pools in the Vienna woods, I felt especially short and chubby next to her Bikini-clad willowy figure.

When Hitler occupied Austria, Paul escaped to his brother Otto who was living in Paris. From there Paul moved on to Morocco where he spent the war years, first herding sheep then dealing in oriental carpets. Many years later, I selected one from his large stock in Frankfurt. He eventually married a much younger woman, a blond Marilyn Monroe-type who spent all his hard-earned money on clothes and knickknacks and who, according to aunt Jenny, had an affair with Paul's Moroccan associate. The family was appalled, but Paul was proud of his young wife to his dying day. He died at seventy, as did my father.

Otto was a journalist. I never met him, but on one snapshot I have of him, he is surrounded by a tipsy, Bohemian looking crowd, wine glass in hand, New Year's hat at a tilt. He looks very hand-some and rather easy-going. Except for Isidor who had prominent teeth and a receding chin, they were all strikingly good-looking. So was grandmother Vera, even during that last year of her life when I knew her.

The Czernowitz contingent also included a large number of cousins, nephews and nieces. Some I still met in Vienna during my first year there, in brief encounters without beginning or end. May this recollection be their epitaph.

Aunt Else was blond, gentle and very pretty, in spite of a gap between her two front teeth and a hip-related limp. I only remember one or two visits at their sprawling, dark apartment, and that I liked her. Her husband was unusually tall and deaf-mute, and her sister Ida loud, short and fat. Cousin Joseph or Jossl came to tea to us for a while, devouring everything in sight almost before you set the plate down. He looked shabby, had red cheeks, a small moustache, and short gray hair. He never stayed long.

Rosa Sterngold was grandmother Vera's first cousin. We visited her and her daughter Rachelle regularly, until aunt Rosa died and Rachelle was deported. I was intensely uncomfortable during these visits. Rachelle had only two topics of conversation—how much she adored her 87 year old mother, a tiny, dried-out and querulous woman, and how she had sacrificed herself for her mother, breaking off her engagement when her fiancé refused to take the mother in. Rachelle, in her fifties, was tall, black-haired, very beautiful and quite overpowering. Her sister Gusta had been an opera singer in Czernowitz before the first world war. I never met her and don't know when and where she died, but I have her photograph. It is one of those opulently posed studio pictures, in shades of brown. She sits very straight and busomy, holding an open book but looking into the distance. She is wearing a dark, pearl-embroidered evening gown with a train, large earrings, a long necklace and two bracelets, and looks even more regal than Rachelle. Aunt Rosa died on Dec. 12, 1940, and Rachelle was deported on February 28, 1941.

To the best of my knowledge, of the whole large clan of aunts, uncles, cousins and second cousins only my father, Paul and Jenny survived the war. And I. And also three of uncle Isi's children, whom I eventually met in the States, long after the war.

Like father, Uncle Isidor had settled in Berlin after the first world war, though he remained there even after Hitler came to power. Probably he felt safe because his wife was "Aryan." One day in 1940 he unexpectedly dropped in on us in Vienna. That was the only time I met him. I recall his being unusually short and talking very rapidly. He seemed friendly and cheerful but very absent-minded. According to aunt Jenny, he was a kind and modest man, unlike his brothers. I don't know why he came to Vienna, but I recall his surprise at father's eagerness to emigrate. Things were much calmer in Berlin, he told us. After a few hours he left again.

Eventually, I learned from his sons that he was arrested early in the war and died in a concentration camp. He left four children, three boys and a girl. The little girl was run over by a drunken driver. The mother was ailing and died toward the end of the war, and a maternal aunt took the boys in. In 1949 they were brought to the United States by the Catholic Refugee Committee. All's well that ends well? Only in Shakespeare.

I met them shortly after their arrival in New York. Aunt Jenny had given them my address. The youngest was eight, the others fifteen and seventeen. While the Catholic Committee was trying to find homes for them, the middle boy was taken in by foster parents, a Jewish family whom he had met on the ocean liner. They were childless and lived on Central Park South. He had always been drawn to Judaism, he confessed to them. They paid for his education, but shortly after he graduated, his foster father remarried and he was on his own. However, he seems to have done well for himself. Now and then he phones to tell me about his various commercial ventures and travels. The first phone call gave me a shock: He sounded very much like my father.

The moment the adoption went through, the Committee whisked the other two boys out of New York, into a Catholic orphanage somewhere in Pennsylvania. I began to receive distraught letters from the oldest. He had promised his aunt to take good care of his little brother, and now he was not able to do anything for him, even though the boy stammered and obviously needed special attention. The orphanage was terrible, he wrote, like a prison. Mail had to be sneaked out to the nearest village to reach its destination uncensored.

I was in college then, on a scholarship, and didn't own a car. But on one of the monthly Visiting Sundays, Mauri Weiner, a former teacher of mine who had become a close friend, drove me to the orphanage. It was deep in the woods, at a spot where, as a German saying goes, the foxes bid one another a good night. The children, dressed in their Sunday best, were very polite but so quiet and unresponsive that it was clear they were afraid to talk to us. Even my little cousin. Nor were we able to speak to the older brother without a nun in earshot.

After the visit I went to the Committee's headquarters in New York to indicate my concern. I mentioned the stammer. The Monsignor was very polite and affable. He assured me that all children were well cared for, that the boy would soon be placed in a good home, and that even the older brother who, to be sure, was going through a difficult phase, was adjusting well. He was learning electronics and would soon be independent.

His words did not reassure me. I felt that I had to do something to help, but all I could think of was to write to Eleanor Roosevelt and ask for her assistance. In a democratic country like America this was after all possible, and she would surely be sympathetic. To my great disappointment I never received an answer. Only much later did I realize that I had had quite a nerve to ask her to take on the Catholic Church because of one distressed and distraught little refugee.

After a few weeks at the orphanage, the older brother bolted and made his way back to New York City. He went straight to the Committee with his complaint, on the assumption that they were unaware of what was going on in that foxhole. He also proposed that they release his brother to his care, once he had a job and a room. When they threw him out, he bought an old wreck of a car, borrowed two blankets from me, planted himself across from the entrance to the Committee's office and, despite my protests and entreaties, went on a hunger strike. I was unable to convince him that in this country people didn't go on hunger strikes. (And they didn't, in those days.) On the third day the Committee had him hauled off to Bellevue hospital.

I'll never forget my visit there. If he was sane—and I was no longer sure—how long would he remain so in those surroundings? It took Mauri months to get him out, despite his vouching for him.

My cousin lived with Mauri and his family for several weeks but was so difficult and demanding that they lost patience and turned him out. Then he apparently did find a job. At some point he moved to another state. He married several times and has at least two children. But he didn't stay in touch with me, resenting, I learned later, that I had given the "family jewels" which the boys had entrusted to my care upon their arrival—a wedding band, an engagement ring and a gold wrist watch, if I remember correctly—to the middle brother when he requested them.

He visited aunt Jenny twice, both times depleting her food supplies and handing her his shirts to wash and iron. Once he invited her to the theater. When she met him there, he had a girl with him and asked Jenny if she would mind going some other time. She was very hurt, but even so she kept in touch with his children, sending them little presents whenever she could. After her death I sent a check to them in her name, but they never acknowledged it.

Eventually the Committee located a home for the youngest boy. They refused to give me the address—it was their policy not to disclose the whereabouts of adoptees. All I knew was that the family lived somewhere in California. Years later he located me. I, too, was living in California then, in driving distance, in fact, and we met.

A few years later I spent a week with him and his wife in Europe. She was in the foreign service, with him apparently just tagging along. I noticed with amazement how well he got on with everybody. He hugged and was hugged by all the guards at the embassy, much of the staff, and every neighbor in a circumference of several streets from their apartment, including the next door bartender, the editor of the local paper, even the old man on the park bench.

He took me to a bakery for croissants and coffee. Handshakes and hugs all around. The man at the next table could have been his long lost brother.

"Hey, *monsieur*, meet my cousin from America, A-me-ri-ca! Talk to him, Liesl, you speak French, go ahead and talk to him, tell him about yourself and about America!"

I shudder but try to talk about myself and about America, and I learn in turn that my cousin is all right, a regular guy. As we leave, after more hugs and handshakes, the two grin and wave to each other.

For a time he worked as a cook on an ocean liner—there isn't much he hasn't tried and walked out on in the course of the years—and so in honor of my visit he prepared an elaborate dinner. He invited embassy personnel and much of the village to their garage apartment. Stuffed artichokes and steak with all the trimmings were served on paper plates, on long board tables, with crates to sit on, in a tiny backyard. To his wife's dismay the feast lasted long into the night and got so noisy that she was afraid the police would come and she would have trouble at the embassy. My cousin, whose voice carries, turned a deaf ear to her entreaties to pipe down even when a neighbor, after angry shouts, slammed his window shut. "If he can't sleep, let him join us, stop worrying!" And in the direction of the shut window, at top volume: "C'm'on, *monsieur, venez, venez!*"

At one point the embassy officially commended him and his wife as the couple who had done most to establish friendly relations with the local population.

During that week he dragged me all over town, from morning till night, despite my protests.

"My feet are killing me, let's get back," I pleaded.

"In a minute, I still want to show you something—just around the corner. Have you ever seen a butcher shop with a marble floor? What d'you say? Isn't it something?"

And then there is something else around another corner, and something else again, and I can't find my way to the bus stop without him.

He is moody and difficult but a good, kind person. I love him dearly, despite the fact that with his black hair, high receding forehead, even features, bushy eyebrows and dark eyes, he bears a striking physical resemblance to my father.

7.

My border permit arrived from Vienna a few days after aunt Irma had come to Ostrau. Grandma was relieved that I wouldn't have to travel alone. Irma's two girls were already in Holland and she had been packing to join them when her father died. Gray-haired, chubby and nearsighted, she was a cheerful and easygoing woman. Her infectious laughter lined her unusually thick glasses with hundreds of wrinkles. A trip begun in her company boded well.

I don't know what became of Irma Pollak, whether she managed to join her children in Holland but was then deported with them, or whether she was still caught in Vienna. After the morning of our arrival I didn't see her again.

So many people appeared briefly in my life during those years and disappeared again, without a trace, without a certainty of any kind, leaving behind nothing but snatches of memories. It was a phantasmagorical world, filled with evanescent shapes that came from nowhere and vanished into nowhere—mere names, faces, question marks. And we quickly learned not to expect answers.

In midwinter a muff would not look suspicious. Even so, I kept my hands in it long before we approached the border, and even afterward I held on tight, worried about losing it. I barely talked on that whole long journey, afraid that my nervousness would give me away, and agonizing over the unasked question of what I ought to do, should the border guard want to examine the muff. But no one paid any attention to me at the border, even though a customs official emptied one passenger's entire suitcase on the floor before turning his back on us.

It took me a while to relax, but eventually I became excited at the thought of the new life into which I was heading on that last day of 1939. To be sure, I barely knew my father, nor did I remember much about grandmother Vera. And there would be no Anna. Even so, I thought, it was bound to be better than what I was leaving behind.

8.

Anna was our maid. Her great gift to me were the wonderful
Czech Christmas carols she taught me. I still sing or hum them
when I want to feel christmassy. On the Holy or Bounteous
Evening, as Christmas Eve is called in German and Czech respectively, I was allowed to eat with her in the kitchen. It was invariably jellied carp, one of grandma's specialties. Each piece of fish
sat in a semicircle of cooked carrot wheels. With it came a slice of
Striezel, that slightly sweet and delicious holiday bread. It was a
perfect combination, and to this day carp has remained one of my
favorite dishes. I indulge in it whenever I am in central Europe.
When I once saw carp at an American fish market, I carried a
piece home in great excitement. It didn't work. Despite my metic-
ulous adherence to the directives of my Austro-Hungarian cook-
book, the fish had a muddy taste. Probably because in Europe it is
raised, but in this country it must scavenge. You can't go home
again, I should have known that.

A vase of tartly fragrant fir branches would stand on the
kitchen table which was covered with a white table cloth in honor
of the holidays. The cut glass bowl under the branches was filled
with nuts, dates and figs for Anna. A white envelope, wedged
between the branches, contained her Christmas money. After supper we sang carols together. On that evening I was allowed to stay
up late, and eventually grandma would bundle me up so that
Anna and I could leave for church. There too carols were sung. My
voice was nothing to brag about, but Anna's pure soprano soared
above all others, and I was very proud of being with her.

Anna must have been in her fifties then. She was of medium
height, very heavy and therefore slow-moving, but with a round
face that was unwrinkled and pretty. In her white kerchief and
apron she always looked neat and clean. Her room was a *Kabinett*,
one of those typical European maids' rooms, narrow and with only
one window. Since the window faced the courtyard, the room was
quite dark. There was barely enough space for the wash stand,
wardrobe and chair. Above Anna's bed hung a crucifix. The

kitchen, on the other hand, was bright and spacious. When I was little, Foxl's bed was under the kitchen table. After Foxl died, his bed stayed there for a long time and became my cave.

Anna was not a storyteller, but we always sang together. In addition to carols, she taught me many Czech folk songs. Some have a good strong marching rhythm and I often sing them *sotto voce* during that last mile of a long hike.

Anna was part of the family as long as I can remember. She saw my mother and aunts Paula and Erna grow up, and she raised me, of sorts. She kept the apartment clean, did the laundry and lit the fire in the bathroom stove for our weekly baths. On Sunday she went to church, but by the time we returned from our walk in the park, she was usually back in her room.

Only now do I wonder about Anna's real life, her real self. She never seemed to go out, take a vacation or have visitors. Yet she must have had parents, a childhood, dreams, perhaps a love affair, moments of regret and anguish like everyone else. Perhaps she prayed during those moments. How I wish I had asked her to tell me about herself, and also about my mother of whom I know next to nothing. Not even on that train to Vienna on December 31, 1939 did it occur to me that I might be leaving behind my last chance to ask questions.

Grandma was shorter and likewise heavy, but not nearly as obese as Anna. Her round, wrinkled face always had a smile for me. Varicose veins made it difficult for her to spend so much of the day on her feet. In the evening she would bathe them for half an hour in a wide aluminum bucket, and that was my chance to sit by her side. I talked to her about how much I missed school and Hanna, though I never mentioned my crush on Professor Kejzlar, or my first date. Something made me hold back, perhaps the feeling that these things were too silly to bother her with or too personal, or that she was too old to understand. I remember once asking her in bed in the dark whether one could get a child from a kiss. She just laughed and asked me where I had heard such nonsense, but then she added that even so I'd better not go around kissing people. That was my sex education.

Grandma never slapped me, never scolded. Even when she laughed at me, I didn't mind. "Look at that child—have you ever seen anyone eat an egg with such relish? She is savoring every spoonful."

Eggs were my great passion. I could have spent my entire life happily eating nothing but soft-boiled eggs and bread with butter and chives.

"You are spoiling her rotten," aunt Erna would reply. I suppose she was right.

I adored grandma but had little affection for grandpa. He was tall, bald, wore a pince-nez and looked very dignified, but I don't remember ever seeing him laugh. He talked little when he came home at night, just ate, read the paper, and went to bed. He never paid much attention to me, and I don't remember his ever being nice to grandma either. I may have subconsciously blamed him for grandma's hard life, but now I think that he was merely quiet, not mean. A timid man, perhaps humiliated by his lack of success. Grandma never showed anything but concern and affection for him.

What were they like when they were young? I can't imagine them in love, full of hope and anticipation. Did he ever take her dancing, give her presents? Did he hold her tight and comfort her when their oldest daughter—my mother—died at age thirty-three of pemphicus, a painful skin disease?

Grandpa has remained a blank. I only see him before me on that last day, sitting in his wheelchair, unable to say anything. But when I kissed him goodbye, he seemed to comprehend that I was leaving, for I saw tears roll down his cheeks. I felt very sorry for him but also relieved that I was able to get away.

It all began shortly after the outbreak of the war, when grandpa had to wait in the school yard most of the day to register with the Gestapo. He was seventy then. For hours the men were made to stand with their arms raised above their heads, were spat on, yelled at and I don't know what else. When he came home, he was not only trembling from the tension and humiliation, but he dragged one leg. That gradually worsened, until his entire left side was paralyzed and he was confined to a wheelchair.

Grandpa's bed was in the corner. Grandma and I slept in the big double bed as long as I can remember, and that was wonderful. It meant that I could snuggle up to her after a nightmare and feel safe. In the middle of the room stood the dining table at which I read, did cutouts or played solitaire, except when it had to be cleared and set for the midday or evening meal. Every morning at seven grandpa and the hired girl would deliver the milk while grandma opened the store. It stayed open till eight at night, but even so there was never enough money. That's why we also had four or five paying dinner guests during those last years. Around eleven grandma came home and started dinner, then she went back to the store while Anna was watching the pots. At one, grandma returned briefly to serve, leaving Anna to do the dishes and straighten up.

After grandpa became ill, grandma had barely time to breathe, so preoccupied was she with him and with money problems. The Germans were threatening to "aryanize" the store, that is, expropriate it, and there were no longer any paying dinner guests: someone in the building had denounced grandma. For a short time Anna's tiny room was rented to a young woman who kept very much to herself, but who was taken to the hospital with pneumonia shortly before I left. I think she died there. Someone else came to collect her things.

The other room in the apartment was aunt Erna's and taboo. Though Erna's recent marriage didn't amount to much, she was now Frau Laufer. I don't know if Herr Laufer succeeded in getting out, but Erna at any rate continued to live with us. Her trousseau, a beautiful mahogany dining room set, was the pride of her room. I sneaked in now and then—through the connecting door so that even Anna wouldn't know—in order to admire it. Once I looked through aunt Erna's drawers. She had beautiful lacey underwear.

Aunt Erna said she was twenty-nine, but eventually it dawned on me that she had been saying that for several years. She was quite attractive. With her short, upturned nose and pageboy she has remained in my memory as the embodiment of the flapper. But she could also be sarcastic and flippant. Was that why she had not found a real husband?

At times I couldn't resist and started reading one or the other of the lending-library books on Erna's dresser. Though I couldn't for the world of me figure out what she saw in those dull love stories, they were just as taboo as her room. She made that very clear to me one day when she caught me in the act.

Anna was gone by the time I left for Vienna. After the Germans took over, she was no longer allowed to work for us, though she would have stayed on even without pay. In her last letter, written on the eve of their deportation, grandma sent Anna's new address and said that we would keep in touch through her. But I never heard from either of them again.

Quite by coincidence, I returned to Ostrava fifty years to the day after I had left, on January 1, 1990. The timing, which only struck me as the train was pulling into the Ostrava station, seemed uncanny. As if to affirm that that period of my life was now truly over and done with. If I didn't understand that right away, it soon came home to me. Our street looked very different, with slick store fronts and enormous display windows. The apartment house was still standing and I recognized the entrance, but it was locked and no one answered the caretaker's bell. The housing registry at the town hall did locate an old entry for the address I gave them, but it was for a Karla Vrublová, not Anna. A sister? Cousin? Why hadn't I found out when there were still answers! On Anna they didn't have anything. As if she had never existed. And Karla was dead, the house torn down. Even the street was renamed.

I was very unhappy during that fall of 1939. All I wanted was to go back to school or at least visit my girl friends. Instead, I had to stay home so that grandpa would not be alone while grandma was at the store. One or the other friend would drop in now and then, but they were uncomfortable in grandpa's presence and did not stay long. I felt trapped and forsaken, and wanted badly to get away from all these restrictions, fears and uncertainties that were closing in on all sides. When the border permit finally arrived, I welcomed it and took leave of Ostrau with a light heart.

Now I find it difficult to believe that I was fifteen then and not just ten or twelve. When I think of my daughter at fifteen, it seems to me that I must have been retarded, or at least a slow learner, as they say nowadays. Or were all of us so protected and spoiled, so wrapped up in ourselves that we remained unaware of how serious what was happening around us was? Why didn't it occur to me that I might never see any of my family again? Was it thoughtlessness? The selfishness of youth? My father's genes? Perhaps all of these, and also the instinct for self-preservation which may have put blinders on us, blinders which brought destruction to some but enabled others to survive. And perhaps being fifteen when it all began, with an intact childhood behind me, enabled me to remain fairly sane and without nightmares when younger children would be permanently scarred.

I resented my father's not sending the money he was supposed to. I recall grandma's writing to him repeatedly about my needing a winter coat. Finally, she somehow scraped the money together on her own. Her great sorrow was that she couldn't afford to take me to an orthodontist to have my teeth straightened. I did not care about that at all, but I was dying for piano lessons. For a while I went to Hanna's house twice a week and she taught me how to read music. I would practise on her piano until her mother came home. When Hanna left for England, that too came to an end. In college, I finally signed up for "beginners' piano" and drove my landlady crazy.

Grandma knew nothing of my musical ambitions. I was well aware that she had neither the time nor energy to listen to my daydreams, and no money to make them come true. Nor did I take them very seriously myself. I liked school, loved to read and had several girl friends. What more could I want? Except for those last few months when I was no longer able to go to school and had to take care of grandpa, it was a very happy childhood that ended on the last day of 1939.

9.

It occurs to me that some of my wartime diaries might still be around, perhaps in one of the boxes stored in the attic and not explored in years. I resolve to check them out when I get back from my walk. Not that I have any illusions—I am obviously no Anne Frank. But who knows, they might supply a few useful pieces for my puzzle, and the voice will be authentic.

"Ostrau, June 14, 1939. Last night they burned down the temple. First they robbed it, then they set it on fire. The Jewish school was stripped as well. All Czechs are indignant. In the twentieth century a country that is more brutal and barbarous than in the Middle Ages! To burn down churches, places of worship, and remain unpunished! If there is a God he will avenge this and will chastise them terribly. And even if there is no God and God is the Ideal, as I keep telling myself, even then Good must be victorious in the end, as a matter of course. And perhaps it is just as well that I am Jewish because, speaking objectively, who would want to belong to such a people!

July 7. To have to remain in Ostrau during the summer is miserable, but aunt Erna has already been let go, so how can I ask for anything. On Sundays we go for walks. Yesterday (a holiday) we were in the Bielau woods.

August 31. Grandma is in great straights because daddy isn't sending any money, and here things are not going well at all. Erna is no longer working at Strebingers, because they were aryanized, so she isn't earning anything. Grandma can't have paying dinner guests any longer either, because the tenant in the third floor apartment has denounced her.

Those last few days have been very tense. All day long the German soldiers march through town and sing the same songs ad nauseam, *Erika* and the awful *Horst Wessellied* in which Jewblood drips from the knife. Everybody speculates whether there will be war or not. And what's worse,I don't know which would be better. Peace means that England and France who were supposed to protect Poland in case of war, have betrayed them just as they betrayed us, and that Poland too will fall to the Germans, entirely or in part. Last week's nonaggression pact with Russia came as a total surprise, and hardly a cheering one. But the opposite case would be just as bad, for the entire border would become frontline territory. Yesterday we heard the first shots. Apparently they were shooting at a Polish plane. It was flying too high. Well, what did they expect?

The critical situation has made many customers leave, and the store is in trouble. Movies are forbidden, and I am glad that the vacation is almost over. I signed up for a sewing class in the convent; today I will find out if I was accepted. If so, I begin tomorrow. Tomorrow is also my last English lesson. Grandma hasn't got the money for it. Too bad, I think I have learned a lot. But I fully intend to continue on my own. I have to quit now, for Anna is making up the bed in the other room and I don't want her to see you, diary.

P.S. I have remembered something else. Imagine, on the 14th I went to visit Hanna's uncle Adolf. I was looking for stamps and got as far as the hospital, so I went in. He was very pleased, but I had to sit down next to him and he petted me like a woman, and I found it terribly embarrassing.

September 2. We are at war, diary! It came quite suddenly, yesterday morning. In a speech at the *Reichsparteitag,* the Führer announced that the Poles had kept him waiting for two days, him, Germany's leader, so that he ran out of patience and gave orders to march in. The Poles are of course resisting, and there is bitter fighting, especially in Upper Silesia. Last night, there had to be a blackout, and people claim that it will be like that every day now. We sat under a covered lamp, since only the kitchen window has a shade. Besides, there too one needs to cover the lamp because of the glass doors to the balcony. And just as I had begun to read after supper, a neighbor rang our door bell to say that she could still see light. So we had to turn everything off and go to bed by flashlight. Incidentally, the entire street was pitch black.

Grandpa went to aunt Paula who owns a radio, and brought back some information. Since Germany has broken the Comintern Treaty by its pact with Russia, Italy will—at least for the present—remain neutral; nor is Japan expected to intervene. Romania supports the Poles, Turkey the British. Switzerland and the United States are neutral, but everybody is mobilizing. No word on where Hungary and Yugoslavia stand. Bulgaria will remain neutral or is so at least right now. I wonder how we will get any news since listening to foreign broadcasts is strictly forbidden.

Zdena dropped in from Michalkovice just as a ten minute air raid drill began. Sirens were howling and everyone took cover in doorways. We watched from the window. This afternoon I will go visit her. She knew nothing of the huge bloodbath in Michalkovice with twenty casualties which was reported in the paper. May the Lord protect us.

September 6. I have begun a new segment in my diary and of my life. Times are too grave to think of petty things.

The war is continuing. Thank God, we don't feel much of it as yet, since all the fighting takes place in Poland. The only reminders are the nightly blackouts and the droning of planes flying over Ostrau. It is funny how easily one gets used to war. It is almost uncanny: everyone shops as usual, theaters and movie houses are not exactly empty, my school in Schlesisch Ostrau has started (the Ostrau schools are on an extended vacation), and a few kilometers away a life and death struggle is taking place, hundreds of people are being killed or crippled. But, nothing surprises any longer, 'stop thinking' is the precept of the day.

I am very homesick for school, not so much the classes as some faces. On the first day of classes I climbed the hill, but when I found out that our class was going to have the gym teacher for math this year, I felt less bad about grandma making me leave school.

Yesterday daddy wrote asking that Erna should obtain the necessary papers so that I could join him in Vienna. Perhaps it would really be best if I were there by November 13, when we are supposed to get our passports. Right now I could howl when I think of leaving, but that too will pass. To face life today you need a lot of courage. Chin up, Liesl and go to it!

September 10 (Sunday). As you see, diary, I am still in Ostrau. And who knows when I will get out. At the police, Erna was told that, since I am Jewish, only the Prague Emigration Authority can issue the exit permit—for entry into the Reich! Since the fourth I have been sewing at the Ludmilla. They run the classes, and some of the girls are nice.

Today we are very worried. All present and former Polish citizens must register tomorrow with the Gestapo—who knows if they won't be shipped off to Poland. Dear God, protect us!

The war continues. The Germans have taken the fortress Krakau, and on Friday night also Warschau. No news from the Western front. If it were only tomorrow and grandma and grandpa back home unharmed!

September 22. How little time has passed and how much has happened! That Monday night both grandparents returned from the registration dead tired, but everything had gone well. Their personal data had been taken down, that was all.

However, there has been another crisis. All Jews, the newspaper announced on the sixth, must appear at the Gestapo, alphabetically—the As on the seventh, the Bs on the eighth etc. Of course everyone was fearful and we were glad to be so far back in the alphabet. Fräulein Alt reported that you had to hand over radios, cameras, typewriters, jewelry, bank books and cash. Though not much can happen to us since we don't own anything, we were hardly reassured. On top of that, they first said everyone from fourteen up, but then those under twenty were sent home.

Aunt Erna was the first to go. It went relatively well. Other than their having to stand with their fingers in their ears (!) for about two hours, not all were molested. Incidentally, there was an amusing episode, and we all had to laugh when we heard about it, for unless you laugh you would have to cry.

Hans L. was one among the many who had to carry the confiscated radios into the basement. Down there others were sorting them. As he comes down and hands over a radio, he suddenly hears a familiar voice: "Servus, Hans, so that's where you are hanging out!" He looks up and sees his brother Paul's grinning face. When Paul some fifteen minutes later comes upstairs, he sees his brother—standing in the corner. As punishment, of course.

Less funny was the encounter of Mr. R. with the Gestapo. An SA-man avenged himself for a complaint which R. had lodged against him some fifteen years earlier. For a week R. could not show himself in the street, he was so swollen.

The only form of address there is *Saujud*, Jew-pig. If you fail to offer a polite greeting to the guard at the door (he is barely twenty), you have to go upstairs and back down three times, and greet each time. An old lady asked for some courtesy when they kept pulling at her hat, so they locked her in the cellar for twenty-four hours.

My grandparents' turn came on the 19th. Since it was raining, some were told to wait in the cellar. That way, the first turned out to be the last to get home. They were gone from seven in the morning to one-fifteen in the afternoon. That we were very tense, goes without saying. Their People's Bank savings book for six hundred crowns was confiscated, but we would never have seen that money anyway. The Weiss family was worse off. They had to leave aunt Paula's jewelry, their radio, camera, Walter's bicycle and five hundred crowns.

The fighting continues. We learned that Warschau was still broadcasting in Polish days after the Germans had hoisted flags and celebrated the victory. Now Russia has mobilized and marched into Poland. The Czechs think the Russians will attack the Germans, but that may be wishful thinking. There is a great shortage of food. Ostrau is amply supplied with everything except butter, eggs, milk, meat and bacon, and who cares that the prices have just about doubled; or? As of last week soap even requires a coupon; in other words, neither coupons nor soap are in evidence. Oderberg, Karwin and the entire surroundings are starving.

October 5. Please, diary, don't be angry with me, but I rarely feel like writing now. On Saturday, the 23rd, was Yom Kippur, the Day of Atonement. It is the greatest holiday of the year, a fast day. This time it was a sad holiday. No services were permitted, the stores had to stay open (for otherwise the Gestapo would have had one more reason to confiscate them) and since grandma had to cook, all of us fasted only until noon. You can imagine how we felt.

The war is over. That is, Poland has ceased to exist. The Germans took one third, the Russians two thirds. Grandma is very worried about our Krakau relatives. Of course, one can't get any news. It would have helped if at least Krakau had fallen to the Russians. Onkel Salo and aunt Nuscha have undoubtedly lost the store. Only God and they themselves know what they now live on.

On the Western front, the fighting continues and, since the newspapers and radios are totally silent, we assume that the Germans are not doing well, or at least have no victories to announce. But we really can't find out anything, now that they have successfully stripped all Jews of their radios. These, by the way, are being sold to Germans for a song. Too bad that we can't decide to buy a radio and even more's the pity that we are not eligible. Ha, ha.

Ration books have been issued and in the store accounting has become a nightmare. There is constant aggravation, with customers who neglect to hand in their registration forms, with the baker whose rolls weigh 35 grams instead of 40, and with me who sticks her nose into all that though it is none of her business.

Since movies are off-limit in the entire Protectorate, I go to the theater more frequently. Standing room only, of course, and even then it's not always worth the money.

Daddy writes that I'll be able to join him once our passports arrrive. Though I know that my life won't ever again be as good as it is here, I am looking forward to Vienna and to seeing the lovely

Votivkirche again. I'll confide in you, my diary: I feel terribly sad about not being able to go to school and even more so that I won't ever again study with Professors K. and F. A man and teacher like K. is hard to find. But enough of that, Liesl, are you starting again? Once you are away, you will forget that too. Chin up and onward.

October 13. It is Friday, the thirteenth. Other than my breaking a sewing needle, nothing bad has happened so far. But I am surprised at myself for being able to joke. What is going on is beyond all imagining. Every day brings new terrors. I wonder if we Jews will ever be left in peace.

Two days ago everybody had to register again, this time from fourteen up. And do you know what the heading was, in big bold letters? "To all Jews who want to emigrate" or some such. We do? Why don't they just leave us alone? Yesterday the newspaper announced that on Tuesday all men, from 14 up, are to assemble in the riding school, and on Wednesday they are supposed to leave! Nobody knows whereto. Some say, to a retraining camp in Wolhynia, others speak of Lithuania, to build barracks for Jewish resettlement. Many claim that the men will not be allowed to maintain contact with their families, but others have heard that families will be able to follow in three months. In short, one could despair.

Aunt Paula is of course desperate. She cries all day for Uncle Robert, and in addition she fears that they might take Walter as well. Uncle Robert assured us today that he was to be made Commander in Chief, starting salary 200 RM per month, to be raised soon. We could hardly laugh at his jokes. When aunt Paula upbraided him, he said that he had plenty of time for worrying and it cost the same money. There he is of course right.

We are also concerned about the store. From two other Jewish stores so many supplies were requisitioned that they could do nothing except close up.

October 28. Another two weeks have gone by, and much has happened. On Tuesday, the seventeenth, the men were shipped off, straight from the riding school. Luckily, grandpa was sent home, but he is quite ill and arrived at home more dead than alive. Aunt Paula is of course in despair, and she makes life hard for herself and everyone else. The mood was dismal. Half the town left for Prague, the other half is thinking about it. On Sunday, the twenty-second, grandma suggested that Erna and Paula go to Přívoz with her and get some advice. I took the street car to Zdena and had a good time there.

When I got home, my mood changed immediately. Erna was packing and I was told that she, Paula, Walter, Mrs. Krummholz and Erwin were taking the train to Olmütz, to head on from there. They left that evening. On the next day, Monday, the order went out for all single women, including those whose husbands had been sent away, to report on Wednesday to the riding school with one suitcase per person. The weather was awful; it poured, wasn't warm either, and none of that helped improve the mood. There was a great rush for the Prague trains. Karla too wanted to leave that evening. We were glad that Erna and Paula were gone. On Tuesday grandma went to see Mr. Krämer and learned that the transport had been postponed. Everyone was jubilant and spread the good news, and even the sun appeared and *"blickte durch der (entlaubten) Zweige Grün,"* as Schiller would have put it—peaked through the green of the (bare) branches.

On Wednesday the second transport of men left. We were allowed to send a crate to those who had left before. Grandma packed a quilt for uncle Robert, several coverlets and some canned food. Whether this will reach him is of course a different question. Erna telephoned from Olmütz, wondering what to do. Grandma didn't know either. Besides one can't say on the phone all one thinks. The following day Erna phoned again—and knew as little as before. In short, yesterday both were back. Walter arrives today.

And that's it for today.

November 20. A month has passed and has brought much sadness. Grandpa has suffered a stroke. His left side is paralyzed, and the doctor says it is a blood clot in his brain; therefore the nerves don't function. But the disaster is that grandpa has also been impaired mentally. He has lost his memory, eats a bite, then stops, and has forgotten the next moment that he should continue eating. His vision is very poor as well. In short, he is badly off and makes life even more difficult for himself and the others than it is already. Aunt Paula who is desperate anyway because almost all men have been heard from except Robert, is now even more depressed, because grandpa lets go completely. He deplores how much work they have with him and torments them even more by talking all the time about dying. All I can do is pray that God may help him. But I can't even do that: Liesl, you want help from a god in whose help you can't believe? A god whom you view as only an ideal? No, you voice inside me, I know you are right but you must not be right. That God in whom the others believe is supposed to be merciful, and He will help me.—How is that, you refuse to believe in Him and yet you do?—Well, then *you* must help me, Ideal, in which I believe, Truth, Justice, whose victory I rely on, Love which contains mercy. Are you silent now, you voice inside me, have I silenced you finally? Well then, may my conscience keep me from digressing from the path which my mentors have pointed out, keep me from losing courage and make me kind, good and patient!

For, diary, I am not good at all. I get annoyed at grandpa and keep forgetting that he is a sick man. The doctor says it can take a few weeks and even months, but I don't believe that grandpa will ever get well again, nor does grandma. Poor grandma, this is very hard on her. At night she has to get up three or four times when grandpa needs to relieve himself. She must dress and undress him, and he makes himself very heavy, leaning on her completely instead of trying to walk. If she will only be able to stand this. She doesn't want to take him to the hospital for he wouldn't be well taken care of there, and so her drudgery will hardly lighten up. I know I am thankless and unloving but I am still young—I want to live, not sit home with grandpa all day without being able to have any girl friends visit or go see them, nothing, nothing. And after four I can't even read or write because the lamp is covered with blue paper. I can at best play solitaire and be bored. It is ugly of me to want to leave right now but I feel trapped, everything around me is depressing and full of hidden tears, so much misery and sorrow.

On Saturdays and Sundays I am allowed to go out. On Saturdays we usually go to the theater. One evening I was in the gallery of the *Národní Dům* where the trade school had its dance class. If times were different, I too could go to school, and also learn how to dance. A while back I went up to my school for a free theater ticket, and when the professor heard that I was not enthused about sewing, he tried to talk me into coming back to school. He is still an optimist. If only I too could still be hopeful! But even if things should change, studying is over for me. I will be one of thousands to have only eight years of schooling—no education, no knowledge. But where there's a will there's a way, and I have the will: I will learn in life's school, and hopefully not fail.

On the 19th I celebrated my 15th birthday. I celebrated—diary, do you understand what I am saying? Karla offered to host the party. I hunted up raspberry juice, we baked coconut cookies which, since there is no coconut flour, we made out of walnuts, and Miss Čermák loaned me her grammophone. Renée Arm brought a few records. It war really fun. Karla gave me scissors and *Monte Christo* which I am now tackling. On Friday, Draha came into town especially to buy me a present; she went back that same evening. Karla handed me from her a nice pin, a compact and face powder. Erna said that I shouldn't spoil my good skin with powder, and so I have the compact just for show. Zdena has not yet given me anything, but she is having a photo of Kejzlar and Fiala made for me. Erna hunted up silk stockings, quite an accomplishment nowadays. Aunt Paula even managed to get gloves and a scarf for my gray coat. Daddy only sent a picture-postcard, which struck me as odd.

Last Sunday was Ilse Rosengarten's birthday, and so the grammophone had to do duty again. Having those Saturdays and Sundays helps a lot. Now I would be glad if I could still go sewing. We always complain and are dissatisfied until things change for the worse. To be sure, I was never dissatisfied with school. I knew that that was the best time of my life. And it could have lasted another four years if...

On Wednesdays, from six to eight, I take a typing class together with Karla, and that is quite interesting. It's on tonight, and I am looking forward to it.

December 6. Diary, the sun is shining again! Imagine, two days ago a cable came for aunt Paula: "AM WELL WITH MINNA KISSES ROBERT—ALLEMAGNE DELAYED IN USSR."

Diary, the happiness cannot be described. Grandma began to cry from joy, aunt Paula likewise. It was high time for the telegram to arrive, for Paula was a mere shadow of herself from sorrowing. It is dated 10/29! Uncle Robert has been safe for five

weeks, and we were so distraught. But now all is well. Even so, I
wish I were in Vienna, for grandpa is terribly difficult. My God,
he is ill, I mustn't reproach him.

December 15. Diary, these are sad days. About a week ago we
heard from aunt Rosa in Krakau that uncle Salo, her and grandma's youngest brother, died on September 30. He was very ill—he
had only one kidney and an open sore. Grandpa's brother also
died not too long ago. And yesterday grandpa Weiss was buried.
He died on the twelfth. But if one is eighty-seven, it's nothing to
be surprised at. Aunt Irma has already arrived from Vienna so
that aunt Paula is a bit unburdened. Note that aunt Irma, who
was informed only two days ago, is already here, and dad still has
not achieved anything. I am sure aunt Irma would have had me
in Vienna long before this.

By the way, the British radio is supposed to have announced
that if Hitler's voice is heard on the radio once more, they will give
him all their colonies. Can this be true? Or are the Germans
spreading the rumor in order to agitate against England?

Sunday, December 24, 1939. Something awful has happened to
me. If I only think of it, I feel rotten. But I must report in
sequence.

On Saturday, daddy wrote that my border crossing permit
must be at the Ostrau *Oberlandrat* by now, according to the
Vienna Police Presidio. I went there myself, somewhat scared, but
I went. I was indeed told to come back the next day, but they are
closed on Wednesdays. On Thursday it wasn't ready either.
However, much to my amazement, it was really ready on Friday.

Since that was the last school day before Christmas vacation,
I immediately climbed up the hill to say goodbye to my friends.
Unfortunately, I could barely talk to Kejzlar or Fiala. Zdena
promised to drop in that afternoon, and we went shopping together. In the Aso department store we met a fellow from Michalkovice
who joined us and suggested we see a movie together. But I don't
even want to think of that."

10.

The sky has changed to a dull gray. It is drained of even the slightest bluish shimmer. Instead, dark bands streak across much of it, as if in pursuit of one another or of me. Where have they come from so suddenly? A few sunny patches are still dotting the fields on my left, but the righthand side is steeped in deep shade, with only a few low-growing shrubs showing dark outlines, and an equally somber grassy knoll.

The white fence next to me is punctuated by shrubs and vines. Their pattern resembles a carefully spaced arrangement of white letters and dashes against a green backdrop—a message which I am unable to decipher. A clump of tall wildflowers, some white, others purple, are leaning against the white slats, as if in search of support against any sudden gusts of wind. They resemble long-stemmed pinks but are fuzzier and a little dissheveled. They look both hardy and graceful.

Across the road a tall unpainted fence catches my attention. In that muted setting it looks alien and forbidding. Each of the thin, densely spaced wooden posts comes to a sharp point at the top—spikes with the raw look of wood which has been cut recently. Unyielding like rows of lances, the fence squares itself around the house. The house almost touches the left side of the stockade, as if it were trying to break out. There is something odd about all of this, though it takes me a while to pinpoint it. The north side of the house is painted white, but the façade is unpainted and as inhospitable-looking as the fence. There are no dogs or horses in sight whom that tightly fenced-in yard might be meant for, but a jungle gym suggests children. It has irregular, almost bizarre outlines—a ladder here, a pole there, a slide, and several odd curves and bulges, all in strong, clashing colors—yellow, orange, blue, green and purple. The colors are even more incongruous than the mottled house and the raw picket fence. Has it always looked like that? If so, how come I haven't noticed it before? Ornament or trap, designed to fence in or fence out?

Fenced out I was on that Saturday afternoon when I took the elevator to the fourth floor but then was unable to open the door to our apartment. It took me a while to realize that the bolt was secured. An oversight, I thought, and rang the door bell. There was no response, even to repeated rings. Grandmother Vera was spending the afternoon visiting Rachelle, and I knew that the other two families were out as well. Father must have absentmindedly secured the bolt. I went back downstairs to ring the outside bell. Once he recognized my voice, he would let me in. Only when the intercom didn't come on did I realize with a shock that he was locking me out deliberately. He must be in there with someone. A woman. Frau Stella? I couldn't think of anyone else.

During my first few months in Vienna, Frau Thiemig was a frequent visitor. Grandmother Vera never discussed her with me, but I recall her mentioning that my father and Herr Thiemig had been old friends and chess partners. I didn't meet him. He must have been gone by the time I arrived, while his wife had remained behind, either to wait for needed papers or to settle their affairs. One always tried to get the men out first.

Frau Thiemig was extremely attractive, in her thirties, full-bosomed, with shiny black hair raised into a high Spanish-style bun, with wide cheekbones, long dangling earrings, very white skin, beautiful teeth, rouged cheeks, deep red lips and flashing black eyes. She was obviously a flirt, though father treated her as he did everyone else, chivalrously but dispassionately, without dismounting from his pedestal of calm superiority. She never said much to me. I found her intimidating but could not take my eyes off her. She would visit now and then, presumably to see grandmother Vera, and then grandmother Vera would serve tea. When father arrived, we sat around the tiny table for a while, then he escorted her home.

By the time I found myself locked out, Frau Thiemig had already disappeared from the horizon. Perhaps she had succeeded in emigrating, or she was deported—at any rate she was never mentioned, and I accepted her disappearance as I had accepted her appearance, without questions and without much thought.

Frau Stella turned up later. She was very different, younger, probably in her late twenties, blond, tall and willowy, and so pale that she seemed to be ailing from some mysterious illness. I remember her slightly bulging eyes, her low husky voice, and a charming and as if apologetic smile between dimples. I liked her a lot until the day much later when she—or her husband— refused to let us escape through their apartment.

Because her husband worked for the Jewish Community, they were protected, though eventually they too were called up for deportation. Only Frau Kleppner returned from Auschwitz, even thinner and more willowy, and with a number tattooed on her arm. I don't know if she came back to my father.

Whenever grandmother Vera was not at home, it was my task to serve the tea. Not until father locked me out did I realize that they must be having an affair. As I stood there not knowing what to do, I was angry and embarrassed, but also elated. At that moment, my grudging admiration for my father's superiority—everyone I knew looked up to him—dissolved in distaste for his behavior. Suspicions about his integrity had already surfaced during an earlier episode, but at that time I had repressed them. Now I found them confirmed.

He would not marry again, he had said to a circle of friends in my presence, because he "didn't want to give the child a stepmother."

"Aren't you lucky to have such a solicitous father!" This was addressed to me, but before I could say anything he cut in:

"What does she know! She takes anything one does for her for granted."

Though I had resented his treating me like an inanimate object, I had also felt guilty for letting him down.

I don't recall where I went that Saturday, but I stayed away until evening. When I finally returned home, everything seemed normal. Except that father never inquired why I was coming home so late, and I didn't say anything either.

Strangely, my resentment was directed only at him and not at his women friends. I never caught him *in flagranti* again nor did I try to ascertain whether he was having affairs with the women around him. Much later, when Frau Litzi became our housekeeper for several months, I did wonder if she was my father's lover, but since I was fond of her and she seemed to like me too, it did not matter.

Frau Litzi supplied us with black market edibles and cooked for us. Come to think of it, they probably did sleep together. That would make for a more credible explanation for her presence than father's statement that he wanted to give me a break from cooking and shopping, which I had chalked up as greatly to his credit, even though it seemed out of character. At any rate, Frau Litzi had black-market sources and was an inventive cook, while I found it very difficult to concoct anything palatable with what little was still officially available.

Frau Litzi was hefty but well-proportioned, with a double chin, an ample bosom, voluptuous curves and swinging hips. Her hair was short, curly and auburn red. Though like the rest of us she had little to wear, she always managed a rakish scarf, a ruffle or a necklace. The bright red lipstick accentuated her small but sensuous mouth. She had something of a gypsy about her. I couldn't decide whether she was vulgar or had flair. Perhaps the borderline between the two is merely a matter of taste.

I not only found Frau Litzi exotic and fascinating but was totally devoted to her, because she didn't treat me like a child. Instead, she made me her confidante. For hours she would talk to me about her life and her lovers. There had been many. Usually she was the one to jilt them, on the principle that it hurt less if you did it to them than if they did it to you. When I asked her if it was really important to remain a virgin as long as possible, she answered with her usual half diffident, half rakish smile: "When the right man comes along, you regret not being one."

This wasn't here nor there but she wouldn't say more. She was neither young nor pretty; therefore her conquests cheered me greatly. I never forgot her statement that she had never regretted anything she had done, only what she had left undone. It seemed a good principle.

She too was gone one day, but since she seemed a survivor by nature, I like to think that she made it.

Frau Litzi was with us in 1944, just before the daily bombardments started and everything began to fall apart. By then we had long been evicted from our nice apartment across from the Swedish embassy, just below the picturesque Strudlhof steps. It was a beautiful apartment, with its view of the Liechtenstein palace and gardens. Of course, I knew that we were there on borrowed time, what with the steady stream of German refugees arriving from the war zones. The apartment below us had already been requisitioned. It housed a young woman from the Ruhr who had been bombed out and resettled in a choice location because she had two small children. Probably also because her husband was a high-ranking airforce officer. She was tiny, had sandy hair and a flattened nose. I remember her as the only non-Jewish person in the building who acknowledged my greeting with a smile and kind word.

One evening—it must have been in 1940 because we lost the apartment in September of that year—the doorbell rang. The German woman's husband stood there in full uniform. Our uneasiness didn't abate even when he asked politely whether he could come in. We ushered him into our *Kabinett* and grandmother Vera offered tea. He declined. He had come, he said, to urge us to leave Austria as quickly as possible. He had seen one of those "resettlement" camps: people were being shot in them, often immediately upon arrival.

This seemed totally unbelievable, though we didn't say that but only thanked him for the information. After he left, father and grandmother Vera wondered aloud what could have made him concoct such a horror story. In the middle of the twentieth century, and in Central Europe at that. It went without saying that we would leave Vienna as soon as we could, but that wasn't as easy as he imagined. Since the defeat of France and the entry of Italy into the war, emigration was reduced to a trickle. Only Shanghai and some Central and South American countries were still possibilities, via Siberia and Japan, and that only if you had connections and money, lots of money. Which we didn't have. And go into hiding? Impossible. For a day or two, friends might take us in, but for months and without ration cards? Could he want our apartment for friends of his own? Whatever—all we were able to do was lie low and hope that the war would soon be over.

Now that information on what really went on at that time is available, I realize how subdued his warning was in comparison to the mind-boggling reality: there was Hitler's public promise of January 30, 1939, that the result of a war would be the total annihilation of the Jews; Himmler's decree in late 1941 prohibiting all emigration of Jews because plans for a "final solution" were under way; the proposal, of December 1941, by *Generalgouvernement*'s governor general Hans Frank, to exterminate the Jews through starvation and other measures, because they constitute 3.5 million *"für uns äußerst schädliche Fresser"*(13/290)—extraordinarily harmful parasites; the creation of special *Einsatztruppen*, killing squads, which by April of that year reported to Himmler the execution of 481,500 Jews and by June, of 700,000; the use of mobile gas vans in many of the killing centers as early as November 1941 while crematoria were being built in Auschwitz—five of them, capable of "processing" twelve thousand victims a day. By the end of that year, two and a half million people had been shot, starved or gassed. And we were talking of twentieth century civilization! But we might have gone mad or committed suicide had we been aware of any of this.

And yet, our naïveté was excusable. A report on the transport to Riga of January 19, 1942, when 70-80 people were selected for a work detail and the rest shot in a birch copse, contains this chilling description: "All shootings are carried out in such a manner that they are barely noticed. ... Even the remaining Jews believe that those in question were simply resettled. ... In Latvia, the number of Jews remaining in Riga was reduced from 29,500 to 2500." (10/35) And when, on August 8, 1942, the Geneva representative of the World Jewish Congress sent a cable to the American Jewish leader Rabbi Stephen Wise substantiating the Nazi plan to exterminate "the Jews of Europe," it was held back by the State Department "in view of the fantastic nature of the allegation." (18/44-45)

After our apartment on Strudlhofgasse was confiscated, we spent two years on Wipplingerstraße, close to the famous Anker clock. The apartment, in fact, the whole house belonged to an elderly Romanian couple. They were able to take us in since their third bedroom had not yet been assigned. The room was large enough for three beds, and so I left the Mehrs with a heavy heart. I had felt at home there, far more so than with father and grandmother Vera. In the second bedroom lived another elderly couple, Herr and Frau Dr. Schreiber. I recall very little about the apartment's owners, Herr and Frau Hofrat Winternitz, but I see the Schreibers vividly before me.

Herr Dr. Schreiber, a chemist, was tall, thin, white-haired and slightly stooped. His wife was very short and neither fat nor thin. Her quick movements had something mousey, and so did her long, pointed nose and the small sly eyes under barely visible pale eyebrows and lashes. She wore her hair in a bun. When loose, it was thin but so long that it reached the small of her back. It was still naturally light-blond though she must have been close to or even above sixty.

Frau Doktor had, unless I am much mistaken, no degree of any kind, yet there was nothing she couldn't do or didn't know. Since I wasn't able to attend regular schools, my father arranged for her to tutor me. English, math, chemistry, cooking, baking, cake decorating, you name it. He claimed that I would finally learn something practical instead of taking those useless retraining courses offered by the Community. Of course, a few months later they were discontinued anyway.

Frau Doktor was an odd person, but she taught me a great deal. I learned to use my ingenuity and common sense, to improvise when necessary or desirable, and not to give up easily. However, some of that I learned only when I visited her in Karlsbad during the summer of 1946, after she had come back from Auschwitz.

On September 7, 1942, we moved into an apartment of our own on Untere Augartenstraße, and there we lived until the end of the war. Frau Litzi's reign took place in that small, dark, two room apartment.

11.

A torn paper bag next to an overturned garbage can displays what the racoons and dogs have refused. A half-eaten hamburger, still partly wrapped, must have been overlooked. I remember the shock when, at my first meal in an American cafeteria, I said to the man behind the counter that I didn't want any bread, and he took the plate which he had already set out and emptied it into the trash can. Perhaps it is inevitable that people who didn't experience war or a similar calamity lack a genuine appreciation of food.

Automatically, I scrutinize the spilled trash for something still usable—a habit likewise acquired during the war or perhaps learned from Frau Doktor. That lack of pride served me well when I arrived in the States in 1947. I quickly discovered the Goodwill and Salvation Army stores, and as a result managed not only to live on my scholarship but to save enough for summer visits to aunt Jenny in England.When Auschwitz was liberated, Frau Doktor dragged herself to Karlsbad in Bohemia, now known as

Karlovy Vary. She was down to less than a hundred pounds and had decided to head for Karlsbad because it was a spa. She was sure that its waters would cure her dysentery. She made it and they did. When I visited her in 1946, she had regained some of her chubbiness and much of her strength. Her wits she had never lost.

She invited me partly out of gratitude for the food packages I had sent to her to Theresienstadt, partly to suggest various joint business ventures which she wanted us to launch together. One of them, I recall, was establishing a language school for children. It seemed a good idea. But on my way to Karlovy Vary, I had spent a night in Prague with a young couple, friends of Viennese friends. Though both were medical students, their shelves were full of Marx and Engels, and much of the evening they were out distributing leaflets. At that point I decided that, no matter how much I loved Czechoslovakia, rather than return I would try to emigrate to America. Though I didn't know it then, the Communists were already the country's leading party. In February 1948, they seized power and turned Czechoslovakia into a communist state.

Frau Dr. Schreiber was a survivor in every sense of the word. When she arrived in Karlsbad, no relief agencies were in place, Jewish or otherwise. She went from trash can to trash can, picking up pieces of wire, buttons, old pans—anything and everything. On a self-made board table she spread her wares, selling, trading and bartering. Since everything was in short supply, she soon did well enough to rent a small store. By the time I visited her, she had sold the store and was involved in several new projects.

I heard from her once more, about two years later when I was already in the States. It hardly surprised me that her letter came from Florida. She was importing down quilts and suggested that I become her New York representative. I had an office job and was taking a college preparatory course at night. I declined, and she didn't contact me again.

12.

The Leopoldstadt is Vienna's second district, locale of the former

Jewish ghetto, and on the whole a rather poor, rundown neighborhood. As the Jewish apartments in other more desirable locations were requisitioned, most of the Jews still legally in Vienna by 1943—and their numbers were dwindling rapidly—ended up in the Leopoldstadt.

Untere Augartenstraße 25 had an unusual and, as it turned out, for us very fortunate layout. It consisted—and still does—of two buildings of the same size, each five stories high, one behind the other, linked by a courtyard, one side of which you had to cross to get to the rear building. Part of the courtyard was taken up by a low structure which likewise connected the two buildings and was accessed from the courtyard. Perhaps it was a tool shed—I was never inside. Our apartment was on the third floor of the rear building. It faced Haasgasse which runs parallel to Untere Augartenstraße. From Haasgasse there was a direct entrance into our rear building, but though from the outside the huge wooden double door looked like a perfectly normal access, on the inside it was bricked up. During the battle for Vienna, this fluke may have saved me and my father.

The French doors of our bedroom opened onto the flat roof of the storage shed, as did the doors of the corresponding apartment in the front building, the residence of Frau Stella and her husband. Perhaps they had helped father find the apartment. One of our two rooms—no family was entitled to more than one room—was rented out to Nellie Goldhagen, like us a Romanian, and a gentle, sweet woman. I would have liked her for a stepmother, though she may have been older than father. Anyway, by then he had struck up a friendship with Grete Klüger who lived, with mother and sister, around the corner from us at Förstergasse 7. I was fond of Grete as well, so much so, in fact, that I once warned her not to marry my father because he was a cold and inconsiderate egotist who would make her unhappy. At first Grete smiled, but then she said very seriously that she would keep my words in mind. She was spared that decision, if little else.

The Leopoldstadt occupies about half of the island between the Danube Canal and the Danube. It is linked to the Inner City by a series of bridges across the Canal, and if you blow up the bridges, the island becomes a fortress. Probably that was why in 1945 the Germans decided to defend it. The Red Army had already taken most of the city without encountering significant opposition, but when it reached the Danube Canal, it found the bridges blown up and the Germans entrenched.

During that last engagement, the Germans were shooting at anything in sight, including their own people. We didn't know that until we left the cellar during a lull in the shelling. As we stood under the arch which opened into the courtyard, there was a sudden flash, a deafening roar and a cloud of thick dust. Ears blocked and eyes burning, we raced back into the cellar.

Only several hours later did word get around that one man had been hit, in the stomach. Though he was not Jewish—by then we were the only Jews in the building and our door was starless—there was no way to move him to a hospital or get help. All night long we heard him moan in his cellar cubicle. The moaning stopped just a few hours before the Russians marched down our street. "Then they will say we did it," the Russian officer commented upon seeing the body. He was inspecting the cellar for hidden German soldiers and weapons. My father did the interpreting.

Strange as it now seems, during five long years of war and persecution, it had never occurred to me that I might be killed, not until that day. The thought that "once the war is over everything will be different" helped me even through the desperation of the final months. But when the Germans fired at us, with the Russians just a few blocks away, I suddenly realized that I might not survive, could still be killed even now when the end was within reach. The roar of that shell with which the war burst into our courtyard and picked a victim, entirely at random, woke me to the realization of what war really meant, and how fragile and accidental life was. It was as if I had grown up at that moment, finally, at age twenty and from one minute to the next. And it did not feel good.

On that day, the SS went from house to house in our neighborhood, knocked on every entrance and asked the *Hauswart* whether there were any Jews left in the building.

The *Hauswart* was no ordinary caretaker, though he locked and unlocked the outside entryway, and kept hallways and stairs clean and lit. He was also the building's official guard and spy.

The spouses usually assisted. They watched everything and everybody, keeping a sharp eye out for suspicious activities—a radio that might be tuned to a foreign channel, or the repeated appearance of an unfamiliar face, which could indicate black market transactions or the presence of someone in hiding, a "U-boat." Everyone was at the *Hauswart*'s mercy. Some residents put up with plugged toilets and dripping faucets in their attempt to lie low and escape notice. Others tried to stay in his good graces by supplying him with food and textiles, even cigarettes and tobacco from the black market. Though this involved considerable risk, usually no questions were asked. Of course, he could turn on you any time something rubbed him the wrong way.

The *Hauswart* reported to the *Blockwart*, his superior, usually a party member. He, in turn, kept the Gestapo informed about such matters as the whereabouts and activities of the handful of Jews still living in his block.

Who was left during those last two years? Jewish spouses in mixed marriages and their offspring who counted as Jewish unless baptized by November 14, 1935, the target date established by the Nuremberg Race Laws; the employees of the Jewish Community and, after it was disbanded in November 1942, of the much smaller caretaker administration, the *Ältestenrat der Juden Wiens*, Council of Elders of Vienna's Jewry; likewise the workers of affiliated establishments such as the Jewish hospital, orphanage, clothing exchange, soup kitchen and cemetery; finally, a handful of Jewish foreigners like the Klügers and us, though I don't know how many there were in addition to the five of us.

The fact was that in the early war years, most foreign governments were protecting their Jewish citizens. However, on September 23, 1943, the following "urgent communication" was directed by the Head of the Security Police and the Security Services to all Gestapo Centers: "In agreement with the Foreign Office, all Jews remaining on German-administered territories after completion of the so-called repatriation drive [*Heimschaffungsaktion*], can as of now be included in deportation arrangements if they are citizens of the following countries: Italy, Switzerland, Spain, Portugal, Denmark, Sweden, Finland, Hungary, Romania, Turkey. Since for diplomatic reasons the deportation of these Jews to the East cannot yet take place, the concentration camp Buchenwald will serve as temporary quarters for male Jews over fourteen, the concentration camp Ravensbrück for Jewesses and children." (10/13-14) In October 1943, 4 Jewish Italians, 3 Romanians, 6 Hungarians and 28 Turks were sent to Buchenwald. But even that tells only part of the story: they came for us long before September 23rd—in early June.

Still in Vienna were also those few whose protected status had been abrogated but who, by luck or foresight, were not at home when the SS came to round them up for the next transport. If their luck held and no *Ordner* was posted at the door to nab them upon their return, and if the *Hauswart* was not aware of the action and therefore not on the lookout for them, they were safe till the next roundup. A few succeeded living that way from transport to transport, though most were either caught eventually or went underground.

Finally, until 1943 you were also protected if you worked for the Community as *Gepäckträger*, *Ordner* or *Jupo*—assignments which were truly pacts with the devil.

Gepäckträger or porters would carry the luggage of people selected for deportation from the apartment to the van (50 kg were allowed, aside from hand luggage), unloaded it at the assembly center, and reloaded it on deportation day into the freight cars designated for the transport. *Ordner* or *Ausheber* were Jewish assistants to the SS on their roundups, ostensibly there to help people pack, but actually to prevent their escaping after the SS officer in charge had left, and before the trucks returned, several hours later, to collect them. Here is an example of the SS's truly diabolical ingenuity: early in the war, the president of the Community requested that his staff as well as people in possession of emigration papers be exempted from transports. The request was granted—on condition that he vouch for it that all those earmarked for deportation appear at the assembly center on time, and that he supply the staff required to accomplish this.

There were 15-20 *Gepäckträger*, about a hundred *Ordner*, and 6-8 *Jupos*—that sorry lot of Jewish policemen who tried to save their own hides by spying on and denouncing other Jews. They didn't have to wear the star, but everyone knew who they were and feared them. According to Egon, at least one of them—one of the worst, he said—was gassed in Auschwitz. Another was arrested after the war and committed suicide in his cell.

Egon: I met him recently when, in the wake of my walk, I began collecting people and information on the war years. An old friend in Vienna with whom I reestablished contact, told me that Ditha, another member of our wartime circle, was living in Connecticut, and so I visited her.

Her husband Egon talked willingly about the past. He was collecting information on the Holocaust, which involved conducting an extensive correspondence with survivors, prompted by his almost fanatical desire to set straight misconceptions and errors in published accounts. He had been a porter. In October 1942, when the mass action ended, he was sent to Theresienstadt and from there first to Auschwitz, then to Dachau. He survived by hiding when the Germans were evacuating the inmates, just before the Russians arrived. Almost all of the 7000 died on that notorious forced march. In the garden of Jerusalem's Holocaust Memorial site there is a bronze monument to them. It shows a closely packed group of emaciated people on the march, the first on the point of collapsing. The monument was donated recently by a town in Upper Bavaria, the first gift to be accepted by Yad Vashem from Germany.

Transports, however miniscule, continued to the end of the war. They had priority over troop movements even when the few still functioning railway lines were clogged with retreating troops and refugees. But since by 1943 few Jews were left, transports were leaving at longer and less regular intervals—whenever a handful of victims was rounded up, a U-boat caught, a mixed-marriage partner available for deportation because the non-Jewish spouse had died or divorced, or some hitherto protected administrator, hospital nurse or "medic"—they were not allowed to call themselves physicians, only *Krankenbehandler*—was declared expendable.

It was as if the machinery, once set in motion, could not stop. Or perhaps those running it kept it going any way they could, in order to avoid being sent to the front. Auschwitz had been liberated for weeks while we were still preparing for the battle of Vienna, and the last, minimal transport from Vienna arrived in Theresienstadt two days after Vienna was taken by the Russians. The "death march" from Dachau began eleven days later, on April 26.

13.

I take a deep breath and look around. The sky has darkened noticeably and I am not even halfway. I'd better speed up. The red hydrant by the small white farm house is dripping. Should I alert someone? I feel awkward about meddling. There is after all no water shortage, and a fire is quite unlikely in this verdant, succulent greenery. Also, if I stop now I might not make it to the bank on time. If it's still dripping when I come back, I'll do something about it. Then I blush: Be honest—it's just an excuse in order not to get involved, isn't it? Next time—in this case it's no big thing, but what if there is no next time? At what point does an excuse turn into a betrayal?

For a long time I thought of them as "betrayals." Such as Zdena's denying me. In retrospect, though, that was only a miniscule betrayal, perhaps no betrayal at all.

Zdena had become my best friend after Hanna left Ostrau for England. One day we went to the movies together, a week before my departure for Vienna. A friend of Zdena's came along as well. The entrance to the movie house sported a big sign saying *Juden unerwünscht*. Zdena asked me in a whisper whether I was willing to ignore the sign—the movie was supposed to be very good. Yes, I was quite willing, as a matter of principle, in fact. It was absurd to claim that all of a sudden there was a difference between being Jewish and being "Aryan"—whatever that meant—and I didn't give a hoot about being welcome or not. Zdena agreed. I am not sure whether she was any more aware of what was involved than I was, though I may have underestimated her. In view of the circumstances, I was probably blaming her unfairly.

I had changed schools that last year in Ostrau, as did most of the Jewish children whose families spoke German at home and who had therefore been enrolled in the German school. After the Austrian *Anschluß* in March 1938, the atmosphere in Ostrau's

German *Mädchen-Reformrealgymnasium* had become very unpleasant. Teachers started raising their arm in the Hitler salute, and many of the girls were wearing *dirndls* and white knee socks, the uniform of the *BDM*. It was the girls' equivalent to the *HJ*—pronounced *HAYOTT*—the Hitler Youth. When the Germans marched into Czechoslovakia the following spring, the German school immediately expelled all Jewish pupils. In the Czech school, Jews and non-Jews were united in their hatred of the invader.

At first I found the Czech school very difficult. In the Jewish elementary school one year had been conducted in German and the next in Czech, so that we learned the subject matter in both languages. But three years in the German secondary school had eradicated much of my literate Czech. At home we spoke Czech only with Anna, and I had adopted her *Kuchelböhmisch* or "kitchen Bohemian"—a mixture of colloquialisms and local brogue. Nor were the few swearwords I had learned from her of much use. I still remember them, though. *Ježíš Maria* was the most common one. More satisfying, perhaps because of its sound quality, was *krucifix,* and also *pšakrev* which is actually Polish and means dog's blood. Those two could really be spit out to a wonderfully liberating effect, even if I couldn't utter them in front of grandma, however indulgent she was otherwise. Oh yes, there was also *potvora*, the bitch, and *ta kolera*. To refer to people by that dreadful disease indicated that they were utterly vicious and despicable. Anna would cross herself every time she used the Lord's or His Mother's name in vain. This, I assumed, undid the harm. Since I was not Catholic, I didn't need to cross myself.

Anyway, swearwords were of no help in the Czech school, not even with the other girls. My primitive Czech frequently subjected me to ridicule, mainly from our homeroom teacher. He was an unattractive man, so round-shouldered as to seem hunchbacked, with an enormous bald watermelon head, an unusually long stubbly chin, and a crafty grin. Everybody feared his sharp tongue. We called him *strašidlo*, the scarecrow. I still remember how humiliated I felt when, upon my asking for permission to leave the room, he pretended not to understand and made me repeat my question three times in front of everybody, until I realized that I was using the slangy *nadůl* instead of the literate *dolů*.

Zdena's presence helped greatly to make school less formidable. She was pretty and popular, and from the moment I arrived, she included me in her circle. But what made the Czech school really wonderful was the presence of Professor Kejzlar, Antonín Kejzlar, called by us Kecal or Tonda. The names of the other teachers are gone but I remember his. Tonda was our math teacher and I had an enormous crush on him. Tall, handsome, fortyish, with piercing black eyes under bushy eyebrows, he was the only *pan professor* to wear a white doctor's smock. He looked rather haughty and could be quite ironic, but he was never mean or sarcastic like the scarecrow.

Professor Kejzlar's smile, his rare smile, was like the sun. I thought him brilliant, quite unlike the other teachers. Though not very interested in math before, I now threw myself into it with the determination with which you dive into an Alpine lake, knowing that it will take your utmost to conquer the cold currents. I spent hours on my math homework, neglected everything else but wouldn't quit until I had obtained the correct results.

My day of triumph came as we were struggling with an especially intricate problem which none of us was able to solve, not even the teacher's pet, a colorless blonde with short sandy hair and freckles, by the name of Mikulčáková. (Why in the world do I remember that name when I have forgotten so many others? Guilt? Shame? Perhaps gratitude.) The assignment was due in a week. Every day we compared notes, only to learn that nobody had got anywhere, except that the pet claimed she had not had time to look at the problem. This of course raised our suspicions. It was just like her to have the answer and not let on, so that she wouldn't have to tell us how she had gone about it.

On the evening before the homework was due, I worked till all hours, and suddenly it clicked. My exhilaration knew no bounds. For once she was not going to be the only one to please him, for once I wouldn't be a little monkey but out front! I arrived in class at the last possible moment that morning, to avoid having to share the solution with the others.

It went even better than anticipated. After the usual routine of handing Tonda the class book to enter the day's absences, Mikulčáková asked him to excuse the entire class for not having done the assignment. There must be something wrong with it, it couldn't be solved. The fact that even she had not managed it came to me as a total surprise, but without a moment's hesitation I stood up and announced that there was nothing wrong with the problem, that I had worked out the proof.

Did the class hate me at that point or were they delighted that the pet was shown up? The only thing I took in was his surprised and appreciative glance. As if he were seeing me for the first time, which he probably was. Have I ever regretted the incident? Not really. Even though in retrospect I find it embarrassing.

My victory was short-lived. Hanna, who had changed schools together with me, was weak in math and I tutored her in exchange for piano lessons. On an important exam she got an A. This would have pleased me enormously, had I not received a C! It was an undeserved C: when recopying a problem, I had omitted to include the divisor. Though the divisor was fully visible in the crossed-out section, Kejzlar had marked the entire problem as wrong. I felt not only humiliated in front of Hanna but also indignant at Tonda's pettiness. In addition, the bad grade would ruin my otherwise good prospects for an A in math—the only grade I cared about because the term before Tonda had only handed out one A.

I tried to talk him into giving me at least partial credit. He listened silently to my long explanation: that I was tutoring Hanna, that the fact of her success showed that I too must know the subject and that, since I had everything right except for that one little oversight, he ought to reconsider the grade. When I was through, he said: "If you cross something out, that means that you don't want me to consider it. If a barber were to cut his customer's throat, he could also call it a little oversight, but that wouldn't bring the customer back to life." Oh, how I hated him.

I had two other encounters with Kejzlar, one personal, the other indirect, and they became my treasure trove.

Since the Czech school stood on a hill across the river, in Schlesisch Ostrau, the walk to school took a good half-hour. After Hanna had left for England, I would meet Erna and Hana (her name was spelled with one "n") on Masaryk Square every morning. We would walk on together to Karla's place—the three were cousins—and whistle under Karla's window until she came down. Together we would then head across the bridge and up the hill. (To my great disappointment, everything looked very different when I visited Ostrava fifty years later. Only that footpath up the hill seemed vaguely familiar. My daughter and I trudged up, but we found a huge, brand new school. You can't retrieve the past, I should have known that! Especially when you are looking for it. Though when you least expect it, you may walk right into it.)

On the day the Germans marched into Ostrau, the four of us were walking to school together. Silently and glumly trudging up the long hill, we were trying our best to ignore the endless convoys of German tanks which thundered past us into town.

When I entered the long hall of the classroom building, I saw Kejzlar's white coat at the far end of the corridor. He was coming toward me. Though he looked right at me, I neither greeted him nor lowered my eyes. I held his gaze until we had passed each other. I was quite sure that his eyes understood mine, read in them the sadness and dismay which both of us felt. Later I thought that there had also been pity in his eyes for me and my fate, but at the moment of the encounter I didn't know that I was to have a fate.

On that day we were supposed to take a math exam. Everyone except me was convinced that Tonda would cancel the exam. I knew him better. Mine was the best grade in class, a C. And, after an oral presentation, I received an A for the course.

When the border permit finally arrived, I went up to the school to say goodbye. To my surprise, the scarecrow was very friendly, wished me good luck and asked me to let him know how I was doing. Tonda was a real beast. When I said that I had come to say goodbye, he asked how much time that would require. Though Zdena assured me that he must have been joking, I was hurt, almost hurt enough to be glad to leave. In spite of this—and I was annoyed with myself for being so weak—I sent him a note from Vienna. Much to my surprise, he replied almost by return mail. A picture-postcard with two lines of writing and his signature conveyed his thanks for my note and offered best wishes for the new year and for fulfillment of all my hopes. The picture on the card showed the smoke stacks of Ostrau belching fumes. Perhaps that was meant to console me.

When toward the end of the war the bombs were falling on Vienna, I left a suitcase with my most treasured possessions at my friend Inge's house, where I thought they would be safer than with me. Their maid made use of the confusion of those final days to abscond with assorted things, among them my case. I shrugged off the loss of the collapsible umbrella, even that of my beloved burgundy wool dress, but I could not forgive her for the loss of Tonda's postcard. I didn't hear from him again.

Zdena and I sat down in the movie house. I had the aisle seat, on the right aisle if you were facing the screen, about two thirds down. Just before the lights dimmed, I recognized the little brother of one of my former friends from the German school. He looked at me, so I smiled and waved. He was about ten and seemed to be alone. While my eyes were still on him, he got up and walked over to the usher. I saw him talk to the man and point in my direction. The usher said something, the boy nodded, and the usher started out toward me. When he reached our row, he bent down and asked me whether I had my *Ariernachweis* with me. Someone was claiming that I was Jewish. No, I don't have it on me but my friend here knows me—and just then Zdena mumbled under her breath: "Leave me out of this!" Thereupon I offered, with an offended expression, to go home and get my identity card.

The usher apologized for the inconvenience but insisted that I do so. I left with head held high, though I was inwardly burning with indignation, shame and pain. What hurt most was not the behavior of that despicable kid nor that the usher had listened to him, but that my good friend Zdena had let me down. For a long time I couldn't forgive her, and it didn't occur to me that my denying my Jewishness could also be seen as a betrayal, perhaps more so. Only much later was I willing to acknowledge that her prudence might have been justified.

Then and there I resolved that I would never be a coward, never deny my friends. On several occasions in Vienna when more was at stake than being turned out of a movie house, that decision could have easily undone me, and it was none of my merit that it didn't.

Perhaps I was so cocksure because as a Romanian citizen I did not have to wear the star. When my Jewish friends were only allowed to travel on the open rear platform of the street car—and that with a special permit—I insisted on standing there with them, disregarding the many disapproving stares and remarks. I had heated arguments about this with my father, but I didn't yield. By sheer luck, I was never confronted, attacked or arrested.

Even more foolishly, I continued to go to the movies, banking on the fact that since I had not gone to school in Vienna, nobody could recognize and denounce me. At first I went alone, then with Inge whom I had met in an English course at Berlitz. Since I was not sure whether Inge's father was a Nazi—he owned a sausage casings factory and they seemed well off—I hadn't told her that I was Jewish. She only knew that I was Romanian and therefore exempt from the compulsory labor service which affected Jews and non-Jews alike.

Nor did it occur to me that I might be jeopardizing Inge as well, should we be stopped together. I simply split my life into two separate halves. One was my close friendship with my Jewish friends. We would meet on weekends at one of our respective homes, later on at Ilse Mezei's office in the Jewish Community building, and at the Jewish cemetery. My other life involved going to the theater, opera and movies, either alone or with Inge, once even to Ellmayer for a ballroom-dancing lesson. It was a stubborn attempt to lead the normal life of a typical teenager, at least as long as life in Vienna was still "normal" for those who didn't have to wear the star.

Was my association with Inge also a kind of betrayal? I would like to think of it as a purely instinctive if foolish protest against that arbitrary label which was suddenly dictating what I could and could not do, but I suspect that it was mainly thoughtlessness and a childish craving for "fun," for an escape from the worried faces all around, the daily chores, and my father's oppressive presence. As I look back at those years, it seems to me that I somehow suspended growing up in 1939 and didn't resume it until 1945 or even later—upon reaching America two years after that.

How Jewish was I? Probably as much or as little as most of my friends. I went to the Jewish elementary school where we struggled through the Hebrew alphabet and memorized the names of innumerable Old Testament judges and prophets, only to forget them the moment religious education was no longer compulsory. My grandparents went to the synagogue on the high holidays and

I of course with them, and at Passover grandpa conducted the family *seder*. Walter and I would argue for days as to who should recite the *ma nishtano*—I was the youngest but he was the boy—until grandma declared that both of us would read it, first Walter, then I. On Friday evening, grandma would come home from the store early to light candles and say the appropriate prayer. It was in Hebrew which I didn't understand, but the sounds still ring in my ears.

That was just about all I knew of Judaism, though on my school certificates my religion was listed as *mosaisch* and, if asked, I would of course have declared myself Jewish. But if questioned further, I might have tried to explain that I didn't really believe in a personal god, only in the "ideal" toward which it was imperative to strive, namely to be good and kind like grandma.

The question could be extended into the present: how Jewish am I? Or rather, am I Jewish? Still an atheist or, at best, an agnostic, I have great but not uncritical sympathy for Israel, yet am far from considering it my "homeland" or "my" country. I take pride in the fact that I don't pay heed nor seek to find out who around me is Jewish and who is not, and yet I am somehow drawn to Jews, usually feel more at home with them than with non-Jews, take pride in their achievements, and smart with their failures. I am often impelled to volunteer the information—especially to non-Jews—that I am Jewish. Out of solidarity? From an acknowledgment of the importance of tradition, ethnicity? But how so since I profess no allegiance to the Jews as a group, no adherence to their customs and priorities? Do I abhor antisemitism directed at Jews? Of course I do. At Arabs who, after all, are likewise Semites? That gets a bit sticky, though I make an effort. Am I then Jewish only by Hitler's standards, by having had Jewish grandparents and parents and not having been baptized? A discomforting conclusion which, even if correct, is hardly adequate: the phenomenon Hitler has also imparted on my Jewishness a fervor, depth and loyalty which it would probably not have had otherwise. So be it.

In the German school, most of my girl friends were Jewish, but that was mainly because we had come from the same elementary school and stuck together. Religion was not an issue until the Czech and Moravian *Sudetenland* seceded to "join the Reich," at which point the white-kneesocked crowd began to avoid us and we them. In the Czech school I don't recall anyone paying attention to who was Jewish and who was not.

After the Germans occupied Ostrau, Jews were required to take Israel or Sara as their middle names. We received Identification Cards with thumbprint and a photo with the left ear exposed—as if we were criminals. Passports had to have a big red "J" stamped inside. This, I read to my dismay recently, was instituted at the request of the Swiss police chief who wanted to stem the influx of Jewish refugees into Switzerland.

When I arrived in Vienna, I was surprised to find that none of this applied to us Romanians. Nor did our ration cards have J-marked coupons, which would have limited our shopping hours and excluded us from receiving clothing coupons and special allotments. More important, father collected our ration cards at the regular local distribution center and not at the *Zentralkartenstelle für Juden* on Taborstraße, thereby avoiding being on the list from which the Gestapo made its deportation selections. Finally, we didn't have to wear those demeaning yellow cloth stars when they became obligatory in September 1941, nor to display a star on our apartment door when that was prescribed in April 1942. You had to pay ten *Reichspfennig* for the star, and you were allowed to purchase only three altogether. Right over the heart it went, with *Jude* emblazoned in its center in large black letters, as if to mark the spot for Hagen's spear.

Not wearing the star must have confirmed me in the belief that I could do anything I wanted. On the other hand, once I had Jewish friends, it didn't seem right that I was spared this humiliation as arbitrarily as they were subjected to it. Perhaps it was that feeling that made me insist on being seen with them in public.

One time Ditha forgot her jacket at my place. For a while I studied its bright yellow star, then I put it on and went out. While I was in our neighborhood I covered the star with my purse, then I bared it. I wanted to know what it felt like—perhaps I also wanted in some minor way to make amends for my privileged status.

It was an unnerving experience. I may have imagined it, but it seemed to me that everybody was either staring at me as if I were a freak, or looking away deliberately, pretending that I didn't exist. In a defiant mood I stopped an older woman and asked for directions to a nearby street. "I don't know," she mumbled and hurried off. Two teenagers smirked and said something as I was passing. Though I didn't catch the meaning, I was sure that the remark had been pejorative and directed at me.

I stopped at a shop window, not to glance at its display but because I was startled to see my reflection wearing a star. As if I as a non-Jew was seeing a Jew for the first time, and also seeing myself for the first time as a Jew. Then I noticed that a saleslady inside was motioning to me to move on. She had an angry, mean face. I began to cross a small park, but when I saw the sign ONLY FOR ARYANS on the nearest park bench I quickly retraced my steps. In my hurry to get home I forgot to cover the star. I rushed upstairs in a sweat and tore off the jacket. I felt like an escaped convict, subhuman, branded. How could my friends stand it, how could they live in this city and among these people day after day, and not lose their self-respect or become violent?

Just then the doorbell rang. I hid the jacket in case it was Inge but it was Ditha, its owner. With amazing equanimity she picked it up, put it on, star showing, and left.

Inge shared my love for opera and we spent hours lining up for standing-room. Sometimes her friend Annemarie would join us, to my great discomfort. Annemarie was at first in the *BDM*, and later she sported a party badge. Her presence made me extremely uneasy, though she seemed nice enough. I accepted her because she was Inge's friend and I was afraid to lose Inge if I rejected Annemarie. It only occurs to me now that my associating with Annemarie was also a betrayal, probably much more so than not admitting my Jewishness to Inge.

Years later, long after Inge had obtained my American address from my father and we reestablished contact, I confided in her. No, she hadn't known that I was Jewish and not "just" Romanian, but she couldn't understand why I had made a secret of it. When I mentioned that I had suspected her father of being a Nazi, she laughed: "Come on, he was from Yugoslavia and hated the Germans! He wouldn't have dreamed of joining the party. In fact, when our classroom teacher signed everybody up for the Hitler Youth, he made such a fuss that he got me excused. How? I don't remember, but I think he invented a health problem. Too delicate for all those extra-curricular activities or something like it. That was all there was to it." That was all there was to it. How simple. And we had lived side by side with our respective secrets for four years, neither of us confiding in the other.

That conversation turned what had for a long time amounted to "being friends" into a genuine friendship. It also made me realize that it will never be possible to explain to a non-Jew what being Jewish meant during those years.

The conversation with Inge cleared the air in another way as well. I began to enjoy my visits to my father in Vienna, which before I had dreaded. I could even go past Frau Wilma's wool shop on Wipplingerstaße without hard feelings. I told myself that the time of betrayals was over, and I believed it—at least until Waldheim became president. Now I know that it's never over. A word gets redefined until it becomes unrecognizable, and only the dictionary with its unshakable memory enjoys the joke.

I don't know where and how my father met Frau Wilma, nor what their relationship was. No, nothing personal—probably black market transactions, since that was the only way he could make a little money after Mr. Guttmann, the wealthy Romanian whose financial adviser he had been, died. Frau Wilma assured us that, any time we needed a hiding place for a night or two, we should come to her and she would take care of us. But when the day came and my father sent me to her, it was the wrong night. So sorry, not today, but do try some other time!

Was Frau Wilma merely as naïve as Inge, didn't she understand that there might not be another time? Possibly, but today I am aware of how many variables there were. Perhaps she was really unable to put me up that night because of visitors in whom she couldn't confide. Or she suddenly realized that hiding a Jew might mean arrest, concentration camp, even execution.

Most people would have looked the other way to start with, would have tried hard to remain ignorant in order to avoid a confrontation with danger or guilt. She had at least offered awareness and sympathy, and thereby conveyed much-needed reassurance. That was almost as valuable as genuine help, at least up to the moment of an actual crisis. And that moment might never come. Would Jews have been more willing to risk their lives?

Some undoubtedly did, though I know of only one—Harry's father—and he paid dearly for his courage. Even the *Jüdisches Nachrichtenblatt* kept exhorting its readers to lie low, not to endanger others. Here is one example of its many regularly reiterated admonitions: *"Mahnung an die für jeden Juden unumgänglich gegebene Pflicht des bescheidenen Auftretens"*—an exhortation to all Jews to abide by the uncontrovertibly imposed duty of modest demeanor (7/Jan. 8, 1943). Recapitulation of various prohibitions was always followed by a reminder that disobedience would have *"empfindliche Straffolgen"*—serious punitive consequences (June 4, 1943).

I was, of course, willing to take all sorts of risks, but that was only because I had not yet woken up to reality and had not, in my thoughtlessness, grasped the fact that my heroics could jeopardise my life and the lives of others.

When during our first reunion Inge told me that Annemarie had died quite young and after a long and painful illness, the thought of divine retribution flashed briefly through my mind. Then I recalled my reasons for parting company with God—if I had ever been close to him—and that it was hardly fair to bring Him into this now. I was even able to feel sorry for her. Would I have been any wiser, had I been in her shoes? Every stand one takes leaves a mark, on others and on oneself. Not having choices simplifies life greatly, but it also precludes judgment. I was on the point of asking Inge how she had felt about associating with Annemarie who, after all, never made a secret of her loyalties. I didn't ask. Friendship is a rare and fragile thing.

On all those escapades with Inge into Vienna's amusement world it never occurred to me that someone might see me with my Jewish friends, and then recognize me in a movie house or the standing-room line at the opera. Nor did I take in the fact that since roundups at public places were frequent, I, who had no identification other than my J-less ration card, could get into serious trouble. My father exploded every time he found out that I had been at the movies or the opera. He called me an imbecile and threatened that if my irresponsible behavior got me arrested, he would not lift a finger to help me. I just laughed it off and some gods up on high must have laughed with me, amused by so much stupidity.

14.

On the right-hand side just before a two-storied white Victorian, the sidewalk begins, and I cross back to that side of the road. The house belongs to a long-haired black dog, part spaniel part something else. He is on the front porch no matter what time of day I walk by, and we are old friends. When he sees me come, he barks loudly and indignantly.

"You're a good boy," I call out as I approach. "It's all right, quite all right!"

Thereupon he ambles over toward me, still barking fiercely but wagging his tail with equal ferocity. I stop in my tracks and wait. He barks until he reaches me, then he cranes his neck and sniffs at my hand. These ceremonies completed, he tilts his head into petting position. We have as extended a session as I have time for, after which he trots back to the house and lies down on the porch, head raised and eyes on me. I usually turn my head and promise: "Good boy! I'll see you soon."

But on that day he wasn't there. I looked around, called—his name is Cocoa—but nobody appeared. Could something have happened to him? The house looked deserted. As I walked on, I was suddenly uneasy. He is an old dog. Perhaps he has wandered off without his collar, was found miles away, taken in, given a new name, and is now vainly waiting for the familiar combination of sounds? Nonsense, he knows where he belongs. But he is an old dog. What if he has died? Like that morning when Foxl was lying on his bed under the kitchen table, very still and rigid, and grandma said that he had died in his sleep. Then she carried him away. I didn't dare follow or ask what she was going to do with him. Instead, I crawled under the table where his mat still smelled of dog, buried my face in it and cried. I was seven then and it was my first death. Perhaps the most real death of all.

The stretch beyond the house used to be wilderness until quite recently, with blackberry brambles and wild roses. Now some of it has been cleared for a housing development, and a long semicircular road cuts into it, as if carved out with an enormous curved knife. Big signs advertise twenty-five lots for sale. Two almost identical, very plain houses stand across from each other, some twenty feet up the access road's far end. The rest of the property looks as desolate as if it had gone through an air raid.

One cheering thought though: the project was begun over a year ago and only those two houses are standing. People seem to be baulking at the undoubtedly overpriced lots, so perhaps we will be able to preserve our rural tranquility. In fact, I have personally benefited from the enterprise because, in addition to the horseshoe access road, a paved footpath was laid out along the main road. Even better, instead of following the road closely, it weaves picturesquely through the wilderness in several wide curves. After a slight rise it disappears between clumps of shrubs, veers off into a grove of tall trees and dense undergrowth, crosses a creek, and only then reemerges near the other end of the access road. The main road is invisible for much of that stretch so that I can try to imagine the droning of cars a dance of bees and flies.

But I can't. The present interferes in the shape of a woman jogger who appears from behind the first bend and smiles a "hello" as she passes. We haven't met before and I marvel at this friendly greeting from a total stranger.

As if to end the adventure with a special flourish, the path traverses a graceful wooden footbridge shortly before it ends. Despite the temporary look of the unpainted wood, there is something incongruously dainty, Japanese about the little bridge. Before the area was landscaped, the small runoff creek had turned much of it into swampland. Now the creek is shored up and tamed by the new bridge. But as I cross, I notice that the water is still stale and muddy, and the tree branches which are piled up along both banks smell of decay and decomposition. The small ravine in the Wienerwald must have smelled like that when they found the body of Renate's mother there, several months after the end of the war.

Just beyond the bridge the path ends. I turn left and after some ten yards am back on the main road.

15.

Now that I am again out in the open, I see that the sky has disappeared almost entirely behind what looks like several layers of dirty bunched-up cotton wads. Only a few bluish slits split the cloud cover. Will the weather hold at least until I reach town?

Behind a fence on the left side of the road graze several cows. I don't know the name of the breed. I guess I am still not asking enough questions. The cows accept the traffic with total equanimity. Their tails brush it off the way they brush off obstreperous flies. Further away two horses are frolicking on a succulently green meadow. Paradise may still exist, but only the crickets know how to express it.

Though the shoulder is uncomfortably narrow here, I have stopped swinging my umbrella, which I had done before to make my presence known. The echo of an old fear is resonating within me, or of an old wisdom: Don't call attention to yourself, lie low. Even a wrongful accusation can taint. The man without a shadow. The sign of Cain. A scarlet J. To be sure, the letter is invisible right now but who can tell for how long or whether to everybody? I must pull myself together—this walk is unnerving me.

Not much further the regular sidewalk resumes, harbinger of civilization. Perhaps just as well. Today I am not doing very well in my attempts at communing with nature.

Civilization means neatly trimmed lawns instead of sprawling pastures and casual fences. On the left side, one last meadow is fringed by clumps of healthy looking shrubs, then there too the manicured lawns take over.

The cottage on that side of the road sports a large FOR SALE sign. The house, white with green shutters, is well-scrubbed and polished. Even so, it has a forlorn look. The blinds are drawn, there's no car in the driveway, and something intangible casts a pall over the entire scene. Closed, finished. Everyone gone.

Is it better to end with such finality, to live with the knowledge of a death accomplished, whether successfully or grudgingly but in any case definitively? Like grandma's letter informing me of grandpa's death a few weeks after I had arrived in Vienna. Her own death was not even a "passing away". It consisted only of one last family letter, written on September 23, 1942, the eve of their deportation. In it, grandma, Erna, Paula and Walter all said their goodbyes and assured me that one day we would be reunited. It was a matter of being brave and prepared, and they were brave and prepared, bags packed, ready to go.

In a nightmare, you see a loved one slowly disappear in the distance while you stand paralyzed, unable to follow or call out. Long after the figure has vanished, its outline is still before you, frozen in its movement, unreachable but also without the certitude of real disappearance, of death. Perhaps grandma has remained so alive in my memory because she didn't die before my eyes, not in a letter and not in an eye-witness account.

Or is this disbelief in death as simplistic as our disbelief in the horrors of the camps was when that well-meaning German officer tried to warn us? I was told that even in Theresienstadt most inmates didn't believe the rumors about the extermination camps until, on December 23, 1944, 400 Jews were brought in from a Slovak camp. They were well-informed about the horrors of Auschwitz, yet even then some believed them demented (9/169). Cowardice? Delusion? Self-preservation has many faces.

Recently, I was in Israel, for the first time. That trip too was to some extent a consequence of the doors which had opened during my walk. They opened even wider on that visit, by allowing my deeply buried Jewishness to well up and give me a new sense of self. But that's not why I am mentioning it.

After much soul-searching, I decided to visit Yad Vashem, the Holocaust Memorial in Jerusalem. Though after the first few rooms the historical exhibit proved too much for me and I hurried through it not looking right or left, I did stop once more. Displayed on a lectern was a large open book, the *Wannsee Protocol*. It contained the minutes of a conference held at lake Wannsee in January 1942, with *Obergruppenführer* Reinhard Heydrich, Head of Reich Security, presiding. At that conference, fifteen top Nazi administrators established the legal basis for the annihilation of Europe's eleven million Jews. Yes, their plans encompassed eleven million, broken down country by country, including the Soviet Union and the British Isles (16/5-6). I suppose we ought to be grateful that they could only lay their hands on six million.

Equally chilling was the announcement that "in Slovakia and Croatia...the most essential problems have already been brought near to a solution. In Romania the government in the meantime has also appointed a commissioner for Jewish questions. In order to settle the question in Hungary it is imperative that an adviser on Jewish questions be pressed upon [in the German text: *aufok-truiert]* the Hungarian government without too much delay. ...In

France the registration of the Jews for evacuation can in all probability be expected to take place without great difficulties. ...In some countries, such as the Scandinavian states, difficulties will arise...and it will therefore be advisable to defer action in these countries." (16/9) Finally—"the Foreign Office anticipates no great difficulties as far as the South-East and the West of Europe are concerned." (16/10)

The entire project was delineated in sinister legalistic euphemisms. The terms used were "resettlement," "natural decline" and "the final solution" when what was meant was deportation, death from forced labor, sickness, starvation, and genocide. Eight of the fifteen participants had PhDs. The minutes were recorded by SS *Obersturmbannführer* Adolf Eichmann.

Above the Historical Museum is the Hall of Names where files of those murdered during the Holocaust are kept. You are invited to add the names of your loved ones so that there may be a lasting record of them. That felt good, and I revived. The two floors above the Hall house an art museum containing drawings by children and grownups from and about Theresienstadt. With a pounding heart I read the names and ages, half hoping, half fearing to find someone I knew. I didn't. On my way back to the exit, I noticed the Archives building and hesitated. Inside they might have exact records on where and how grandma, Erna, Paula and Walter had died. But did I really want to know? Or was it cowardice not to face reality? The same sense of obligation that had made me go to Yad Vashem now made me enter.

Yes, they had complete lists of the Jews deported from Czechoslovakia. They were arranged alphabetically—which letters did I want to see? I asked for S for grandma Silberstein, W for Paula and Walter Weiss, and L for Erna Laufer. The assistant brought me three fat manila envelopes, filled with loose sheets of paper. Columns of names, followed by birthdates and transport information, were typed in alphabetical order on consecutively numbered sheets.

I sat down in the reading room and pulled out the thick batch of S-lists. I found the Silbersteins easily—there was over a page of them—and began to look for Sophie. But there was no Sophie: Silbersteinová Malvína was followed by Silbersternová Anna. No double space, no indication of a gap. As if something or someone didn't want me to know. I reached for the V-Z envelope and had another shock. After a paginated batch of Vs came a newly paginated batch—of Zs! No Ws whatsoever. The assistant went back into the storage area to check but returned empty-handed. He had given me all they had. I reached for the Ls, convinced that I would not find anything either, but I did. Lauferová Erna, born July 25, 1902, arrived in Terezín from Ostrava on September 30, 1942, sent on to Treblinka on October 5, 1942.

Even so, as I was leaving the building I felt that I had been right to come. Months later the local Red Cross office called me in to tell me, after a few gentle preparatory remarks, that my cousin Walter had been sent from Theresienstadt to Auschwitz on February 1, 1943.

16.

The sun is back. It has torn a big hole into the clouds. Perhaps the weather is going to hold after all. Just ahead and still hidden by shrubs, something brilliantly blue comes into view. When I get closer, I see that it is a spectacular display of light blue iris in full bloom, a row almost nine feet long and over three feet high. They are beautiful and my spirit rises. Behind them a clump of birch trees paints a network of intersecting shadows onto the sidewalk. *"Und die Sonne blickt durch der Zweige Grün/ und malt auf die glänzenden Matten/ der Bäume gigantische Schatten."* Amazing that I still remember *Die Bürgschaft*, Schiller's pæan to friendship! That goes all the way back to grade school.

It was a great moment when Michael Kornblüh and I were asked to recite the poem to the class, after we told our homeroom teacher that we had memorized it.

Michael was my first love. He knew it, too. In fact, he had set it all up. He would sit in his seat, chin in hand, and stare in my direction until I felt his eyes on me and turned toward him. Then he would look away nonchalantly while I blushed. The moment I looked away, he started all over again. This went on for several days. I didn't know what to make of it, but I felt strangely elated. During the break he would deliberately turn round to see if I was there, then turn away again. By then Walter had begun to distance himself, and we no longer walked to school together. But my relationship with Walter had never been like that anyway. Did I now have a real boyfriend?

The relationship changed dramatically the day the teacher asked Michael to read a stanza from *Die Bürgschaft* aloud. During the break I mustered all my courage:

"Michael, you read that beautifully!"

"It was nothing," with a deprecating gesture.

"Oh, but it was! You sounded as if you knew it all by heart."

"Well, I know much of it."

"Really? How come you memorized it?"

"Just so. It was fun, that's all."

I memorized *Die Bürgschaft*.

"Michael, would you like us to prepare it together, each doing a stanza? We could recite it for Titi." Only her nickname has stayed with me.

"All right, as long as I don't have to waste much time on it." Then, generously: "We can rehearse tomorrow during the big break and see how it goes. Just make sure you know it properly."

Our performance was duly admired. Even Walter told me that it had been neat. Euphoric, I began to memorize other Schiller ballads, *Der Taucher*, *Die Kraniche des Ibykus*, *Kassandra*. It seemed to take less and less effort. I even began *Die Glocke*, despite its length. But by then Michael had lost interest. He was not even staring any longer. Though the romance was over, the poems have stayed with me, mementos of my first love.

The second romance came quite a few years later. I was four-teen, but to my sorrow looked much younger. I hadn't had a date yet and no male had ever invited me to promenade with him on the Korso, Ostrau's favorite young people's hangout. Perhaps that was why I admired Zdena so much. Whenever the two of us would walk up and down the Korso arm in arm as was the custom, young men she knew stopped to talk to her. Though she never neglected to introduce me, they didn't pay much attention to me, and I did not know what to say to them. Was it because I didn't have older brothers whose friends would have provided me with practice? Or because I had never had to "make conversation" with Walter? Or did I just look too young and unattractive? Even talk-ing grandma into a permanent wave—and they were torture and expensive—didn't seem to help.

Luckily I loved school. There I had no difficulties expressing myself, in fact, I found it hard to keep quiet. Only on my last report card did I manage an A in conduct. Dr. Jekyll and Ms. Hyde. Did others also have more than one self?

Some of my social education was now taken over by Karla. She and her two cousins, Hana and Erna, had attended grade school with me but then switched to the Czech school. When I arrived there, we resumed our friendship. All three were tall and very grown-up. Erna, heavy-set and wearing glasses, looked especially mature. She already wore hats and dated. Hana was shy and lanky, with a black pageboy, very blue eyes, white skin and freckles. She usually followed Karla's lead, and so did I. I liked Karla best. She too wore glasses. Her straw-blond hair was very straight and her cheeks very red. Though she was not pretty, this didn't seem to bother her in the least. She was always full of energy and ideas. Once we borrowed a gramophone and a few records, and she gave me a dancing lesson. She also introduced me to cigarettes and beer, neither of which I took to, but it was good to know that I could handle them if I had to. And one afternoon, Karla introduced me to her cousin Erich.

We were walking on the Korso together when he approached. He had arrived from Berlin only a few days before. I didn't notice that he was addressing me as *Fräulein*, and so I used the familiar *du*. He seemed a bit perplexed but continued to walk with us. When we parted, he suggested an outing to Michalkovice for Saturday. Next day Karla mentioned that Erich was twenty-five, and I was horrified at having addressed him with *du*. I must apologize the moment I see him again.

Saturday morning Karla came by to let me know that she couldn't come along on our walk—I forget the reason. I wasn't sure whether it was all right for me to walk alone with Erich, and if he would even come under these circumstances. To be sure, he didn't show up. I was convinced it was because I had said *du* to him. Terribly disappointed, I took the streetcar to Zdena's.

That evening Karla dropped in.

"Erich told me that he was delayed, and when he came to pick you up you had left. He thought he would catch up with you on the road to Michalkovice but didn't find you, so he just went walking by himself."

I could have kicked myself. Once again I had blown it. Now I would never be able to apologize and probably never see him again.

I did, though. Karla told me that Erich was giving her cousin Erna English lessons, and grandma agreed to let me join in. After the first lesson, he asked whether I was free to walk the following afternoon. Of course I was. And I never did apologize. During the lesson he addressed me now with *Sie* now with *du,* and I said *Sie.* And in English it didn't matter since there was only "you." When walking, we both used *du.* We chatted but I remained tense. I could tell that I was not really intelligent enough for a man of twenty-five, no matter how hard I tried. After we had eaten our sandwiches, we lay down under a tree and looked at the sky. Then he asked whether he could kiss me. I said "yes" and he kissed me, once, lightly, on the mouth. Then he said "thank you." I don't know what I had expected but I was very disappointed. Why did people make so much of kissing? It was nothing very special, no revelation, only a kiss like any other, like grandma's or aunt Paula's, except that he had kissed me on my mouth and they usually didn't. And did the "thank you" indicate that he was pleased or had he just been polite? Should I not have agreed to his kissing me? Or protested at least a little? My disappointment was eased by the realization that I had not been missing much.

On the way home Erich treated me to an ice cream cone. After some protesting, I let him pay, again unsure whether that was the right thing to do. When we parted he said: "Thank you for the pleasant outing. I'll see you on Monday at our lesson." Though he used *du* I was convinced that he wouldn't ask me out again.

The lessons were good and I learned a great deal. But when grandma stopped them because money was tight, I didn't really mind. I had begun the sewing course by then and it kept me busy. Shortly after that, Karla left for Prague. I don't know when Erich left but in any case my second romance was over.

17.

The train reached Vienna at ten-thirty in the evening. There was still time to toast to the New Year in aunt Irma's apartment before we went to bed. Around ten the next morning my father arrived. The first moments were awkward. He seemed very much a stranger, shorter than remembered but very good-looking. With his high, receding forehead, black, slightly wavy hair, regular features and dark, bushy eyebrows, he reminded me a little of Tonda. His speaking manner was similarly calm and deliberate, and that too I liked.

Father explained that three families had been assigned to our apartment so that he and grandmother Vera only had the *Kabinett* to themselves, the former maid's quarters. Since that held barely enough space for their two beds, I would sleep at the apartment of good friends of his who lived close by. It wouldn't be for long anyway. Our passport situation ought to be resolved soon and then we would leave Austria.

At first the arrangement seemed strange and made me uncomfortable, but the two women were friendly and I soon felt at home with them. More so, in fact, than with father and grandmother Vera. Both spoke German with an attractive Hungarian accent which I soon slid into and which must have mixed oddly with what father called my "Czech singsong."

The mother, Frau Mehr, was in her late fifties. She was short and pudgy, but not really heavy. Her hair was gray and curly and pulled back into a low bun, her face was round and somehow washed out, almost expressionless. She spoke very softly, usually with an apologetic smile or an embarrassed shrug. Magda was short as well but thin, with long, very light wavy hair, a small, triangular face, a large nose and thick glasses. Her voice was loud and high-pitched. There was something old-maidish about her, though she might not have been thirty. She was a heavy smoker and seemed propelled by a tense, restless energy. She was often impatient with her mother but always nice to me.

The Mehrs were very hospitable—almost every evening father and other visitors would come for tea and conversation—and yet they seemed strangely subdued, as if permanently frightened or depressed. I felt sorry for them without knowing why. I don't think father had an affair with Magda, even though she quite obviously found him attractive. It might have done her good.

I lodged with them for eight months and was quite happy there.

Frau Mehr reminded me a bit of grandma. Though I was supposed to be "at home" for breakfast by eight-thirty, I often overslept because they never woke me, considering sleep important for a youngster. On those days, they would invite me to have breakfast with them, and I accepted happily. This made father very angry. We don't need anybody's charity, he said.

Life in Vienna was different from anything I knew. Grandmother Vera was tall and white-haired, an imposing woman who must have been very beautiful in her youth and still was. She was hard of hearing and spoke so quietly that it took an effort to understand her. Her movements were slow and majestic. Her head trembled a little when she was agitated, and she was often agitated.

Of the three other women who used the kitchen, Frau Schratter was a real shrew, a *Biskurn*, as the Viennese would say, nosy, overbearing and rude. Her hair was very straight and short, like white straw. The round metal frame of her glasses gave her face an owlish look. Her mouth was pinched even when she wore her dentures, and you could hear her loud, shrill voice from one end of the apartment to the other.

In contrast, her daughter Grete never raised her voice. Even so, she always sounded tense, as if she had to use all her will power not to explode and tell her mother what was what. Grete was in her thirties and exceedingly heavy, and her tread across the large hallway made the walls shake. Her hair was grayish brown, tied into a loose, low bun, and it always looked as if she had just got out of bed. It was hard to catch her side of an argument because she kept her voice down, but eventually she always seemed to acquiesce to her mother's demands or commands. After any such altercation her face would turn very red and she would stomp out of the kitchen across the hallway, through her parents' room and into the *Kabinett* which she shared with her husband, slamming every door. She didn't reemerge for hours, and an ominous silence would settle over the house.

Both husbands were quiet, polite and hardly in evidence. Nor was the third family, the Rieglers, a couple with two sons in their twenties. The father was tall, pointed and thin, the mother short and round. They made perfect illustrations for a Dickens novel. She was a cook at the Jewish hospital, which meant that she came home at night with bulging pockets. I don't recall what he did, but both seemed hard workers. They left the house early and returned late.

Frau Riegler's aunt—at least everybody referred to her as *die Tante*—was a tiny, toothless and shrivelled old woman who came every day to clean their room, make their beds and cook for them. With great agility she climbed the four flights, not trusting the elevator. On Fridays I would watch with fascination how skillfully and rapidly she braided two loaves of *challah*, the sweet white bread used for the Friday evening candle-lighting ceremony. Often she would save a handful of dough and braid a tiny loaf for me, as long as I promised not to tell Frau Riegler. The sons kept irregular hours. Ostensibly they were "porters" but most likely also black marketeers. Since the Rieglers' room was adjacent to our *Kabinett*—with the connecting door locked from our side—we heard much arguing at night, the mother calling them good-for-nothings and potential jailbirds. Grandmother Vera claimed that the entire Riegler clan were thieves. She kept marking her flour and sugar containers and swore that someone was dipping into them in her absence.

Grete's father as well as her husband were working at the Community, which protected both families. The Rieglers were likewise safe because they worked for an affiliated establishment. I lost track of all of them after we had to vacate the apartment.

Grandmother Vera liked to talk about the past, and since father was rarely at home, I was her audience. She spoke of her pampered childhood—the Gherzans were a wealthy Jewish family in Odessa—and of her unhappy love affair with a Russian officer of the hussars whom her father wouldn't let her marry. My grandfather was much older than either of the sisters he married. Men tended to fear his sharp tongue and ascerbic pen, according to aunt Jenny, but he was a great ladies' man and could have any woman he wanted. He doted on his five boys and they adored him. Any window they broke he paid for without a word of reproach, for "youth must have its fling." However, he ignored the girls, Olga and Jenny, and so apparently did their mother.

Vera was probably not only unhappy but bored. There was enough money for maids, wet nurses and governesses, and she must have had too much time on her hands. She consoled herself with dressing to the height of fashion, giving tea parties, going to balls. Aunt Jenny recalled how, dressed for the opera or the theater, she would put in a brief appearance in the nursery so that the children could kiss her hand and wish her a good night. Even so, during the war Jenny regularly sent some of her hardearned money to her mother, in a complicated transaction which involved transferring the money from England to a certain Dr. Sandmann, a former suitor of Jenny's, who was in France. Upon notification from him, his mother, who lived in Vienna, would bring the corresponding sum to grandmother Vera. Even so, Jenny was never able to talk without bitterness about her mother and her own loveless childhood.

By the time grandmother Vera married again, all children had left home. Apparently that marriage wasn't happy either, though she never spoke of it or of her second husband. His name was Margosches. I have one photograph of the two together, both middle-aged, very dignified and proper looking. He is wearing a monocle, her mouth is set. Neither of them is smiling. I also have several photographs of grandmother Vera alone. They show her in magnificent gowns with pearls and feathers, beautiful and haughty, and with a pained line around her mouth.

Grandmother Vera was always nice to me and I liked her. However, I found it very embarrassing and gradually more and more upsetting that, whenever she was not talking about her past or the neighbors, she would invariably complain about my father. How he showed no appreciation for what she did for him, how she saved the best morsels of food for him, shortchanging herself, and that he accepted everything as his due, without thanks or a kind word. Nor did he ever give her pocket money. If "Janderl" didn't send her money now and then, she wouldn't know what to do.

At first I defended father but gradually I began to side with grandmother Vera because my experiences were similar to hers, and I began to feel sorry for both of us.

Father had assigned our duties as follows: grandmother Vera had to cook and do the laundry, whereas I was to shop and take care of the accounts. It was a thankless job which lead to constant friction.

"You're out of money already? What did you do with it? Are you putting it aside for yourself or are you being cheated? And have you made sure that mother is paying for her share of the food?" Of course I have, though I hate to ask her for money because she has so little. She is entirely dependent on the pittance she receives from the Community, and on what aunt Jenny sends. Nor can I help her out. All I get is one mark pocket money every three months, which is nothing. Every time I need toothpaste I have to come begging.

Father also made me quit Nelly Grossmann's fashion design course which I had begun to take in March, and which was my great joy. It's a waste of money, he said; you can draw at home just as well. Luckily, he didn't stop my English classes with Nelly's sister, despite his remark that if I took a dictionary and memorized the words alphabetically at two letters a day, I would know English in less than a month.

Zdena was sending long letters urging me to come back. How I wished I could!

18.

When father heard about my sewing class at the Ostrau convent, he signed me up for a course in pattern-making. That was right after my arrival in Vienna. I can't recall if this was one of the Community's retraining courses, but in any case it turned out extremely useful. By learning how to make dress patterns to individual measurements, I was able to make my own basic pattern and, with its help, accomplish successful old-into-new transformations throughout the war. After the course ended, my instructor, Fräulein Hermine Rosenfeld, suggested—and my father gladly concurred—that I stay on as an apprentice, one of two non-paying and unpaid helpers.

Like everyone else, Fräulein Rosenfeld had to take Sara as a middle name, but she defiantly left Sara behind whenever she could. She also insisted on being called *Fräulein*, though everyone else would have been offended at being addressed as "Miss" once they had reached thirty. She did not consider herself a seamstress but kept stressing that she was an *"haute couturière."*

What were the qualifications of an *haute couturière*, judging by Fräulein Rosenfeld? To smirk at the workmanship of anything not produced by her, to brainwash her clients into demanding what she wanted them to demand, into liking what she liked and into paying outrageous prices for her artistic creations. To my amazement, despite her peremptory ways she had quite a following. Her customers were mainly non-Jews who sought her out clandestinely, disregarding the maxim of the day according to which race and religion determined quality. Her Axiom One was: clothes make the woman, even more so in times of war. Axiom Two: Hermine Rosenfeld knows best what suits the customer.

Needless to say, her Jewish clientele was minimal, first because they couldn't afford her, second because they wouldn't take her sharp tongue sitting down, and third because she was not willing to waste time and talent on resewing. She considered it degrading to turn old coats into new jackets, jackets into vests, dresses into jumpers, blouses into scarves and so on, which was the best a fashion-conscious Jew could do in the absence of clothing coupons.

Fräulein Rosenfeld was the stereotypical spinster. Haggard, with glasses balanced on the tip of her long nose, and with habitually compressed lips, she seemed a reincarnation of the widow Bolte in *Max und Moritz*. Except that I was neither Max nor Moritz and therefore suffered. Under the nuns' pragmatic eyes, slips and nightgowns had been stitched up in no time, with little or no basting. If a seam wasn't totally straight, it could be doctored up or ignored, as long as the flaw was not too noticeable. Now everything had to be chalked out, basted, marked and remarked—pinning was taboo—and every seam had to be ironed down before and after basting, once again after it was sewed and a fourth time after it was neatly finished. Every lining had to be held down by tiny, invisible stitches. At least initially, I had to do much of my handiwork over again and again.

I disliked Fräulein Rosenfeld, but I learned much from her, if not exactly what she set out to teach me. I realized that once you knew what you wanted and how you wanted it to look, you could make imaginative improvisation look like quality custom sewing. This proved especially useful during the first years of emigration, when I had very little money but knew how to change a neckline or sleeves of a second-hand acquisition, add a pocket here, a scarf there, raise or lower a waist or hem. The result was almost as good as if I had acquired something new.

What made the apprenticeship bearable was the presence of another victim. Miriam was only thirteen but much more developed than I—"buxom" seems the right word—with a long, thick, jetblack braid, curly ringlets around her ears and dark mischievous eyes. Her sewing was even worse than mine, but criticism slid off Miriam like water from oilcloth. The irresistible faces she made behind Fräulein Rosenfeld's back often got me into trouble.

Since we spent hours together every morning, I soon became familiar with Miriam's dramatic life story. I don't recall if she was Jewish since the star had not yet been imposed, but I assume so. However, she was an orphan, had been shunted from relative to relative, sexually abused by an uncle when she was nine and raped by a friend of the family when she was eleven. One member of the clan—the relationship was not fully clarified—had taken a liking to Miriam and suggested adopting her. But whoever was in charge of her tried to undermine the adoption—I don't recall the reasons. They described her to the rich cousin as a real problem child, lazy, unreliable and whatnot, whereupon he arranged the apprenticeship with Fräulein Rosenfeld. If after six months the progress report was satisfactory, he would reassess the situation. I didn't think that Miriam was trying very hard to prove herself, but perhaps that was because she had other things to worry about.

There were actually two additional problems. First of all, she was not sure about the cousin's intentions. He was a widower and Miriam suspected that he might have amorous designs on her, even though he knew nothing of the infamous rape. The other problem was even worse. Miriam had a boyfriend and now her period was late. If anything should be wrong, they would kill her. Unless she committed suicide first.

I, whose sex life up to that time amounted to a few stares and one fatherly kiss, was both appalled and fascinated. And tremendously impressed by Miriam's ability to cope with these horrendous crises without going to pieces. Yet, her talking of suicide worried me since I was unable to tell how serious she was. I offered to ask Frau Mehr or Magda if they knew a physician who would perform an abortion, but Miriam wouldn't hear of it. Every morning my first question was whether her period had come, and every day

I marvelled more at her calm, especially if I compared her to what I had been like at thirteen and still was like at fifteen.

Then came the morning when, as I put my daily question to Miriam, she burst out laughing: "Come on, you silly, I'm not pregnant! I was just kidding."

"Then there's no problem with the adoption?"

"Oh, I made that up too. My parents would make a fine face if anyone tried to adopt me."

"You are not an orphan?"

"No way! I live with my parents and my little brother."

"And what about the uncle who abused you?"

"You don't think I would let anyone abuse me, do you?"

"But then why did you tell me all these stories?"

"For the fun of it. You liked them, didn't you?"

"I see." But I didn't see. I was angry because she had made a fool of me, and bewildered because the Miriam I thought I knew had dissolved into contradictions and left a stranger behind, a very strange stranger for whom telling lies—and what lies!—was a way of having fun.

A few days later she arrived at work very excited and reported that she'd almost been arrested for shoplifting, but had eluded the clerk by hiding in a restroom. There she had pinned up her hair, put on makeup and tied her scarf into a turban. She left unrecognized.

"Oh yeah?" I said. "Good for you."

Not much later, my sewing career came to an end for some unremembered reason, and I signed up for Nelly Grossmann's fashion design course.

Though I never saw Miriam again, the episode kept haunting me. This attractive and vivacious girl had seemed so totally sincere and straightforward that my heart had gone out to her. And all that time, while I admired her and agonized over her plight, she manipulated me and was laughing at me. This was a betrayal much more reprehensible than Zdena's. How could she do this to me—for no reason except a joy in dissimulation, for no purpose other than to make a fool of me? How could I believe anybody if someone as charming and friendly as Miriam could be a liar? How could I ever tell what people were really like and what their motives were? I resolved not to trust anyone ever again, not to expect anything from anybody, so that I couldn't be hurt as much as this denigration was hurting. I didn't realize that the new principle clashed with my very basic need for acceptance and affection, and that it would therefore at best mitigate but not prevent future "betrayals."

19.

The Czech cobbler around the corner listens regularly to foreign broadcasts. He confides in me because I speak Czech. To my dismay, he claims that the war will last at least another year, even though "the Czechs are working at it."

To be sure, things don't look good at all. The war's been on for less than a year and Hitler has occupied much of Europe. The Danes apparently offered little resistance, and although Norway did fight and had England's support, it lost. Holland and Belgium have capitulated, and a few days ago Paris was under German bombardment. Everyone's hope, the Maginot Line, has turned out useless. And yesterday Mussolini declared war on England and France. Now we are trapped without an escape route, and those who fled to some of these countries and felt secure there may be trapped as well. Even the Aryans are uneasy. All these victories are outright uncanny.

Ironically, we have just received a letter from Olga, mailed in Austria and thus uncensored: "Dear brother, Mr. Adler wrote from Shanghai that work permits are on the way for you and Liesl. I have of course requested one for mother as well and hope that he sends it soon. Max has left for Palestine. He sent a note from Bengasi in Libya where they put in a stop. I will follow in a few days." Now that Italy is at war, she may not be able to get out.

Father has been promised a passport by the Romanian consulate. It will come in the nick of time since Romanians without passports are now being drafted into the labor force. Jews are of course assigned the toughest jobs—road work, factories, at best piecework at home "in support of the war effort." Father is talking of our leaving for Romania when the passport arrives, or of somehow making our way to Palestine. Although Romania is neutral, neither sounds enticing.

20.

Intersection and traffic light. Were I to continue straight, I would soon be back among the meadows but to get to town, I must turn right here and head up Main Street. It isn't very "main" yet but will eventually take me into the center of town.

B&S Glass takes up the righthand corner. As I round it, I notice a huge new sign, right by the entrance and mounted on a post rammed into the lawn. It reads: "We thank you for allowing us to serve you." Genuine appreciation or shrewd commercialism? Truth or make-believe? But there's no need to think in extremes— it could well be one of those disarming combinations that are so common in this both generous and self-serving country: Don't miss the opportunity—ample parking—phone orders welcome— fast service—free delivery—all credit cards accepted. How simple life can be! I wonder how many customers of B&S Glass can even imagine what it was like to live with windows covered with blankets or cardboard after a bomb had shattered the glass, or to stand in one of those endless lines between eleven and one, the only time Jews with J-marked ration cards were allowed to shop. How would they feel about having to prepare a meal with nothing but potatoes available? Baked potatoes, potato salad, potato goulash, potato pie.

During my recent visit to Vienna, I discovered in the University library a bound volume of the *Jüdisches Nachrichtenblatt*, The Jewish Community's newssheet. The 1943 issues contained quite a number of recipes. Here are a few revealing samples:

Potato dumplings:
Use potatoes, rye flour, egg-substitute and salt. May be served
  with sugar or cinnamon substitute.

Stuffed cabbage:
Stuff cabbage with barley, serve with potatoes and artificial
  gravy.

Semolina cake:
1 cup semolina, 1 cup liquid, 1/2 cup sugar. Mix and set aside for

3 hours. Mix in 1 package baking powder, some cocoa powder and lemon substitute. Bake. Fill with jam. (All from the January 8, 1943 issue.)

Egg cake without eggs:
Vanilla, water, baking powder, rye flour, salt, sugar. Fry it and you have a complete meal.

Carrot schnitzel:
Grate carrots, mix with potatoes, salt, paprika, pepper substitute, garlic and bread crumbs. Coat with flour and bake. (Both from February 26, 1943.)

Household hints:
To wash woolens without soap use water and a chalk paste. (April 25, 1943)
Potato peel soup makes a good cleaning substance for glass, window frames, stoves, cutlery etc. (July 30, 1943)

No wonder my cooking was nothing to brag about. However, after grandmother Vera was gone, father had to put up with it until Frau Litzi and her black market connections took over.

21.

In the summer of 1940, the Russians occupied the northern Bukovina, and father and I went to the Soviet Consulate to apply for repatriation. When the Germans overran much of the area a few months later, we began to worry that we might now be considered enemy aliens. Luckily, nothing happened—who knows what became of the files at Vienna's Soviet Consulate. Even so, I didn't dare visit the Soviet Union until 1989, despite my American passport, and even then I went sort of incognito, as a member of a group.

During the first days of 1941, the pressures increased drastically. Jews were no longer allowed to use public phone booths or the central telephone exchange. Their own phones had been requisitioned long before, together with all electric appliances, jewelry, furs, typewriters and bicycles. Now their bank accounts were blocked as well, except for small monthly sums which would barely sustain them. They were not allowed to have pets, use public transport, libraries or hair salons, buy newspapers or magazines other than the *Jüdisches Nachrichtenblatt*—I have probably forgotten many other items since I was not affected. I marvelled at how my friends managed to lead fairly normal lives in these strait jackets.

And it got worse. A rumor sprang up that all Jews would be moved to Poland. It seemed too unbelievable to be taken seriously, and at first people shrugged it off. But on the first of February, all retraining courses were canceled as of that day, and a few days later summons to *Prinz Eugenstraße* began to arrive. There, in the former Rothschild Palace, the Gestapo's Jewish Emigration Center had established itself, Eichmann's office "for the solution of the Jewish question." "*Prinz Eugen, der edle Ritter...*" we had sung in school. The noble knight who had saved us from the Turks—where was he now?

This time the news could not be shrugged off: one thousand people were to be relocated to Poland. The summons was the first step, and now the mailman's visit was awaited with trepidation. On the street, people looked askance at one another—the way one looks for the telltale signs of leprosy or the plague.

On February 15, a transport of one thousand men, women and children left "for resettlement" after spending a week at the Jewish school on Kleine Sperlgasse which had been turned into an assembly center. Fifty kilograms of luggage were allowed, but most people had less because they couldn't carry that much. They had to sign statements confirming that they were leaving voluntarily and had donated their remaining possessions to the *Reich*, in lieu of payment for resettlement expenses. Nothing like law and order.

The first transport consisted primarily of people with stateless passports or without any papers. They had received expulsion notices several weeks before, but could of course not leave the country without proper papers. Among them were many old, frail and sick people. It was obvious that few of them would reach the resettlement camp alive.

On Wednesday, February 19, another thousand left. Almost

everyone had friends or relatives among those already deported or those sitting on their bags at the school, waiting to be loaded on trucks and eventually into freight cars. There was absolutely nothing one could do to help them, no authority to protest to or plead with. The phones at the Community rang incessantly, and Ilse Mezei, the switchboard operator, repeated over and over: "No, unfortunately they haven't been called off. I'm afraid the next one will leave on schedule."

After the undesirable aliens had been disposed of, it was the turn of those receiving subsidies, either in cash or as meals from the *Ausspeisung*, the Community's soup kitchen. Then came those not protected by working for the Community or for an enterprise considered indispensable to the war effort. And even these exemptions could be withdrawn at any time. With obvious sadism, the selection process was often turned over to the Community's administration by the simple command that they designate a certain number of previously exempt employees for the next transport. Divide and conquer—not a new idea and not less terrifying for being a cliché.

More reliably protected were those who were married to non-Jews, especially if they had children baptized by 1935. Mixed marriages with Jewish children were likewise safe—though all but the Aryan member had to wear the star—except that their privileged status was terminated if the non-Jewish partner died, divorced or was arrested on a valid or trumped-up charge. Early in 1945, only weeks before the Russians took Vienna, a deportation order was issued for the Jewish-raised children of mixed marriages and their Jewish parent. Fortunately, the Council of Elders managed to stall long enough to prevent their deportation, and some of my friends were saved.

Transports left every Wednesday, week after week. At first we were lucky. Neither grandmother Vera nor father and I were summoned, even though Vera didn't have a valid passport or any other reliable paper, and we worried that she might be viewed as stateless. Our passport had not arrived either, with the hearing once again postponed, now to July 14.

Gradually the first letters began to trickle in. Only the second transport had reached a sizeable Jewish settlement, and that group was fairly well housed and fed. The others complained of hunger, cold, backbreaking labor and other hardships. Everyone was asking for food, clothing, and blankets. People were stripping themselves bare in order to send packages, though it was not at all certain that they would reach their destination. After a few weeks, the Gestapo prohibited all packages.

The *Jüdisches Nachrichtenblatt* carried long columns of death notices, many as tersely revealing as this one, of February 23, 1941:

Pollak, Hans Israel, 43, III. Sebastianplatz 7
Pollak, Marianne Sara, 44, III. Sebastianplatz 7

Just then, having accumulated the required number of clothing coupons, I managed to talk father into letting me have some money to buy material for a winter dress. Magda and her mother had left for Hungary by then, but Anny, a friend of the family, offered to go shopping with me.

We were lucky to find a reasonably priced piece of very attractive burgundy-colored wool cloth. Just in time, too. A few days later, the *Hauswart*'s wife came to collect our food and clothing ration books. Henceforth, Jewish foreigners would be getting J-marked food stamps. That meant the end of clothing rations—later also of meat, eggs, wheat products and milk—and long lines because of the restricted shopping hours.

The seamstress whom Anny had recommended, at first refused to take my measurements. She had been notified to prepare for deportation, and though she hadn't heard anything further in two weeks, she could be called up any day. I talked her into taking the material, just in case a third week might pass without her having to go. Perhaps it would bring her luck. It didn't—two days later the cloth was back in my possession. She had been assigned to the fifth transport. I didn't know what to say except for the clichés we all used and nobody believed any more: "You'll soon be back, the war can't last much longer."

Grandmother Vera's summons arrived during the week of the fourth transport, just after I had bought the material. She was still there to admire it. Father accompanied her to the assembly center in Castellezgasse, carrying her little suitcase. Then, with almost foolhardy courage, he went straight to "Brunner Two," the

Gestapoman in charge of transports. He was feared almost as much as *Obersturmführer* "Brunner One," the First Lieutenant of the SS who was called in on "special" cases. I wonder what became of the two? Were they tried and sentenced, or still around when it was time to vote for Waldheim?

That puzzle piece has likewise fallen into place by now: Brunner Two (Anton), a bookkeeper by profession who had been made State Commissioner for Confiscated Jewish Property, apparently without even being a party member—and who was, incidentally, dispatched by Eichmann to Ostrau in 1939 to supervise the Nisko operation—was convicted and hanged on May 10, 1956. Brunner One (Alois) disappeared and was never brought to trial. He is rumored to live somewhere in Syria (4/528).

Father asked that grandmother be released because she was old and ill, and a Romanian citizen. Brunner Two let father finish. Then he said with a sly grin: "If you are so concerned about your mother, why don't you volunteer to go with her?" "*Zurück, du rettest den Freund nicht mehr, so rette das eigene Leben!*" In Schiller's *Bürgschaft* unselfishness was rewarded; in real life it rarely is. Father returned home and grandmother Vera left for infinity.

This was the first of only two times when I saw father lose his composure. So he wasn't such a bad stepson after all. The other time was at the very end of the war.

Grandmother Vera left with the fifth transport, and people began to pack for the sixth. It seemed as if it would go on and on until the last Jew was deported. But you learn to accept almost anything. People were no longer talking about the transports. They went about their daily business as if nothing were wrong. At most they would answer unemotionally—"No, not yet" or "Yes, I have. My bag is packed and I am ready." Every day revolved around the one excruciating moment—the arrival of the mailman. If he left without delivering a summons, you heaved a sigh of relief knowing that life could go on as usual for another day.

Just then father's passport arrived, issued by the Vienna Consulate. Perhaps the weekly transports had convinced the

Romanian consul that speedy action was needed and so he took matters into his own hands. As a minor, I was included on the passport. Though it was valid for only six months, six months were an eternity just then. It was a life saver, literally. It likewise protected me from the compulsory labor service into which I would otherwise have been drafted.

Initially, father had talked about repatriating to Romania. I don't know what made him abandon that option. Perhaps he was unable to get the required exit permit, or he had doubts about our safety there. After Romania joined the Axis powers on November 23, 1940, there was no telling what pressures the Germans might exert. At any rate, for the moment we were safe in Vienna.

As once before, father's hesitation turned out to be a blessing. Just recently I read that Romania and Croatia were the only two German satellite countries to organize their own "final solution." Between them, they killed 200,000—300,000 Jews, and the accounts of atrocities committed by the Romanian Iron Guard in late November 1940 make your hair stand on end (8/415).

However, when in late 1943 the war turned against the Germans, anti-German forces began to rally in Romania and the remaining 300,000 Jews were not sent to the death camps. After Antonescu's overthrow in August 1944, Romania switched sides officially.

While people were waiting to be collected for the sixth transport, a new rumor spread with lightning speed: the transports were called off. At first we didn't believe it, but soon the Community office confirmed the good news. Their information was reliable since they had to supply the appropriate number of *Ordner* and *Packer* every time a transport was assembled. Incidentally, the reason for the cessation of transports was not a humanitarian impulse but the need to transport troops to Bulgaria, where the German military was massing in preparation for the attack on Yugoslavia and Greece (10/23).

The good news was celebrated as if it were *Sylvester*—New Year's Eve. Strangers were hugging and kissing in the street, offering to share their meals, their precious cup of coffee. Tears flowed freely, smiles were ecstatic. The worst was over and normal life could be resumed. Except by grandmother Vera.

22.

Normal life meant life with father. Actually, it was no longer as bad as initially. To be sure, he continued to make me account for every penny I spent on groceries, and I was deeply hurt that he trusted me so little. He likewise continued to demand the lion's share of our rations—"a grown man needs more than a child!"— and I had to relinquish my weekly egg to him, as well as watch him use up his butter ration within a day or two and then dip into the cooking lard, of which there wasn't enough anyway.

He would spend his days with friends, for all I knew, or play chess or bridge somewhere, while I had to shop, cook, clean, wash, iron and mend his socks. I did all of that quite resentfully, remembering how in Ostrau "the child" had always come first. He was as stingy with me as he had been with grandmother Vera. Inge had to treat me to the movies more than once.

Even so, grandmother Vera's departure drew us closer together, as if we realized that we only had each other now, that we needed one another. I knew that in return for my keeping house for him, father was protecting me and would get us out of Vienna the moment it was possible. When he shouted at me for taking risks, I appreciated it even if I didn't mend my ways. Which I no longer did from spite—if they deport me, you won't have anyone to cook and clean for you!—but only because I felt so sure that nothing bad would happen to me, and because I wanted so badly "to live" while I was still young.

Father also began to help me carry the groceries, at least if they fitted into his briefcase—for he would not be caught dead with a shopping bag. Also, he brought books home for me to read, *Crime and Punishment* and, when I asked for more Dostoevsky, *The Brothers Karamazov*, which launched me on endless speculations about the existence and nature of god, human justice, the problem of evil. Yet, although I took the heavy burden of the universe onto my shoulders, I didn't give much thought to Hitler and to what he was doing to the Jews, Czechs, Gypsies, Poles, the sick, his own people, Europe, and the world. Whatever little of that I knew or suspected, I accepted simply as temporary: all would be well once the war was over.

At that time, I even forgave father—though not without considerable pride in my own magnanimity and with a stubborn residue of bitterness—for a remark which had rankled a long time.

"You are too strict with the child," Magda had said to him, not realizing that I was in earshot. "She has a very sensitive soul."

"Children have no soul," he had replied.

Even though my attitude had improved considerably, I still found it difficult to talk to him and didn't know how to make him talk to me. Perhaps that was part of the problem. Grandma had always listened. Even when she had no time for me I knew where she was, what she was doing and that she loved me and worried about me. Grandmother Vera had not shown much interest in me and my thoughts, but at least she had shared with me her little aggravations, observations and memories, and had appreciated my sympathy. Father refused to reveal any aspect of his life to me. He might be an hour late for supper so that it was all dry and tasteless by the time he arrived, while I worried half to death about what to do should he have been arrested. He would complain about the quality of the food, but it never occurred to him to apologize for being late, or at least to explain. If I asked him where he was going or where he had been, I was told that that was none of my business. Had there been an emergency, I would not have known where to find him or how to get word to him, and now that the Mehrs were gone I had no one to turn to.

23.

Fortunately and almost miraculously, a circle of girl friends always materialized when I was at my loneliest. Not long after one group dispersed, another would surface and fill the void.

Sylvia Walzer, Liesl Obernbreit and Ilse Markstein made up the first group a few months after my arrival in Vienna. I met Sylvia and Liesl in the fashion design course. I doubt that many of those retraining courses provided us with marketable skills, but at least they gave us something to do and a place to congregate.

I don't remember how and when I met Ilse. Perhaps she too attended the course, or someone there introduced us. We hit it off immediately and became "best friends." I felt as close to her as to Hanna and much closer than to Zdena or Karla. Her parents were quiet, gentle people. I felt at home with them, especially with her mother. Until Ilse left for North Germany to work in the asparagus fields—she volunteered in the hope that that would protect her parents from deportation—we spent much time together at her place or mine. That was one advantage of my father's never being at home.

Ilse was dark blond, chubby and very pretty. She radiated warmth, high spirits and solicitude. I could pour my heart out to her, and she always managed to cheer me up. She never seemed to need cheering until her letters from the labor camp in Aschersleben began to arrive, and even then she tried not to complain. Instead, she urged me to allow her to share my worries. But by then her problems were worse than mine had ever been, and I tried hard to convey affection and hope.

It was not easy for our foursome to find something to do and places to go. Parks were off-limit and so were movies, concerts, theaters, museums, public baths, libraries—in other words, everything except the streets, and there you were not allowed to congregate. At that time we had not yet discovered the Jewish cemetery which later became our Sunday recreation spot. All we could do was get together at our respective homes, talk, play games or dance to the tunes we hummed until the curfew—eight in winter, nine in the summer—drove us home.

One day I asked father how to play bridge. I did it mainly to have him talk to me and because I knew that bridge was one of his passions. It worked. He explained the basic rules of the game quite patiently. I conveyed them to my friends, and we began to play. Whenever we had questions, I would ask father how to handle specific situations. At first he was very condescending, doubting that the game we played could really be bridge, but after he had watched us play he admitted that we weren't half bad. He taught us various bidding conventions and a few other strategies, and soon the four of us were an enthusiastic team of pros. Bridge was a godsend—it filled the hours. For that same reason, I have been avoiding it ever since.

When Liesl left for Sweden in June 1941, we recruited Pulli, another member of our fashion design team. Pulli was only her nickname, but I can't recall her real name. What I do remember is that she was quite tall, on the heavy side, but with an interesting face with blue eyes, very white skin, black frizzled hair, a small sensuous mouth and two dimples which restored its innocence. She plucked her eyebrows into a pencil-thin curve which inspired me to do likewise, something I regretted later when they filled in very irregularly. Pulli was quite nearsighted but refused to wear glasses. I remember her eyes as narrow slits under the thin, plucked eyebrows. That made her look oriental, which likewise impressed me. She was so quiet that none of us knew much about her, but she played bridge well and made a good fourth.

After Ilse's departure, we recruited Lilli, another student from Nelly Grossmann's class. She was pale, blond, and orthodox. Her creed forbade her to take part in our séances, but playing bridge was apparently all right.

There were about ten of us in that fashion design course. Sylvia was one of the most gifted, and her fashion sketches had a lot of flair. She was even selling some. I believe Frau Nelly arranged that. My own work was not bad, but undistinguished. I didn't mind. The important thing was that I had an excuse for getting out of the house three mornings a week, and someone to talk to.

In the room adjoining our classroom, Frau Nelly's sister, Lucie Ellenbogen, taught English to a small group. Rumor had it that something else was going on in that room as well, and it didn't take me long to be initiated into "the inner circle."

Fräulein Lucie was able to call up spirits by means of a ouija board. Whether or how she used her "gift" otherwise I don't know. We were of course sworn to secrecy because one could get arrested for such things. Four or five of us would sit around a small round table topped by a cardboard circle. Along its rim, the letters of the alphabet were hand-drawn, with spaces between them. Inside the alphabet circle were two smaller circles, one marked "yes," the other "no." A turned-over glass was placed inside a small center circle. We were instructed to touch the glass very lightly with our fingertips. So did Fräulein Lucie, our guide to the supernatural. After a while, the glass began to describe small, then larger circles, cruising from letter to letter in even, rhythmic movements, stopping briefly at each, then moving on to the next.

They were strange creatures, these spirits that visited us. They would answer our questions with odd and often ambiguous statements. "Will the war end soon?"—"Time brings solace." "Will I be deported?"—"Think of what is close at hand." "Who are you?"—"The king's jester."

The king's jester came quite frequently and usually talked in rhyme, sometimes in riddles. Deciphering the messages was a slow process since we had to piece together each sentence letter by letter. In the middle of an animated conversation, the glass might suddenly spell "I must go," move back into the center and stand stock still.

We were intrigued, although for a long time suspicious that Fräulein Lucie was making it all up, that she was guiding the glass from letter to letter. However, when we tried to steer the glass without her, we found that we were unable to make it move without putting considerable pressure on it, and even then it moved jerkily and unevenly. And since the glass resumed its harmonious circles the moment she put her hand over ours, even if she barely touched our fingers and most definitely not the glass, we were converted.

After a few of these sessions, Fräulein Lucie suggested that we find out whether there was another medium among us to help her. Apparently calling spirits was hard work. We put our fingertips on the glass without her, in groups of three. For most of us, the glass remained totally immobile. However, for one girl, Edith, it slowly began to move. The moment Fräulein Lucie added her own fingertips, it circled very energetically. After a few practice sessions, Edith became a satisfactory second-in-command.

We decided to try our luck at Edith's house as well. First we prepared an alphabetized ouija board similar to Fräulein Lucie's, but the results were disappointing. The glass moved excruciatingly slowly, always on the verge of expiring. Then we tried a small table on which we placed our linked hands, palms down, and asked the table to respond to our questions by jerking once for *yes*, twice for *no*. It did, but its answers were arbitrary as well as frustratingly minimal, and we soon gave up.

Lucie's ouija board kept us occupied for quite some time. Even Lilli who was too religious to indulge in such witchcraft couldn't resist its temptation. Though she stayed away from the table and sat in a corner of the room, she watched and listened. Once, when we asked a spirit—"where are you?" it wrote: "Sitting on Lilli's back." She jumped, much to our amusement. We were not afraid. These ghosts seemed harmless enough and were usually as eager to talk as we were to listen or, rather, to decipher their writing.

In general, information which was based on the past was fairly accurate. "I am Sylvia's cousin Franz"—and indeed, Sylvia had a dead cousin Franz. "Uncle Theo"—who was alive—"is well and will write soon." Very specific questions, however, tended to be ignored or were deliberately misinterpreted, and queries about the future invariably elicited cryptic responses.

When I described it all to Kuno for whom I was working at the time, he just laughed. My father, on the other hand, took me seriously and offered an explanation: "Energy is indestructible and it is possible that all thought continues to exist as energy until it is once more reshaped into ideas or words. The future, being undefined and unformulated, cannot be converted into words." It made sense, sort of.

My father was called by everyone *Herr Ingenieur*, although he only had *Fachhochschule* training and not a university diploma. I am not sure that he ever put his training to use. At any rate, during the war the only way he could earn money was through odd jobs, like finding black market sources for others or, in one or two instances, as a financial consultant. Strange that he should have been good at this even though he never had any money himself. He also liked to write, as did his brothers Otto and Paul, although Otto, the journalist, was then the only published writer of the three. He died in Paris of tuberculosis or pneumonia, I believe. His pen name was Renato Mondo.

During the summer which I spent in Vienna before the war, I remember uncle Paul always narrating one or the other screenplay he had made up and was going to send to Hollywood. And when I left for the States, father made me take along a 35 page manuscript of his on "the origin of the universe," with instructions to forward it to Albert Einstein. I did, with considerable embarrassment. It seems that Einstein even looked at it. He sent me a brief note acknowledging its receipt, and added that he did not consider my father's theory truly innovative. I wish I had kept the note instead of mailing it on to Vienna. Now it is lost.

It seems incongruous that father, whom everybody considered a highly intelligent and levelheaded person, should believe in astrology. But he did, wholeheartedly. Perhaps that was why he also took our séances seriously. He had a big, fat book which I was not supposed to read and therefore perused from cover to cover. Even so, whenever I tried my hand at guessing birthday signs, my success rate was far lower than his.

One séance stands out in my memory. When I asked whatever spirit was communing with us just then—some identified themselves, others did not—whether it had anything to tell me, the answer was: "Stay away from the Danube Canal." Parks had watchmen, whereas the banks of the canal did not. Therefore, they had become a favorite spot for walking and sun-bathing during that year. I tried to scoff at the message, but even though I was tempted to go to the Canal just to see if the ghost would turn out to be right, I didn't quite dare. To this day, I wonder if anything would have happened to me had I gone.

When all retraining courses were cancelled, our forays into the netherworld ceased as well. My English lessons continued for a while longer, until Fräulein Lucie was deported. Frau Nelly, I learned later, died of typhoid. I don't know what happened to Lucie. Pulli and Lilli were likewise summoned into one of the five transports of that spring.

Inside my diary I found a long letter from Ilse, dispatched from the asparagus fields of Aschersleben. It speaks of barracks with lice-infested mattresses, backbreaking labor, minimal rations, heat, blisters, sore limbs, and the hope of seeing me and her parents again. At night she was reading Rilke poems by flashlight, she wrote.

The transports were resumed in September 1941, not to stop until the end of the war, almost four years later. Sylvia was deported with her parents and sister on February 6, 1942, in the same transport as Ilse's parents and before Ilse could return and join them as she had requested. She was brought back to Vienna eight months later and deported soon thereafter. Her parents were sent to Riga, she to Minsk. None of them returned.

24.

On December 12, 1941, Hitler declared war on the United States. "Now he is sunk, you'll see!" said my Czech cobbler friend.

"But how soon?" I asked.

Since grandmother Vera's departure, I could only think of my Ostrau family and whether they would remain safe.

25.

Recently Harry sent me this undated entry from his father's diary:

"September 1, 1941—yellow star compulsory for ages six and up.

May 1, 1942—Jews not allowed on street cars except for special occasions (funerals etc.), and then only on the rear platform of the last car and with a permit from the Jewish Community.

May 6, 1942—19th transport, to the ghetto in Minsk.

May 15, 1942—21st transport, to Izbica.

May 27, 1942—23rd transport, to Minsk.

June 2, 1942—24th transport, to Minsk.

June 5, 1942—25th transport, to Izbica.

June 9, 1942—26th transport, to Minsk.

June 10, 1942—Rothschild hospital cordoned off, all visitors arrested and incorporated into the next transport.

June 14, 1942—27th transport, either to Izbica or Kielce.

June 20, 1942—28th transport, to Theresienstadt.

July 10, 1942—30th transport, to Theresienstadt.

August 17, 1942—36th transport (to Minsk?)

August 20, 1942—37th transport, to Theresienstadt.

September 24, 1942—42nd transport, to Theresienstadt.

October 1, 1942—43rd transport, to Theresienstadt.

October 5, 1942—44th transport, to ?

October 9, 1942—45th transport, to Theresienstadt."

In December 1942, the Viennese newspapers announced that the city was now judenrein—clean of Jews.

Dies irae...

26.

This is what I have been able to piece together, though most of the figures are approximate:

Altogether, about 147,000 Jews left Austria, 360,000 Germany, and 30,000 the Protectorate Bohemia-Moravia (16/4). In 1938, Vienna had the third-largest Jewish community in Europe after Warsaw and Budapest, with approximately 185,000 *Volljuden*, i.e., practising Jews (4/468). About 122,000 succeeded in emigrating, largely through financing from abroad (6/3-5). On October 31, 1941, all emigration was stopped and plans for "the final solution" developed. About 67,600 Austrian Jews were deported or caught in the countries they had fled to, with 2,142 surviving (10/52).

45 transports, each with about one thousand people, left Vienna in 1941 and 1942. In 1943-1945, another 46 smaller transports were dispatched, ranging from 1 to 200 people, 1,900 persons altogether (10/45). 1,747 returned to Vienna at the end of the war (4/525). On March 10, 1945, the deportation of the Jewish partners and children of mixed marriages was decreed, to be carried out in April. Fortunately, Vienna was liberated before the directive was implemented (4/525). In Prague, it was carried out as early as August 1944, with the Aryan wives sent to labor camps or factories and their Jewish husbands to Theresienstadt (9/171).

In October 1942, Vienna had about 7,100 *Geltungsjuden*, non-professing Jews or part-Jews declared Jewish by the Nuremberg Race Laws of 1935, as well as 1,200 *Volljuden*—"full" Jews. The rest of Austria was "clean." The transports of October 1 and 9, 1942 included between 700 and 800 hitherto protected Community employees and their families, as well as over 400 *freiwillige Mitarbeiter*, volunteer workers. Thereby the Community's staff was reduced from 1,068 on January 1, 1942 to 254 by the end of that year, and the number of volunteers from 558 to 80 (1/27).

By the end of 1944, the total number of Jews in Vienna had shrunk to about 3,400. Seventy people perished in the direct hit on the Jewish Community building on March 10, 1945, and eleven were still deported in early 1945 (4/522). After the liberation in April 1945, 219 U-boats surfaced, 74 of them men (4/518). 5,816 Jews, mainly *Geltungsjuden*, survived in Vienna (11/131).

In 1938, Vienna had approximately 185,000 Jews, on September 1, 1939 67,000, on August 31, 1940 48,465 (6/3), in 1945 about 5,000, and in 1988 about 6,000, many of them refugees from Eastern Europe (3/70).

The Ostrau Family

above: with grandma, grandpa and aunt Erna
below: uncle Robert, aunt Paula and cousin Walter

Summer in Ostravice

with the Weiss family and their friends

The Vienna Family

aunt Jenny

grandmother Vera

aunt Olga

cousin Rachelle

uncle Paul

uncle Isidor   uncle Otto

PART TWO:

Brief Interlude

1.

Just beyond B&S Glass stands a white church. With its tall steeple, it is all New England serenity and charm, except that it has a sign saying—"Jewish Congregation." How simple things can be: a change in sign or symbol transforms a church into a temple. Of course, Hitler did it all the time, whether you liked it or not. Even so, *this* fusion of symbols is comforting and, rightly or wrongly, reassuring.

Ditha's aunt Martha was aunt Jenny's longtime friend. Both women left Vienna before the war, while Martha's brother and his family stayed. They were protected because Ditha's mother was not Jewish. One Sunday, father took me along to their home, and that's how I met Ditha and her brother Franz, and through them several young people within the orbit of the Jewish Community. Some were considered *Volljuden* because they had three or four Jewish grandparents. In that case it didn't matter whether they or their parents had been baptized or not. When the deportations decimated their numbers, the percentage of *Mischlinge* of the First Class increased—half-Jewish star-wearers who had either not been baptized at all or only after 1935. That group made up most of my circle of friends during the remaining years of the war.

Ditha and Franz were raised Jewish and therefore had to wear the star. Ditha was my age, Franz two or three years younger. Both were tall, blond, blue-eyed and unusually good-looking, despite a short, sandy-haired, freckled and very nearsighted mother and a dark-haired and tall but heavyset father.

After the lonely months which had followed the dispersal of my bridge group, I was doubly grateful for the opportunity to spend my Sunday afternoons at Ditha's. She was outgoing and even-tempered, except that she was also subject to spells of irrepressible giggles. A great many things set her off laughing and then her round, pretty face would turn beet-red—as if she were ashamed of her sense of humor. She had beautiful teeth, and her radiant smile reminded me a little of Ilse Markstein, whose loss I still felt keenly. But despite Ditha's outgoing personality there was something very private about her, a polite formality which I was unable to break through. I never felt close to her, even though we saw a lot of each other in the course of those years.

I was soon a "regular" at their house. So were Frieda and Theo. Frieda was Jewish, short, stocky, gentle and quiet. Theo, half-Jewish, was not very tall either but slim and, though our age, much younger looking. He, too, was reserved and quiet—except when it came to movies. Film was his great love, and the moment he began to talk about a film he had seen, he was transformed. He would describe settings and plot with such shining eyes and embody the various characters so vividly, with changes in voice and intonation, that we were in turn enthralled and in stitches. It was not just the movie that seemed funny, but also Theo's transformation which took place before our eyes. This was so incongruous with his normal self that the event turned into something very special, highly theatrical in itself. The films which he shared with us may well have acquired a dimension in the telling which they lacked in reality. To this day, I remember Willy Forst's "Bel Ami," but can't recall whether I saw it on the screen or know it only from Theo's presentation.

Since Theo had been raised Catholic, he was a *Mischling* of the Second Class and didn't have to wear a star. His star-wearing father was likewise protected, by living in a *Mischehe*, a "mixed marriage." But in 1942, Theo's mother died of cancer and shortly thereafter Theo's father was deported to Theresienstadt.

Being sent to Theresienstadt was considered a blessing since Theresienstadt was not a concentration camp but, we were told, a resettlement camp for elderly and privileged Jews. Moreover, it was in Bohemia and not far from Vienna. That, too, was reassuring. Terezín's Czech population, some 7000 people including the garrison, had been resettled elsewhere to make room for the Jews. Starting with the fall of 1941, thousands were brought in. The first transports came only from Czechoslovakia, but by June 1942 there were also many from Austria and Germany. In November

1941, the town's 219 houses and its complex of military barracks held about 35,000 people, and in September 1942 the population peaked at 58,491. Yet even these figures tell only part of the story: there was a constant turnover, and not only because of disease and suicide. As of January 1942, transports to Auschwitz and other death camps kept disposing of the overflow (17/84-86).

None of that was known in Vienna, from where Theresienstadt looked like a safe haven. Sure, there was overcrowding and a shortage of food, but packages and postcards could be sent and were acknowledged. Letters from Theresienstadt arrived as well, at least initially. According to them, life was quite bearable. It even included a modicum of self-governance.

In a gruesomely ironic twist, things got better yet. In 1943, after the Germans had begun to have military setbacks and were therefore becoming concerned about international opinion, the inmates were ordered to "embellish" Theresienstadt in preparation for visits from the International Red Cross and foreign dignitaries. A lending library sprang up almost overnight, a Community Center with a stage, a prayer hall, a playground with wading pool, and sports grounds. Flowers were planted and lawns seeded. Stores were reopened and stocked with merchandise. The foreign visitors had no inkling that much of it consisted of the inmates' personal belongings which had been confiscated upon their arrival. People were allowed into the streets without the formerly mandatory passes, and were encouraged to draw and paint in their spare time, play theater and make music. On June 23, 1944, a visiting Commission, consisting of the Danish foreign minister and of representatives of the Danish and Swedish Red Cross (according to 9/118, though 17/87 speaks of the Swiss Red Cross), was able to listen to a performance of Verdi's *Requiem*. After that visit, Eichmann ordered a documentary film to be shot, entitled *"Der Führer schenkt den Juden eine Stadt"*—the Führer gives a city to the Jews (17/86). Forty yards of the film are preserved in the Prague newsreel archives (9/121). Once the shooting was completed, the ghetto's population was reduced to 12,000 (17/87). When the film crew returned in February 1945 to synchronize some of the musical scenes, they were astonished at the changes they found (9/121). What they didn't know was that

Theresienstadt was merely back to "normal."

When I visited Frieda and Theo in Vienna recently, Frieda showed me the printed program for the *Requiem*. The concert took place after much frustration and many crises because musicians, singers and soloists, not easy to come by in the first place, kept being summoned into transports while rehearsals were in progress. At some point the conductor, Raphael Schächter, was promised that the group would not be split up further. The promise was kept, and what must have been a poignant performance took place. So did an abridged command performance, requested by the commandant for a visit by Eichmann and his retinue. Rahm was greatly relieved when the *SS-Hauptsturmführer* showed his approval by clapping: Eichmann was obviously relishing the irony of having Jewish prisoners sing an Italian composer's Catholic prayer for the liberation of the soul (2/97-98). After Eichmann's departure, the transports were resumed. In one of them all musicians were shipped to Auschwitz—together, as promised (2/112).

Those who were able to remain in Theresienstadt to the end of the war or were sent back there from other camps during the final months of the fighting survived, provided they didn't contract typhoid, jaundice, scarlet fever or gastroenteritis, die of starvation, or commit suicide. However, for about 70% of new arrivals, Theresienstadt merely provided a transit stop on the way to a death camp, usually Auschwitz (17/86). Theo's father was not sent on, but he was diabetic and didn't make it.

The compulsory labor service affected everyone over fourteen. Non-Jews of course got the better jobs—with some luck, in their parents or friends' businesses or factories. Jews might land at the garbage dump, where they had to salvage usable objects from the trash. I remember somebody describing how he had to clean animal skins. Unless he watched where he sat down, he was likely to squash a fleeing worm or beetle. Renate's father, a lawyer, was painting Tyrolean eagles on wooden plaques. Luckily, his employer was a resistance fighter who didn't say a word about the many disks Renate and her father spoiled and threw into the Danube Canal instead of delivering them.

Though as a foreigner I was exempted from the labor service, I worked in a handicraft studio for several months. The studio consisted of a large, airy attic room in the Inner City. It was managed by two young Germans, their very friendly German shepherd dog and an introverted small tortoise which had a way of hiding for days. Rolf Kunowski or Kuno, as we called him, looked rather Jewish, but his looks were balanced by his very blond and Aryan-looking girlfriend Sigrid. There was one other employee, Thea, of my age. The two of us painted edelweiss and gentian or small St. Christopher figures on wooden pins and pendants. To aid in the war effort? Make trinkets for the natives? Busy-work? In any case, I got some pocket money out of it.

Despite his delicate built, Theo had been assigned to a road maintenance crew. They repaired broken water mains and resurfaced roads. Though the labor was backbreaking, Theo speaks fondly of that time. The men with whom he worked and ate took him in as one of theirs and became a family to him when he lost his own.

After his father's deportation, Theo's visits to Ditha's house became rarer. I remember his dropping in straight from work a few times, and my being disconcerted at finding the slim, delicate boy grimy and smelling of acrid sweat. Often he was too tired to say much. I doubt that he still had time or energy for movies. That must have been the worst for him.

In 1944, Theo received a summons to report to *Einsatztruppe Todt* which was to dig trenches somewhere near the Hungarian border. The troop, composed of *Mischlinge*, had been established by Himmler after the July 20th attempt on Hitler's life. Perhaps the name made Theo ignore the summons (*Todt* is an old spelling for *Tod*—death), or a sixth sense saved him: the entire group was liquidated once they had completed their assignment. Or perhaps he had merely had enough. He ignored the summons and went underground. Relatives of his mother's who lived on the outskirts of Vienna hid him.

In the summer of 1945, he resurfaced in the special three-month crash course which the City of Vienna arranged for us "disadvantaged" youngsters so that we could be given high school diplomas, and we had a big celebration.

After the war, Theo stayed in Vienna and went to the university. At some point he married Frieda. They are obviously well off, but work very hard and seem to have little time to enjoy their lovely house in the suburbs. When we began to talk about old times, Theo expressed what I too felt: that we had lived through the war as if it were a nightmare which one copes with by going through the necessary motions without being all there, by accepting that it isn't real, that one day we will wake up and shake it all off. If one may judge by appearances, he seems to have shaken it off well. But as I know by now, you can't go by appearances.

During my visit, Frieda pulled out a thick wad of postcards she had saved—the notes we had sent to her at Theresienstadt. Most of them were from Ilse Mezei, and only at that point did Frieda disclose to me that she and Ilse had been extremely close. I had not known, and even the cards gave no indication of it. They merely spoke of the weather, of how much Frieda was being missed, that all of us hoped she would soon be back home, that we were fine and anxious to hear if she was well and had received the most recent package. On some cards there were short, similarly innocuous messages—they had to pass through censorship—written or signed by other members of our group, including me. I had forgotten all about those postcards, but that's understandable. By then, I was totally preoccupied with my clandestine correspondence with Harry.

When Frieda started telling me how lucky she had been, her voice tensed up even forty-five years later. During almost four years of war, her parents had been working for the Community, and the family was protected. However, in October 1943, they were deported to Theresienstadt. Frieda was assigned to "agriculture," which meant hard work in the fields all day but also the opportunity to swipe—"einschleusen" they called it—an onion or a couple of tomatoes and bring them back hidden in a pocket of her apron. The day came when Frieda's parents were told to pack for the transfer to Auschwitz. She volunteered to accompany them, even though her boss urged her to desist: she would be separated from her parents anyway and would not be able to do anything for them. He refused to sign the release, and her petition was denied. But Frieda did not want to stay behind if her parents had to go, even if it was to death, though apparently few people in Theresienstadt were fully aware of the immediacy of that solution. She resubmitted her request, and it was again denied. When the transport assembled, there were not enough railway carriages available to hold everybody, and the group was thinned out: right—left—right—left. Those in the right group go, the left group stays. Both of Frieda's parents were in the left group, and all three survived the war in Theresienstadt.

2.

Lea was another star-wearing *Mischling* with a non-Jewish mother. (The system was complicated: Jewish women married to non-Jewish men did not have to wear the star, Jewish men with non-Jewish wives did unless they had children baptized by 1935. All mixed marriages, star-wearers or not, had to use the Jewish hospital as well as display the star on their apartment door.) Lea was my best friend for almost a year. Though she was very different from me, our loneliness had brought us together. My father would come home only to eat and sleep, and even then he barely talked. Thus, once the chores were done, I was left to my own devices. I read a lot but longed to have someone to talk to.

Lea worked in a dressmaking establishment but was at loose ends on weekends, much more so than I since all public places were off-limit to her. Her mother wouldn't even let her go through town without accompanying her. She hovered over her daughter like a hen over her chick, always afraid that something might happen to her, and convinced that the only safe place was home. Eventually Lea did join the cemetery crowd around Ilse, although she never traveled together with the rest of us. Since she and I were barely on speaking terms by then, I didn't find out whether she had rebelled against her house arrest or whether her mother had relented.

Though reserved and quiet, Lea was good to be with. I could tell that she liked me, and I was comfortable with her. Besides, I greatly admired her elegance and poise. She made all of her clothes and was always well-dressed, well-groomed and well-mannered. Her father was quite elderly, tall, white-haired and taciturn, but kind. An accomplished classical pianist, he often played while I was there, and I loved to listen. Lea's mother, who was much younger, resembled Lea in poise and reserve. She was invariably polite to me and seemed to approve of my visits, at least initially, but I was never comfortable in her presence because her eyes glared critically and condescendingly from under thick glasses.

That things began to go wrong was due to Walter. Walter was half-Jewish too, but starless. That was just about all I knew of him. Thea once brought him along to Lea's house, sometime in the spring of 1942. He was one of Thea's retinue of young men. In addition to him, there were, if I remember correctly, Herbert who at seventeen was a real baby, Hans aged twenty-two who was dull but decent and kind, and Fritz who at twenty-five looked very grown-up and was a promising sculptor. What a procession of names! They flickered into and out of my orbit before they could acquire faces and voices. But strange: the same names kept reappearing—Hanna, Ilse, Walter—as if their bearers were reincarnations of one another, according to some mysterious pattern.

Thea did have a face though, and a strong face at that. She was short, stocky, muscular and tanned. Black curly hair. Large nose. She was also a heavy smoker. Later I learned that she smoked so much from hunger. Her mother was a diabetic and Thea gave her most of her own food. Though Thea looked quite Jewish, this did not deter her from regularly leaving the star at home and bicycling to the Danube Canal or one of the public pools, where her friends might already be waiting. I was invited to join in. Lea was of course not allowed to come so, to make up for this, Thea and I began to spend our Sundays at her place.

I admired Thea for being tough, independent and full of spunk. She had an elaborate plan of how she would go underground when the time came, but when she received the summons during the second set of roundups, she meekly accompanied her mother into the assembly center. That was in August 1942. Herbert and Hans were swept up by that same wave of transports. Fritz had been deported earlier.

After Thea's circle broke up, Walter, Lea and I became a steady threesome. I don't recall if or where Walter worked. He, too, played the piano—mainly jazz, dance music, the latest hits. He had a knack for improvising and incorporating popular tunes into pleasing medleys. That was Lea's and my introduction to the pop scene, and we were delighted when we began to recognize the songs he played and could hum or sing along. At times we danced to his music.

All through that winter of 1942-43 the three of us spent most Sundays together at Lea's apartment. We would play cards or games, talk, or listen to Walter's piano playing. Tall and quite good-looking, he could be a real charmer, though Lea found much to criticize in him: he was unreliable and conceited, not very bright yet smart enough to pursue his own advantage. I was more forgiving, perhaps because it was difficult to be angry with him for long or because, having spent more time with him, I had become accustomed to his ways. He treated us equally casually and was probably not very interested in either of us—just enjoying having a place to go and an audience to perform for.

Lea's mother must have liked him too, for she often invited him to stay for supper. Although she would then ask me as well, she must have been aware that I had to go home and cook for my father. Perhaps it was her fault and not Lea's that our friendship broke up. But I wasn't quite innocent either.

This is how it happened. When spring came, Walter began to ask me out for walks and eventually swims on the Old Danube, as we had done the year before with Thea and the rest of her gang. To be sure, we would only go on weekdays, and continued to meet at Lea's on Saturday or Sunday. I was too flattered by his attention to have the steadfastness to decline. And since there was nothing between him and me nor between him and Lea, why should she resent my going off without her, since she couldn't join in anyway? Also, it was my first real date—if it could be called a date—since that awkward walk in Michalkovice years ago.

One day, while we were sunbathing together by the Canal, I hurt my hand and Walter offered to kiss it. A little later I hit his eye, also accidentally, and he made me kiss it in return. "Now I want a kiss on my eye," I said and closed my eyes expectantly. When nothing happened, I opened them again and saw his face close to mine, eyes closed, lips pursed, waiting. I moved my lips to his and we kissed, briefly, lightly. It was a pleasant experience and when we parted, I asked him if he wanted a good-night kiss. "No, better not," he said. "It might become a habit and that would only ruin our friendship." I felt mortified but learned my lesson. When Walter asked me a few weeks later and quite out of the blue, if I would like to "go steady" with him, I declined without much hesitation, without even asking what exactly he meant by going steady.

When I was with Lea after that first and last kiss, I asked her if she could imagine kissing Walter. To my surprise she said yes, she could. I was taken aback and resolved to act more properly henceforth, not to agree to another kiss come what may, and to be completely honest with Lea in order not to jeopardize our friendship. Simple, right? Only that from that day on Lea's attitude toward me began to change, barely noticeably at first, then at an accelerated pace. Whenever she and I were together and, as before, told each other what we had been doing all week, she only seemed interested in learning—though she could not bring herself to inquire straight out—whether I had seen Walter and what we had done together. I reported faithfully, secure in the knowledge that nothing was happening between him and me, and that it wasn't my fault if her mother would not let her join even the most innocuous outing. But then Lea began to use on me that icy politeness which she was so good at, and I stopped going to her house.

Was that how it came about? Come on, what about her birthday?—Well, what about it? I did, after all, mean well when I reminded Walter of her birthday and suggested that it would be nice for him to bring her flowers. How was I to know that he would arrive with a bouquet of roses, red roses? (Much, much later I learned that he had swiped them from the cemetery!)

Lea became very animated. She kept smiling at Walter, at the same time ignoring me completely except to remind me that it was getting late, and didn't I have to go fix supper for my father. I left angry, hurt, and totally frustrated because, after all, I had been the one to suggest that Walter bring flowers.

On the way home I tried to sort out my emotions. I had been torn between my feelings for Lea and the excitement of having something like a boy friend. I had opted for Lea, and now my magnanimity had backfired. Although I was sure that Walter was not in love with her, despite the roses, to be pushed aside like that smarted. I tried to talk myself out of my resentment by reminding myself that she had much less freedom than I did, not only because of the star but also because of her mother. Let her enjoy her day! Unfortunately, the next time I saw Lea she was arrogant and condescending, and my generosity disappeared in a flash.

No, I didn't tell her that Walter had brought the flowers at my suggestion. I didn't sink that low, but I said something almost as bad, about being glad that they had a good time, and doubly glad that I had refused his offer to escort me home. The moment I had said it I regretted it, but the words were spoken. One wrong doorbell answered, and never can the harm be undone.

I made a few more attempts to approach Lea and make up, but they remained futile. Whenever we ran into each other during the cemetery outings, she would be polite but curt and distant, just like her mother. When the weather turned bad and we began to meet again at our respective homes, she would come but either not talk to me at all or engage in meaningless chitchat. However, when I was sick in bed, she dropped in, much to my surprise. But neither of us knew what to say to the other. Erasers work better on paper than in real life.

On that unfortunate birthday, I had of course realized that Lea had a crush on Walter, despite her constant disparagements of him. Did that awareness make me doubly a traitor? After all, I didn't think very highly of him either, and my lashing out at Lea was not due to affection for him but only to my anger at being pushed aside when I had meant well. On the other hand, she too knew what Walter was like. How could she sacrifice our friendship to him? Was pride more important to her than friendship? What is pride anyway? A display of principles, or of vanities? Or were the two of us just too different for a lasting friendship? Whatever. I once again vowed to stop trusting people and not expect anything from anyone.

Was I thinking those thoughts then or am I only thinking them now? Am I still the same I was then or am I inventing a nineteen-year-old self? Perhaps both and neither. I am slipping with such surprising ease into and out of my old skin! More than that—yesterday's and today's perspectives seem to be fusing into a continuum, an intermediate persona, one that is slightly different and quite a bit wiser than both my earlier and my present self, perhaps because it can incorporate both of them, and draw on past and present with the same detachment and without a need to fully identify with either.

The incident with Lea rankled a long time. Although I eventually succeeded in putting it out of my mind, it was not laid to rest completely until my visit with Theo and Frieda more than forty-five years later.

I met Lea at their house. She sounded so genuinely pleased to see me that I felt almost as close to her as many years earlier. In my immense relief I impulsively took the risk:

"We had a falling out at one time, remember? I have forgotten the details, though."

"So have I. Some silly thing or other."

I still wouldn't let go: "Didn't it have something to do with that character who came to your house for a while, what was his name—Walter?"

"Could be. You know—I ran into him in the street once, quite some time ago. Hadn't changed much. He always was an oddball, remember?"

3.

Two very white birches are rising into a very dark sky from a common base. Slim and delicate, they are wrapped in the same veil of dancing silvery leaves. Twins, separate yet inseparable.

"Why don't you come to Community headquarters tomorrow," Ditha suggested, "then I can introduce you to Ilse and Kurt. I am sure you will like them, and Ilse has long wanted to meet you. I've been telling her a lot about you."

"But is it all right to visit her at work?"

"Don't worry, we'll go to the telephone exchange just before she closes it down. Let's say tomorrow evening at a quarter to six. If you'll meet me by the main elevator, we can go upstairs together. Her room isn't easy to find."

That evening everything that could go wrong went wrong and I arrived at the elevator ten past six. No trace of Ditha. What was Ilse's surname? No idea, but I suppose I can always ask for the telephone exchange.

"Take the connecting hallway on the third floor into the other building."

Doors, stairs, no connecting hallway where it should be, no signs, no one to ask. Finally somebody's steps.

"You are in the wrong building. You have to go back down and take the other staircase. I think it's on the second floor, but you'd better ask again!"

Ask whom? Closed doors and windows, dim lights, outside a cold wind which whistles inhospitably. Should I give up and go home? By now she may have left, and here I am wandering around in circles in this labyrinth.

I persist. Ditha has given such a glowing account of Ilse. Finally voices, new directions, another long hallway, a small wooden staircase that seems to lead into yet another building, another flight of stairs, finally a sign: TELEPHONE EXCHANGE —OFF LIMIT TO ALL BUT AUTHORIZED PERSONNEL. The round door knob refuses to engage the lock and I knock, wondering whether anyone is still here or whether I might be locked in till morning. The door opens and it's Ditha. All is well after all.

"Well, here you are finally! I'd given up on you—what happened? Come in and meet Ilse."

"Sit down, my child. Would you believe it—I have known you for a long time!"

How odd: She looks my age and talks as if she were my mother. But somehow I don't mind. She looks vaguely familiar, but I can't place her.

"You took Nelly Grossmann's fashion-design course, didn't you? I was in it too, for a short time. And now I sometimes see you standing in line for milk. I live on Förstergasse—just around the corner from you."

I am perplexed. She uses the familiar *du* which, when at eighteen you meet someone for the first time, is not really appropriate. And she seems to know quite a bit about me though I don't remember her.

"Yes, I was in that course, but that was ages ago."

"Weren't you also taking English lessons from Frau Nelly's sister?" I nod. "I wish I could work on my English!" She sighs. "I'm so tied up here."

"I went to Berlitz for a while and now I am enrolled at *Sprachschule* Kautezky. They have a very good program, and classes meet in the evening, twice a week, Mondays and

Thursdays at seven, so that you—" I stop in midsentence, remembering that Ilse can't go because she wears the star.

We chat until she gets her sign-off call, switches to the night setting and begins to gather her things. Ditha leaves, and Ilse suggests that we walk home together. I head for the door, but she seems to be waiting for someone or something. Then I hear footsteps and Ilse says:

"There he is!"

She pushes me out the door into the dim hall, turns off the last light and introduces:

"This is my brother Kurt, this is Liesl. Of course you say *du* to each other."

I can't help laughing at this ease, and shake hands with someone I can barely make out in the dark and who says to me: "So you've met my sister? How did you survive?"

"Fine," I say puzzled. Ilse explains with a chuckle:

"We are twins, you see, but all good qualities have been bestowed on me and poor Kurt has to make do with what was left."

"That's just jealousy speaking," Kurt interjects and I can hear his grin. "As you will soon notice, it's poor Ilse who has been sadly neglected by the fairies. Wait till she tries to sing for you! You must know that she's under the delusion that she has a voice. You can hear her squeaking all the way round the corner."

Ilse is not tongue-tied. "Those squeaks are Kurt's attempt at whistling. But you learn to put up with them eventually."

4.

Soon I discovered that most of the young people working for the Community or one of its administrative units tended to drop by Ilse's switchboard room at least once a day. Gradually I met most of them. Even if Ilse was busy, she could be counted on offering a welcoming smile and pointing to the one chair by the switchboard or, if it was already occupied, to the table which took up much of the remaining space. Thus after more than three years of relative isolation, I suddenly found myself part of a large friendly group which accepted me as I was and whenever I appeared, without making demands on me.

Not only was Ilse's tiny office our regular meeting place, but she kept us up to date on what was happening in the neighborhood. That neighborhood was small, like a family, and it kept shrinking every time a transport left, so that the rest of us clung together all the more tightly. Whenever we entered her little room, we could tell by her eyes if there was bad news. But she would also brief us on who was ill and who had recovered, who might appreciate help or a visit, and who was flirting with whom. Like a good Jewish mother, she was always ready to match up her friends with one another, and she did this with a half-conspiratorial, half-bashful smile and the guileless glance of a newborn, so that one could never be cross with her.

These tidbits made up the excitement of Ilse's day, since on weekdays the phone and our visits were her only links to the outside world. She did not have a boy friend, but Kurt and she were very close. You could feel the warmth between them, despite their constant kidding.

The two did not look much alike. Though both were of medium height and build, Ilse's face was long and narrow, with wavy ash-blond hair, light skin, slightly bulging blue eyes under very light lashes, and a large mouth with big teeth which usually displayed an odd and charming half-ironic, half-apologetic smile. She talked quietly, blushed easily and was pretty in a low-key, homey way. Kurt's features were coarser, but he had a more outgoing personality. His hair was dark and curly, almost fuzzy, his face round. He had the same prominent eyes as Ilse, except that his were dark brown and could be soulful like a beagle's or mischievous like a puppy's. His big-lipped mouth looked rather sensuous, but that was a wrong signal. Although he joked with every girl, his flattery was playful and innocent, merely a pleasant game, to which all of us responded in kind. His teasing may have been a bit more pointed and persistent than Ilse's but no one minded, knowing that like his sister he was a considerate and kind individual. He didn't have a girl friend and I suspect that his sharp tongue was to blame. Perhaps also his upbringing. Both were orthodox and very serious about their faith.

I started out toward home with that odd twosome, feeling very intrigued. I had never met anyone like them. The street lights were out because of the blackout, and it was quite dark. Therefore it took me a while to notice that Kurt was lagging behind and talking to another dim figure.

"Of course you know Harry?" Ilse asked and when I declined, she turned back and called into the darkness:

"Kurt, why don't you introduce. Where are your manners?"

"But I only met Liesl ten minutes ago myself," Kurt defended himself. Falling in with their jocular tone, I corrected: "It's been at least a half hour by now!"

I press a hand which I can barely make out in the dark, say "pleased to meet you" to a face I can't see—ignoring Ilse's suggestion to use *du*—then am escorted to my door and invited to visit the exchange any time I feel like it. I shake three hands and disappear in my doorway in high spirits.

And that was how I met Harry.

5.

I have begun my trek up Main Street. In the sky, puffy black streaks are suspended from a slate gray canopy. The wind is back. Will it break up the clouds or explode them? Main Street is very straight but as it climbs, it seems to be heading straight into those black streaks or, if I am lucky, into the one lighter opening between them.

Loud knocks are coming at me from the building next to the church: Short—short—short—long, short—short—short—long. Someone seems to be repairing a porch. But the knocks are sharp like blows.

The knock on our apartment door that Wednesday night in early June 1943 found me sitting by the open window, reading. It was unusually sultry and the daylight was fading rapidly. Having been home alone all day, I was more than ready for company, but when I saw Ditha's face, my anticipation vanished. Something was wrong.

"There's a rumor going round that tonight they may come for the foreigners. Perhaps you and your father shouldn't sleep at home, just in case."

I thanked her for the information, locked up and went to the

Klügers to find father. He was spending most of his evenings at their apartment which was just around the corner—next door to where Ilse and Kurt lived with their mother. Old Mrs. Klüger was around eighty, tall and erect, a real matriarch. Both daughters were at her beck and call. Sylvia was very attractive, with short, dark hair, boyishly cut into a *Bubikopf.* I remember her as friendly but somewhat distant, a *grande dame* with cigarette holder. Even the simplest outfit looked elegant on her. Grete's hair was likewise short but reddish blond, and she had the almost invisible eyebrows and freckles of the typical redhead. Her high cheekbones and broad face were not really attractive, but she had wonderfully kind eyes, a lovely small smile between dimples, and naturally pink cheeks. The Klügers were Romanians like us and, just as had been the case with the Mehrs years before, visitors would congregate at their apartment in the evening to share a cup of tea, the latest rumors and the latest worries. But father never took me along.

He was the only visitor that evening. When I reported Ditha's message, it was met with disbelief. The Germans wouldn't dare touch *bona fide* foreigners, would they, and those without valid papers had been deported long before. Even so, father decided to follow up. He excused himself and went to the phone booth at the corner to call up his contact at Community headquarters. No, everything was normal, they hadn't heard a thing. (When I was perusing the *Jüdisches Nachrichtenblatt* for 1943 in Vienna last year, I found an announcement dated June 4—two days *after* that evening—giving a new, "expanded" definition of who would henceforth be considered "a Jew:" Jewish citizens of Belgium, Bulgaria, France, Greece, Holland, Norway, Romania, Serbia, Slovakia, and of the former Estonia, Latvia, Lithuania, Luxemburg and Poland.)

Luckily, father was a cautious person. When he came home later that evening, he had me fill several jugs with water from the faucet on the landing. Then we waited up until Nelly Goldhagen, our tenant, came home. Father double-locked the hall door and briefed us. "Just in case: should anyone ring the doorbell, you stay put and don't make a sound. Though I am quite sure that nothing will happen."

We nodded.

In the middle of the night I was awakened by loud, insistent ringing, followed by earsplitting knocks. "Not a sound!" father whispered. The pounding continued. Any minute now the door would give way. Just when I thought my heart would burst through my chest, the knocking stopped.

I tiptoed into Frau Nelly's room and slipped into her bed. As we hugged, I felt her heart going as wildly as mine. Despite the heat, we were shivering. Eventually we fell asleep in each other's arms.

In the morning father tiptoed in to wake us.

"Don't flush the toilet or make any noise," he whispered. "They may have left an *Ordner* outside the door to catch us when we return home."

We dressed as noiselessly as we could. Then he waved me toward the glass door which opened out of our bedroom onto the flat roof of the courtyard shed. The Kleppners' apartment in the front building faced that same roof. Father's voice was so low that I could barely make out his words:

"Walk across the roof, knock on their door and ask if we could leave through their apartment. Then we can take the front staircase and get out of the building unseen."

I went across and tapped lightly on their door. After an eternity, Frau Stella's face appeared at the window. She raised it just enough to hear me. She would have to check with her husband, she said. The answer was no. It was too risky.

I went back inside and reported to father. He didn't say a word. I wonder what he was thinking. I knew my own thoughts, of course. With bitterness I noted how quickly my list of betrayals was growing.

For another hour we sat in silence. Outside everything was totally quiet. Finally, I tiptoed on bare feet to the hall door and pressed my ear against it. I couldn't detect any sound of breathing. Very slowly and cautiously I lifted the peephole cover and peered out. I didn't see anybody.

"Listen carefully," father said. "Tie a kerchief round your head, take the shopping bag and your change purse, and go as far as the corner store—as if you wanted to shop. Don't turn round but on the way back check if there's anybody waiting by the front entrance."

The front entrance was deserted.

We quickly packed pajamas and toothbrushes, my father into his briefcase, Nelly and I into shopping bags, and headed for the streetcar stop. On the streetcar my heartbeat slowed down.

At the Romanian Consulate General we found four or five others. I knew only one of them, and just barely—a young man named Martin Katz. Another ten or so, the Klügers among them, had spent the night with friends or not opened. All others had been hauled off, over a hundred.

The consul general was indignant. The Germans had no right to arrest Romanians. It must be a misunderstanding. He got on the phone with Berlin and Bucharest, but to no avail. Stay out of it, he was told; forget it.

The consul general was a decent man. He returned to us visibly distraught. The only thing he could do for us, he said, was to let us stay at the consulate until the transport had left.

The staff treated us well. They spread mattresses in the basement for us and fed us. The biggest treat, as far as I was concerned, was the two-egg omelette the janitor's wife brought me. My father made me take off the coral earrings which had been my mother's and which I always wore, and gave them to her. I was sure he could have found something else to give, but I was too scared to offer an argument.

Father also did something which, in retrospect, turned out to be a stroke of genius. He went to the consul and urged him to protect the possessions of those Romanians who had been nabbed.

"It is Romanian property and should be safeguarded for its owners until they return," he insisted. "It must not be appropriated by the Germans."

"Do you want to argue it out with the Gestapo?" the consul asked.

"I can try," father replied, "if you'll give me an authorization to speak for the consulate." The consul had the appropriate paper drawn up and my father departed. I was sure I would never see him again, but an hour later he was back.

"It's all settled," he reported. "Their houses and bank accounts won't be touched."

"Why don't you keep the authorization," the consul said. "I might need your services again."

After the transport had left, everybody went back home. Most of the remaining Romanians applied for exit visas and eventually left for Romania, Frau Nelly among them. We felt protected, for the moment at least, by the note from the consulate.

When it was all over, I went to Lea's house to let her know that we had made it. Although she had acted quite stand-offish lately, I was sure she would worry. Her mother kept me at the door. "Lea is busy and can't see you."

"Could you tell her..." and I reported. Even then she didn't invite me in. "I will tell her but you'd better not come here again. They might be looking for you and you would endanger us." Then she closed the door on me.

A few weeks later, my father made two equally brilliant if less daring moves, and did so in the nick of time. Somehow, he got the consul to certify that both he and I were only half-Jewish. How he managed that is beyond me. The consul general's name was Radu Flondor, I think. Perhaps he had known my grandfather in Czernowitz before the first world war. Also, since Czernowitz was now Russian and out of reach, he may have been willing to risk it. At any rate, father obtained the document and, as a result, regular J-less ration cards were restored to us, as were clothing coupons. By that time there was little to be had, even on unrestricted ration cards, but they made good IDs, especially for the *Hauswart*. And on December 23, 1943, father handed me my first very own, full-fledged Romanian passport, with the swastika stamp of the Germans granting me permission to reside on the territory of the Reich excepting border areas until December 23, 1945. Religion was not mentioned, and there was no "J."

When we returned home three days later, I felt as if I had been away for years. It was hard to believe that nothing had changed, that the streetcar was going up and down Untere Augartenstraße, that people were standing in line outside the grocer's as usual, and that our apartment was untouched. No one seemed aware of what had been happening and what had almost happened to us, and of course I couldn't tell anybody.

As I was approaching our building, I noticed two men at the corner engrossed in conversation. Both wore stars. They looked up as I was passing, and when I turned my head, their eyes were still on me. One of them was fairly young, of medium height, slight, with a wide forehead but pointed chin, black hair and deep set, black eyes under bushy eyebrows. Although he was rather handsome and I have always liked black eyes, the penetrating gaze he gave me frightened me. In the context of recent events, I sensed danger. Was he an *Ordner*, posted to keep an eye on our house and report our return? When I dared make my way to Ilse the next morning, told her of our narrow escape and also spoke of my fears, she calmed me down. Harry had mentioned seeing me, and my description sounded right, so it must have been him. And that was how I found out what he looked like.

6.

The dark streaks have not disappeared. On the contrary, there now seem to be more layers of them. However, the wind has again subsided.

The big building across from the Jewish church displays a large sign saying "Dorsey Memorials. Founded in 1923." Next to the building, a number of tombstones are lined up on the succulently green lawn in informal rows, as if gathered for a rehearsal. Some are light gray, others dark gray, a few reddish brown. None are black—could that be an indication that the journey into the beyond is not a trip into darkness but only toward shadows, or a return to the earth? Nor are any of the tombstones topped by crosses—can all be meant for Jews? Or am I still seeing the world too much in terms of the colors of fear and death, yellow and black?

Three of the grave stones stand by themselves on the other side of the driveway, close to a picnic table. Picnic with your dead—*morituri te salutant*. Better yet: life out of death, *le roi est mort—vive le roi!*

After Thea had introduced me to the Danube Canal I spent many an afternoon there alone or with her and her entourage—they would hide the star—and eventually with Walter. But now, with Ilse Markstein gone, the bridge club dispersed, Theo recruited for road work, Thea deported, the Danube Canal declared off-limit by my friendly ghost, Walter out of the picture and Lea's door closed in my face, I couldn't think of anything to do on

Sundays except stay home with a book.

Meeting Ilse Mezei changed all that. Sunday was cemetery day, she explained to me. Whoever was free, secured from the Community office the required streetcar permit—Community employees had one anyway and I, being starless, wouldn't need it. After lunch we would board streetcar number 71 and head out to Vienna's Central Cemetery. Gate Four, the Jewish section, became our home in the country, our summer resort. It was green, had trees and, right by the entrance, long before the first row of graves, there was a wide open space for sunbathing and ball playing. And no warnings or interdictions of any kind: Gate Four extended its welcome to all Jews, living and dead.

At first, picnicking, singing, playing cards, games or volley ball on a cemetery felt weird, and I was surprised to find that even Kurt and Ilse who were orthodox participated. Then it occurred to me that the dead could hardly object to our presence. If anything, they might welcome the company of the living. An unanticipated feeling of solidarity and of belonging rose up inside me, and I began to feel at home on the cemetery.

We made ourselves useful as well. That, in fact, was the ostensible reason for our being there. In one corner of the cemetery a vegetable garden had been planted by the Community staff to supply its soup kitchen, hospital and orphanage. Every dry Sunday we began our visit at the *Grabeland,* as it was called, raking, weeding, watering or harvesting. Some of it was hard work, but Kurt and Ilse would not let anyone get away without putting in time. And Dr. F., who was in charge of the cemetery, followed our doings both there and during our "time off" with *Argus* eyes and off-color remarks. That seemed to give him a vicarious pleasure.

In retrospect it seems strange how carefully everyone was watching everyone else's amorous inclinations. As if there had been nothing else to think and talk about. Perhaps there was not—or at least we all pretended that there wasn't, and after a while that seemed a natural state. And teasing one another about real or imagined conquests and crushes was not only fun but also somehow reassuring. For all that, we gave Dr. F. a wide berth. We did not mind the twins' kidding, but no one wanted to give him cause for gossip. He would see to it that it made the rounds of the Community, and it might reach our parents and get us into trouble.

According to Kurt, Frieda was interested in Theo who was interested in Trude who was interested in Harry. So were Ilse and Renate, and actually I was trying hard not to let them suspect that I too was drawn to him. The fact was that Harry with his large, flirtatious black eyes seemed as close to a Don Juan as anyone I could imagine.

"It's terrible," he would complain, shrugging in mock dispair. "The girls won't leave me alone. I don't know what to do!"

"Stay away from him," Ilse warned me. "He's not to be trusted." I was sure she was right.

The next time I saw Harry, it was during a visit to the hospital. While I was sitting on a patient's bed he entered, wearing a white hospital smock and carrying a lab report.

"I didn't know you worked here!"

"Yes, I assist my father. He's one of the staff physicians."

I told him what had happened during the preceding week and that I had taken him for an informer. He listened with a smile, his eyes on mine. No, not on them but reaching deeply into them, speaking to me in a language which I had not heard before and yet seemed to understand. They were telling me that I looked well, that the white jacket set off nicely my wine-red pleated dress, that the matching shoes—I had dyed them myself—were not lost on him. I wasn't sure he had heard a word I said.

When I stopped talking, he suggested: "Why don't you come and have a look at the lab where I work." His voice was low and husky but melodious. I remembered Ilse's warning.

"Some other time," I said. "Today I'm in a hurry."

"That's too bad," he said, his eyes still inside mine. "I hope that other time comes soon!"

"Let's hope so." I tried to give my words a flippant ring and turned back to the bed. I would stay far, far away from him, that was for sure. He was much too good-looking, the last person to trust, even if I hadn't resolved never to trust anyone again.

I walked home, proud of my steadfastness. I was humming the drinking song from *La Traviata*.

7.

Father was at the door when I arrived at home. Since this was his time to be at the Klügers, I was taken aback. "Has anything happened?"

"Not yet. But there are rumors of a transport being assembled, and it might be wise to stay away from home. I'll sleep at the Grünbaums, but they don't have room for both of us. Go to Frau Wilma and ask her to let you stay at her place. If you hurry up, she will still be at the store."

"Are you sure she will agree to it?"

"Of course. She is indebted to me, and she has assured me that anytime we need a bed we can count on her."

I took toothbrush, toothpaste, nightgown and clean underwear, put them into my shopping bag and walked across Augarten bridge, along the Ring as far as the Votivkirche, my favorite church, then turned into Währingerstraße where Frau Wilma had her yarngoods store.

She was busy attending to customers but waved me a cheerful hello, and I sat down and waited. But when she heard my request, she shook her head.

"I'm sorry but today is not very good. Can you go somewhere else?"

"Of course I can," I lied. "Don't worry."

"So long then."

Where could I go? I couldn't think of anyone. Only Walter came to mind, though I had not seen him in weeks and had never been at his home. Moreover, we had quarreled, for Thea had left her bicycle to both of us and Walter had appropriated it. Nonetheless I trudged into the seventh district. By the time I found the house, it was getting dark.

Walter didn't invite me in. Instead, he came out on the landing. Through the open door I could hear voices. They had visitors.

"Do you think I could spend the night here? They might be looking for the remaining foreigners tonight, and the place where I was supposed to stay can't have me."

"Let me check with my mother."

A long wait on the dark landing, then the rejection.

"We have company and my mother thinks it's too risky. Sorry.

And how are you otherwise?"

"Fine, thanks. So long."

That was the last time I saw Walter.

I couldn't think of anyone else to try, and by now it was quite dark. I walked home, filled two jugs with water and double-locked the door. I checked out the flat roof outside our bedroom, but there was no corner where I could hide from searching flashlights. All I could do was sleep on the floor so that the bed would not look slept in and, should the bell ring, slip under the bed and hope that they wouldn't break down the door or, if they did, not look under the bed.

It was a long night, but nobody came.

When father heard that I had slept at home he was furious. "Why didn't you come to the Grünbaums?"

"You said they only had room for one!"

"How can you be so stupid? You could have slept in a chair if necessary." That hadn't occurred to me.

8.

Main street is now rising quite steeply. On the left-hand side a huge maple sports such brilliantly red foliage that for a moment I wonder if Fall is on its way. Can there be so little difference between one season and another, is time as arbitrary as all that?

An unusually loud bird whistle interrupts my thoughts. It seems to come from the maple and is so persistent, almost a shriek, that I cross the street to investigate. I discover the source of the screeching with a shock: a cage is suspended from the porch roof of the house by the maple. Inside, on a perch, sits a large gray bird, too large for the size of the cage. It has whitish wings, a yellow head, and a round red spot on each cheek. It screeches at me so insistently that I am convinced it is attempting to tell me something. I try to calm it down by talking to it in a soothing voice, but it continues to shriek. Finally I walk on, feeling helpless and guilty.

That night they had ignored the few remaining foreigners, but father decided that Vienna was becoming too dangerous. Since he had been promised a passport, not from Bucharest but by the

Vienna consulate which seemed far more reliable, he applied for the necessary exit permits. The Klügers were likewise still in Vienna. Most of the other Romanians who had survived the night of the hard knocks had left, legally or illegally.

Time passed quickly with preparations for our departure. Only when I visited Ilse after several days' absence, did I realize how hard it would be to leave all this behind. The cramped telephone center had become a real home to me, and Ilse's and Kurt's kidding always revived my spirits.

As usual, Ilse had a lot of news. Frieda was going to the hospital to have her appendix removed. Also, she, Ilse, had found someone for Renate who was right for her because he talked just as much as she did—Harry.

Ilse's news took my breath away. After my break with Lea, Renate and I had begun to spend a lot of time together. Since she was under fourteen, she was still exempt from the labor service and therefore free most of the time. Also, although she was supposed to wear the star, she would often leave it at home or cover it with her purse.

Renate was very athletic and enterprising. We played ping-pong at her place, went rowing on the Old Danube, and practiced acrobatic stunts during the Sunday cemetery outings—to the admiration of our friends and snide remarks from Dr. F. who saw a traveling circus in our future.

But though well-developed and looking very grownup—more so than I did—Renate was not even fourteen, and quite immature. She would be an easy prey for Harry. I couldn't understand Ilse's pride at her diplomatic success. She explained that she had not only introduced the two but had mentioned to Renate that Harry was interested in her. That had done the trick. And indeed, when I watched them the following Sunday on the *Grabeland*, it was quite obvious that Renate kept following Harry around and would sit down next to him whenever she could. I reminded myself that this was none of my business, and that I'd better keep quiet.

When I dropped in on Ilse a week later, both Kurt and Renate were there. The twins were needling her mercilessly, with Kurt inquiring with an expression of genuine concern whether Harry was a good kisser, and whether Renate felt different after she'd been kissed. Ilse was urging Kurt, with an equally innocent expression, not to embarrass Renate who had undoubtedly not let Harry kiss her at all. Ilse solicitously inquired whether Kurt might be jealous. Renate didn't respond to any of that, she just smiled. I couldn't tell if it was an embarrassed or a happy smile.

She and I left together and I asked her what this had been all about. She gave a somewhat confused explanation from which I pieced together that Harry had surprised her by trying to kiss her, that she had resisted and was still upset. I sympathized, remembering that at fourteen I hadn't been any more experienced. I was also annoyed at Harry's thoughtless behavior and decided to tell him off at the first suitable opportunity. Since I would be leaving Vienna shortly, I reasoned, he could not suspect any hidden motive on my part.

Soon the appropriate occasion presented itself.

After Frieda's appendix was out, her hospital room temporarily displaced Ilse's office as our meeting place, to the annoyance of the other five patients who shared the room with her. But the nurse was nice to us and only dislodged us if the noise level was too high or the number of visitors rose above four.

I recall the day when I had a portfolio of my old fashion drawings with me. I was taking them to the *Dorotheum* for an appraisal, in preparation for our departure. Renate was visiting, as were Frieda's parents, and everybody wanted to see the drawings. While I was busy explaining titles and themes, I suddenly felt Harry's eyes on me. He had come in quietly and was standing by the door. I excused myself and went over to him.

"Could you spare me a minute?" I was still using the formal *Sie*. "There's something I'd like to discuss with you."

He gave me a surprised look and moved toward a far corner of the room. The others were chatting and discussing the drawings.

"Listen, Harry, why don't you leave Renate alone? Remember that she is only fourteen. Don't you see that she is too young for a flirtation? Besides, she is too good for one."

"I don't know what you are talking about." He was likewise using *Sie* and managed to look very blank. I gathered that I could not make him see reason unless I changed tactics.

"She is telling people that you tried to kiss her and of course didn't succeed. Do you like being made a fool of?"

That seemed to do it. He looked at me thoughtfully.

"Come on, Liesl," the others shouted, "don't you want to hear our compliments?" I went back to them. Renate offered to walk me to the *Dorotheum* and we left together, with everyone saying how sorry they were that I would be leaving Vienna.

Harry was standing by the main entrance. The three of us shook hands, then Renate and I walked out.

"Thank you!" he suddenly called out after me. When I turned, I saw him looking at me with that same thoughtful glance. I nodded and felt relieved. I was sure I had done the right thing.

"Why was he thanking you?" Renate asked.

"Nothing important. I had a message for him." It wasn't even a lie.

9.

On the following Sunday I took my brownie camera to the cemetery and, after a good deal of coaxing, managed to get everybody together for a group picture. At least I would have a memory of these happy days. Lea reached for the camera and offered to take another snapshot so that I could be in the picture. I was delighted. Did she want to make up for her mother's behavior on that awful day? As the crowd began to disperse to the garden plots, I suggested to her that we take a walk together, and she agreed. What a relief! Perhaps we could again be friends. Then I noticed that the only other person still waiting around was Harry.

"If you have nothing better to do, why don't you join us? We are going for a walk." I felt generous.

He shrugged with a resigned smile. "I guess there isn't much else left for me to do."

"If you find it such an unpleasant duty, we will gladly release you from it!" I said pointedly and turned to Lea.

She whispered: "Let's go faster and get rid of him."

"I didn't want to be rude," I whispered back, "but I guess I shouldn't have said anything." Just then I noticed Renate coming toward us. We speeded up, took the first turning into the trees and soon lost track of them.

During my next visit at the hospital, Harry appeared behind

me so suddenly that I was startled. When we shook hands, he would not let go of my hand. Again his eyes seemed to be dipping deeply into mine, a little like Michael Kornblüh's had, many years before. But now I felt as if I were stretched out in a boat, eyes closed, drifting happily, aware that it was time to row back but unable to move, unwilling to move. Then I came to. Come on, I said to myself, what's all this? You'll be leaving in a few days. This is not the time to start something. Especially not with someone as conceited as he is. Do you want to be added to his list of conquests? And do you want him to think that you talked about Renate only to draw him toward yourself? Pull yourself together and act properly.

"May I escort you down?"

"No, thanks, I don't want to impose any unpleasant duties on you."

"Why unpleasant? There is nothing I would rather do!" He was smiling and didn't budge.

"Are you sure? Not so long ago you agreed to accompany me only because you couldn't think of anything better to do!"

He laughed softly. "Don't you know that I am never serious? But to be honest, I don't much care to walk with two girls at once—can you blame me? And you have to admit that Lea was anything but enthusiastic about my coming along."

I too laughed. "Nor were you, once Renate showed up!"

"Renate? Why do you have to bring in Renate? Next Sunday I'll walk with no one but you if you want me to!"

"Much obliged. But what makes you so sure that I'll want to?"

"It would be a pity if you didn't."

There was no way of getting at him, try as I might.

"Never mind. Besides, I must be off—I don't have as much free time as you seem to." I tried to sound as flippant as I could manage. But his only response was, with a disarming smile: "I hope I'll see you soon!"

10.

"*Servus* Frieda, Ilse, Franz, have you heard that our departure has been postponed? They have stopped issuing exit permits until further notice. My father was told that it may take another four to eight weeks."

"That's great! Aren't you glad?"

"I don't know. I had already begun to look forward to the trip, but I'm also happy that we can spend the rest of the summer together. What a perfectly gorgeous day!"

Everything was in bloom, the grass very green, the sky very blue, the sun just right, and around me nothing but cheerful faces, all of them showing pleasure at my staying.

Then I remembered an errand. "You'll have to excuse me for a few minutes, I must take care of something. Anyone like to come along?" And, with a smile, in an undertone to Harry who was standing close by:

"You still owe me a walk!"

"Of course," he said. At that moment Renate ambled over: "I'll come along, if you want me to."

"Sure," I nodded, "why don't you both come," and moved over so that Harry was in the middle.

It turned out that he loved classical music and was quite an accomplished pianist, and so we talked about music. Renate did not participate but suddenly gave a short laugh and called out: "What are you doing?"

In answer to my questioning glance: "He keeps stroking my hand! What a funny idea."

I laughed inwardly, an angry laugh. Serves him right, why doesn't he follow my advice and leave her alone! Can't he ever resist flirting? I must stay away from him, no doubt about it.

When I returned from my errand, the two, who had been waiting outside the building, proposed that we take a walk together. I declined.

"I want to get back to the others. And," I couldn't refrain from adding, "I don't want to disturb!"

To my surprise, Harry seemed genuinely annoyed. "You are not disturbing, quite the contrary. So don't talk nonsense and come with us."

What game was he playing? I had never met anyone like him. Trying to keep my composure, I said with a laugh while turning to walk away:

"Not everybody likes to walk in threes. So long."

"Come on, don't be a spoil-sport!" Renate's voice was trailing after me.

I didn't turn back, though I really wanted to stay and was quite sure that she meant what she said, that she really didn't mind sharing him with me. Was I unusually naïve, or were both of us so unsure of ourselves, or were we both pretending, perhaps even unaware that that was what we were doing? When, during my recent visit to Vienna, I saw her for the first time in almost fifty years—and it was a good encounter—she mentioned that she had been very jealous of me then. It came as a great shock. How could I have been so blind?

But then, perhaps everyone is pretending when in love. Pretending not just or not only to others but to oneself as well. Or was I, as so often, complicating a simple issue? Maybe ours was merely the typical adolescent response to a new and puzzling emotion. But if that was so, did our spending our adolescent years in that incongruous, abnormal environment make perpetual adolescents of us? At least of me? Sometimes I think so.

The rest of the afternoon was filled with weeding and cultivating, joking, talking and singing. I was pleased with myself because I had remained steadfast. No, I wasn't going to run after him the way Renate did, and I didn't need any complications now, shortly before my departure. Definitely not.

When I walked over to the hydrant for a sip of water, Renate, Harry and Harry's friend Ischu were sitting on a bench close by. Ischu was a little older than the rest of us. He had finished his medical training and was working at the Jewish hospital. By then, it had already been moved from the impressive Rothschild building into the rundown former Jewish elementary school on Malzgasse.

I remember very little about Ischu. Were it not for my diary, I might have forgotten him altogether. Harry has. Renate, however, remembers:

"Ischu was one of the few really decent people around at that time, and it killed him. When he was asked to become an *Ordner* he refused, even though he knew that that meant deportation. He didn't come back."

As I was approaching the bench, Harry called out to me:

"Liesl, you must tell me why you were in such a hurry to get back. The two of us have been racking our brains all this time whether anything we said offended you. Please sit down, there is room here between Renate and me—Renate, move over a little."

"Thanks, but I can't stay long. No, you didn't offend me. Is it so difficult to understand that I wanted to join the others rather than disturb the two of you?"

"A frank statement," Ischu said.

"Nonsense," Renate defended herself. "Both of us wanted to have you along."

"That's good to know—next time I'll come. But let me try a riddle on you which I have just heard. Ready? How does one wash a tiger?"

"What?" said Harry. "No idea."

"A real live tiger?" Ischu wanted to know.

"A totally alive wild tiger," I confirmed.

Ischu tried. "Well, let's see. You take a long pole, tie a towel around it and push it carefully through the bars—"

"If there are bars," Renate interjected. "What about a tiger in the desert?"

"Are there tigers in the desert?" Harry inquired. "All right, I give up. So how does one wash a tiger?"

"By risking one's life!" I said, and with wry faces everyone laughed.

"Help!" Renate moaned. "Is that supposed to be funny?"

"If you can laugh, it's funny," I defended my tiger and jumped up. "But I really must get back to the others."

"No, you don't," Harry said. "Now I have a question for you," and he held on to my arm.

"Well?" I remained standing.

"A water lilly grows daily by one hundred percent, that is, it doubles its size."

"That's impossible." Ischu stated categorically.

"Quiet, this is a math problem, so don't interrupt!" Harry threw him a reprimanding glance. "A water lilly doubles its size every day. On the fortieth day it covers the entire pond. When does it cover half the surface?"

On the twentieth, I wanted to say but that seemed too simple so I held back. There must be a catch. If it covers half the pond on the twentieth day, on the twenty-first—

"On the thirty-ninth day," I called out.

("Was that really all you kids could talk about during those awful times?" A friend who read these pages asked me.

"Yes, that was all we could talk about.")

"My compliments," said Harry with an appreciative glance. "Most people try the square root or some other complicated mathematical operation."

"Yes, my father did, and he is usually very sharp," Renate concurred.

"But now I really must get to work. Your laziness is contagious." I could feel the sparks. It was high time I left.

Harry pulled me back down on the bench.

"Just when we are having such a good time you want to leave. I will defend you if they accuse you of shirking."

"Are you sure that your defense will do the trick?"

"Liesl, what is it you want? Have I done anything to you that would justify your being so mean to me?"

Again his eyes held mine, but I didn't blink. "I don't want anything," I said. "I just don't want you to think that I am running after you."

He gave me a long look. "No, I won't think that. You have much too bad an opinion of me."

"All the better," and I ran off before he could pull me back down.

All the way home I was humming, elated at the wonderful day it had been. But at home I stepped before the mirror and gave myself a good talking to. Hadn't you decided to avoid him? Is that how you go about it? You know that he likes you but have you forgotten that he likes every girl? These verbal skirmishes may be fun but they are dangerous. And you know it. What is it you want? Draw him away from Renate and ruin your friendship with her too? Don't be a hypocrite, stop all that nonsense right now. Promise?—I promise, I promise!

11.

When I went to the Klügers to look for father, aunt Anny was there. Of course, she was not yet my aunt. Uncle Max married her long after the war, when he was quite sure that Olga wasn't coming back. Seeing her, I knew that something unusual must have happened. Anny didn't show herself much in the inner city or in the second district now that she had become a U-boat.

My father motioned to me to sit down and not interrupt. But Anny had either already told her story or wasn't going to. It must have been a scary one. She was so agitated that her hand could barely hold the tea cup Grete had offered her, and she set it down without drinking.

Anny was not related to us but ever since she had helped me buy the burgundy dress material, I was fond of her. Perhaps also because she too had come from the Protectorate Bohemia-Moravia, the former Czechoslovakia. Last year, when I visited her in Vienna for the first time in many years—she was 84 and quite frail—I was relieved to find her mentally still very alert, so that for once I could ask long overdue questions.

She had lived in Bohumín in Moravia (that's Oderberg in German) till 1941. When her brother, a prominent Viennese scientist whom even the Nazis had not touched, died suddenly of a heart attack, she came to Vienna. His son Paul, whom Anny called Bibi, was in a work detail in Waidhofen, in Upper Austria. He was not molested, but his mother and little sister were arrested shortly after the father's death.

Through six transports, Anny managed to delay their deportation. She bribed the SS official in charge by pressing into his hand a matchbox which contained three diamonds. He promised to get the two released. In the meantime Anny used all her skills to procure the necessary papers so that they could leave for Italy once they were free, and hopefully move on from there.

While his family was in detention at the Sperlgasse school, Bibi wanted to come back to town and volunteer to go with them. He only desisted when it transpired that men could no longer accompany women and children but would be shipped off separately. Despite her efforts, Anny did not succeed in saving the two. They left without arriving anywhere: the entire group was liquidated on the train.

Shortly before they were deported, Anny became suspicious that the rescue operation was dragging out too long. She went to see her SS contact, and was told that he was on the phone and that she should wait. But then his wife appeared and told Anny that he had had to leave, and would she come to a different address the next day. Anny decided that something was fishy, and that it would be advisable to go into hiding. She notified Bibi to return but not go home. Instead, she took him to a hiding place she had scouted out for him—attic space belonging to the apartment of his former high school Latin teacher, Frau Professor Matthä, and her mother. The mother's sister lived there as well, but she could not be trusted. Bibi spent three years in their attic, with water jug and chamber pot on the stairs, coming down only when his teacher signalled to him that the aunt wasn't in. One day in 1944 when a search for war resisters was on, they hid him inside a deep fireplace. There he found two others—a resistance fighter and a nobleman. When they returned to their respective hideouts, their black footprints had to be quickly wiped off the parquet floor before the sister would return.

For herself, Anny was not able to find a permanent refuge. She remained footloose, roaming the city or its outskirts during the day and sleeping at different places at night. Being a cosmetician, she had lined up several customers whom she catered to in their homes, and that provided her with enough money to survive, and with a few hours of shelter each day. Only a few close friends knew that she was in hiding. After nine o'clock when in all apartment buildings the hall lights were turned off and entrances locked, her friends let her in so that she could spend the night with them. She alternated her visits in order not to endanger anyone more than absolutely necessary, and to cover her own tracks.

Anny had several close calls. Once, in need of money, she took her fur coat to a dealer. "I need a thousand marks. You keep the rest." The woman asked her to come to her apartment for the money. "I'll get it right away. You just wait." But when Anny heard her making a phone call in the next room, she picked herself up, called out that she couldn't wait and took off. The other woman tried to detain her, then followed her. Anny jumped on a moving street car, took off her jacket, hid it in the shopping bag, put on a head scarf, jumped off the street car—and knew that she must never again show her face on Kärntnerstraße.

I asked her whether she remembered that evening at the Klügers, in the late summer of 1943. Was that why she had been so distraught then? No, that was something else and yes, she did remember. As she told her tale, slowly and graphically, I sat spellbound, unable to tear myself away, although it was getting late and I was expected at Inge's for supper. Anny remembered every detail as vividly as if it had happened the day before. The pitch and volume of her hoarse, tremulous voice kept rising, and I began to worry that the excitement might bring on a heart attack.

"You are the first to ask," she said to me. "Bibi gets angry if I try to talk of those days. He doesn't want to hear about any of it. But don't you think that these things must be told? And I can tell you some unbelievable experiences."

"Yes, I want to hear everything, and I will make sure it gets told."

That evening she had been visiting Bibi. While in his room, she heard an unfamiliar voice below, in the front room. Later she learned that the visitor was the secretary to Cardinal Innitzer. By the time he left and she was able to get out, it was close to ten o'clock.

When she reached her friend's apartment, she found her ironing, too worried about Anny's absence to go to sleep. By the time she had finished ironing and both women were ready for bed, it was close to midnight.

"Could I open the window just for a few minutes and get some fresh air before we lie down?" Anny begged. "I am suffocating."

They turned off all lights, pulled up the blinds and opened the living room window. Breathing deeply, Anny was looking out over the quiet city when she suddenly heard the rattling of an engine. It was one of those ominously familiar covered vans, and it pulled up in front of the building she was in. Three men in uniform approached the entrance and one rang the caretaker's bell.

"Ella, they are here!" Anny whispered, grabbed the few gold coins she had hidden in a jar, her purse, jacket and shoes, and raced out of the apartment and up to the next floor just as the boots began to stomp up the stairs. She heard them ask for her by name and her friend's answer that she knew her but had not seen her in quite some time. They searched the apartment, then two left while the third stayed put. Soon they returned, dragging somebody up the stairs with them. Anny could hear his gasps and realized that they must be hitting him. Yes, he was sure he had seen her go in and out of the apartment repeatedly. Through the open hall window, Anny heard her friend explain, remarkably calmly, that Anny worked somewhere in the suburbs in a factory or at a large war concern—she didn't know exactly which—and that she did drop in now and then. One time it had got late, the steetcars were no longer running, and so she had invited her to spend the night. She doubted that Anny would show up this night, it was much too late, but they were welcome to wait.

Anny decided that it was high time for her to disappear. On tiptoe, she made her way down in the dark, past the loud voices. By the front door she put on her shoes and began to fumble for the lock. Just then her other set of keys, those to Bibi's apartment, dropped to the tile floor with a crash. Upstairs someone pushed the button which turned on the hall light, and the light enabled Anny to unlock the door and let herself out.

She was walking down the street when the truck caught up with her, its searchlight combing the sidewalks. Slowly, swinging her hips, she walked on, dangling her purse. She was thirty-six then, blond, tiny and delicate. They drove past her.

At the first phone booth she stopped to call one of her faithful customers and inquire if she could spend the night with her. "I have missed the last streetcar and it's too far to walk home. But it will take me a good half hour to get to your place."

"Sure," was the simple answer. "Phone when you get here so that I can come downstairs and unlock the entrance for you."

Men began to follow and proposition her. Finally, there was one who looked like a gentleman and she accepted his offer to accompany her. As she switched her purse to her outer arm, he said with a smile:

"That's a good idea! After all, I might want to rob you."

When she announced that she had arrived and thanked him for his kindness, he would not let her go until she agreed to see him again.

"Look, it's so dark you don't even know what I look like," she tried to ward him off. But he kept insisting until she made a date with him for the day after next.

She found another phone booth but when she opened her purse, she had no change. Bending down, she probed the floor in the dark, just in case somebody had dropped a coin. Nothing. Desperate, she stopped a passing young couple and asked them for a coin to telephone.

Her friend was already waiting in the entrance and ushered her into the apartment. Only there she broke down and began to sob.

When Anny married uncle Max and became a family member, I was glad. Aunt Olga had managed to spirit Max out of Italy. He ended up interned in Switzerland and survived the war there. But when he returned to Bergamo after the war, there was no trace of Olga. Massimo, as he now called himself, remained in San Giovanni Bianco, leased an inn and managed it for some ten years, hoping that one day Olga would surface and find him.

Among the papers that Anny turned over to me after his death, I found an undated *"Declaration"* by an Italian couple, Anna and Cesare Ghisalberti from Bergamo. Here is the literal translation:

> "We the undersigned, parents of Second Lieutenant of the Alpine Troops Carlo Ghisalberti who was arrested by the Germans on 28 November 1943 for refusing to join the army of Mussolini's Republic; and transported to the Headquarters of the German SS Command (at Collegio Baroni di Via Pignolo) are attesting that Signora OLGA CEIGER, using her acquaintance with a high official of the German SS and not heeding the danger which approaching him meant, unselfishly assisted our son by arranging to get to him letters and food, and attempting (unfortunately not successfully) to obtain his release."

Once again Olga must have been playing a dangerous game. It didn't undo her then, for I also found one of her own cryptic notes, locale unspecified but dated 21 March 1944. It, too, was written in Italian, to some unnamed women friends—*mie carissime amiche*—and announced that Olga hoped to go into hospital and be operated on for her ulcer, that she expected to have "the toiletries and clean laundry by Thursday," and would they tell dear Signor Lenti where she was. (Could that have been a call for help?) She was hoping "that my good friends will take care of me" and would they convey her apologies to her friends on Via

Locatelli for all the worries she had caused, although, as they knew, this was not her fault. Since the note only came into my hands after Massimo's death, I was unable to ascertain how he had come by it.

During one of his visits to Vienna, Massimo accompanied my father to Frau Wilma's store. When Anny walked in, father introduced them. Massimo invited Anny to a cup of coffee. She refused. She had to get back to work. Always resourceful, she was managing a small handicraft shop at the time. Ten minutes later, a waiter arrived at the shop carrying a tray with coffee and cake—"ordered by the gentleman outside." When she looked up, Massimo raised his hat, bowed and walked away. It took another year of courting before she agreed to marry him, but once she did, she didn't even resent his talking about "my Olga." She nursed him faithfully until he died, at ninety-two. She was eighty-three then.

12.

Mrs. Mezei, the twins' mother, was a secretary at the Community's central office. The twins and she lived at Förstergasse No. 5, around the corner from us but in the same block. Since the Community's headquarters were in the first district and quite a walk from Untere Augartenstraße, I began to drop in on Ilse for short after-supper visits at their apartment instead. To my surprise, I found Harry there almost every time I came. It turned out that he was supposed to deliver the daily hospital report to the Community office—he had even been allocated a bicycle for that purpose. Instead, he took the report to Kurt on his way home from the hospital, and Kurt would take it with him to work the next morning. Harry, too, lived just around the corner, on Haasgasse, and so he usually stayed to chat until curfew time.

Once I knew the pattern—he always came around eight-thirty—I tried to leave earlier so that Kurt would have no occasion for off-color remarks and Harry would not think that I was waiting for him. Whenever we did meet, I made sure not to show how thrilled I was at his presence.

During the week that followed that special Sunday at the

cemetery, I paid another hospital visit. Frieda had been discharged, and I no longer recall whom I went to see. A man whom we knew only as "Herr Paul" was sitting at the reception desk. He was middle-aged and self-important, and loved practical jokes. When I asked for my pass, he seized my hand and pulled me along, explaining that someone had been looking for me. I had no idea who that might be but offered no resistance in order to avoid a commotion. At that moment a door opened and Harry emerged.

"Here he is!" Paul shouted triumphantly. "Harry, this young lady has been asking for you."

He seized Harry's hand, placed mine in it and disappeared with a huge grin.

"Good morning," I said as casually as I could and tried to pull my hand out of his. "You know Paul, so I don't need to tell you that I was not really looking for you."

"I know, but it's nice to see you anyway!" Why do you fight me, his eyes were asking, you know that I like you and you like me, why don't you let things take their course? I told myself that he probably gave this line to every girl, but my resolve was weakening. What if he really meant it? Then I got angry with myself, and that broke the spell.

"You'll have to excuse me. I've come to visit a patient. No, thanks, I know the way. So long!"

He let go of my hand. I felt his eyes on me until I turned the corner. Only then was I able to take a deep breath and relax.

The following Sunday, Renate and I were exercising together on the cemetery meadow. Harry was not there, which made life much simpler. It was his "Eva Sunday", according to Ilse. In response to my surprised look, she explained:

"Every other Sunday he plays duets with a certain Eva whom none of us know." I noted her sly smile, but it didn't faze me. Not yet.

13.

When I dropped in at the exchange on Wednesday, Kurt, who was one of the Community's messengers, was there as well.

"Are you planning to switch to *du* with Harry before or after the first kiss?" he asked out of a clear blue sky, with a big grin and cunning look. While I was still groping for an appropriate response, Ilse reprimanded him:

"Keep quiet, Kurt, or it will be your fault if Liesl's father goes to see Harry's mother!"

"What in the world are you talking about?"

Ilse mentioned, with many interruptions on Kurt's part which made her tale even more disjointed, something about a walk *à deux*, about trouble at Renate's house, trouble at Harry's house, Harry angry with Renate, Renate unhappy. It was impossible to establish exactly what had happened, except that it had nothing to do with me, which was reassuring.

On Sunday, I realized that something was indeed wrong. Renate was mumbling that life was awful, how the best way out would be suicide. Alarmed, I suggested that she join me on a walk.

This is what had happened: as on many Sundays—and Renate got much kidding for it—she and Harry had gone for a long walk through the cemetery. But on that Sunday, he had indeed kissed her. She reported the occurence at home as she reported everything. Her father took his hat and marched off to talk to Harry's mother, over Renate's horrified protests. She did not know what he had said to her, except that now Harry was angry and avoided her.

I felt sorry for her but also relieved. Her reaction confirmed my impression that, although she enjoyed Harry's company, she was not looking or ready for a real relationship. I tried to console her by telling her that the whole matter was trivial and didn't mean much, and that she shouldn't encourage Harry nor take him seriously.

As I was talking, I didn't immediately notice that Renate was steering me into a side lane until I recognized the two figures coming toward us—Harry and Ischu. They were engrossed in conversation and would have passed us without looking up, had not some demon made me call out:

"Hey, you two! Are you sleepwalking in broad daylight?" But when I noticed the look Harry gave me, I didn't wait for an answer but pulled Renate along. The whole thing was beginning to get out of hand. Moreover, the episode with Lea was still smarting. Not again, I kept telling myself, you mustn't do it again. Except that this time there was no doubt that Harry was trying his best to draw me toward him, and that I found it harder and harder to resist. At that moment, I wished we would get our exit visas the next day and leave.

Having contributed my share of labor, I returned to our spread-out blankets. They were empty, and I stretched out. A little later, some of the others joined me. Kurt had brought along a thin paperback with "1000 Questions" and we began to work on the answers. Ischu and Harry had settled off to one side. During a lull in the conversation I heard Ischu say:

"Look, Harry, here comes Renate! She looks like a stray dog which has lost its master!"

"Doctor, your remarks are totally out of place!" I bristled.

Ischu looked up, dumbfounded. Then he began to laugh.

"Remember, Harry, I told you from the start that Liesl would make a much better partner for you than Renate! Why in the world did you have to pick Renate?"

"If you don't stop talking nonsense this minute I will really get angry!" I snapped.

He got up and walked away, now truly offended. All of us were, after all, making similar cracks all the time and no one took them seriously. No wonder he was at a loss to understand why I had overreacted so badly. I, of course, couldn't explain. It took me quite a while later in the afternoon to pacify him. For once, neither Kurt nor Ilse commented, but my afternoon was spoiled.

Wednesday night I dropped in on Ilse. She was ironing. I sat down on the window sill and watched Kurt, whose task it was to carry the irons to and from the stove to reheat them. When Ilse left the room, I reached for her iron. Work is always more fun at someone else's house.

Kurt was giving me the news of the week. Casually, he stated that Harry had mentioned not seeing me at Ilse's for several days. That reminded me to look at my watch. It was a quarter to nine, high time to leave. But it was already too late. As I was heading for the door, the bell rang. Ilse went to open and Kurt mumbled:

"You have achieved the purpose of your visit."

Before I could think of anything appropriate to say, the two had entered. We conversed for a while, then I decided to take the bull by the horns. It seemed the right moment.

"You know, Harry, you are the only one with whom I am still *per Sie*. How about switching to *du*?"

He gave me one of his intense looks. "Gladly! That's where you can tell the age difference between Renate and you, Liesl."

"What's that supposed to mean? I'd just as soon not be compared to Renate!" I had only wanted to take the wind out of Kurt's sails, and if Harry misinterpreted my gesture, I was again in trouble.

Harry looked away without answering and I got up to leave. "I must get home. It's late."

"I have already been asking Ilse why *Sie*"—he corrected himself—"*du* show yourself so rarely. Didn't she tell you?"

I ignored the question. So you are using Ilse as a go-between, are you!

"I must leave too," Harry added. "Wait for me."

When we stepped out onto the landing, the light was already turned off for the night.

"I hope the downstairs door is still open," Kurt said. "Shout if you need me to come down and let you out. Harry, take good care of Liesl. It's very dark!"

"Thanks, but I can take care of myself," I called back toward Kurt and removed Harry's arm from my shoulders. It required considerable self-discipline because I suddenly had the ridiculous wish that he would keep his arm there and never take it away again.

I compressed my lips. It was so dark that I could only grope my way down step by step, with one hand on the railing. His arm returned, but now to take my elbow and guide me. Again I brushed it off. "Thanks, I am doing all right."

"But Kurt can't see us," he said in a barely audible whisper.

"That makes no difference to me," I whispered back and felt like crying. "Kurt, it's open," I called from below toward the third floor, "good night!" Then I took off like an arrow. Even so, I did not sleep well that night.

During the next few days I was too busy to see anyone and also determined to stay away from Harry. On Sunday it rained so that the trip to the cemetery was out anyway. But by Wednesday I could not stand it any longer and went to the telephone exchange.

I learned that Renate and Harry had made up, that she could

again be found wherever he was, appeared in Ilse's office every morning at eleven in order to run into him on the stairs, and that Harry chatted with her but didn't seem particularly interested. Renate, nonetheless, appeared perfectly happy. I had been right, then—all she wanted was to be with him and talk to him.

On my way home I tried to take stock. She had what she wanted, so perhaps I no longer needed to hold back on her account. But did I really want to get involved just before my departure? On the other hand, perhaps it would be all right exactly because it was not for long? After all, I wouldn't want to get seriously involved with such a Don Juan. But what about his triumph? Another success to be chalked up, another name added to the list. But I was not serious either, was I? I knew better than to fall in love with such a *bel ami*. But wouldn't it make going away all the more difficult? I didn't know what to do and decided to lie low, await developments and, when the time came, let my common sense guide me. Common sense, indeed.

14.

On the right, a long, ornate black wrought-iron fence sets off a mansion-like three-story building which sits in the middle of a spacious and well-manicured lawn. Without sun, the green is very deep, self-contained and sedate, while the house looks just as imposing as its railing. Red bricks, black shutters, a high gray mansard roof with dormer windows. Dignified and unassailable, a safe haven. I wonder what kind of people live there. A porch winds around the house, forms a second, tighter barrier, right now softened by a spectacular wall of purple rhododendron in full bloom.

A fat robin stands motionless on the lawn, his eyes on me. In contrast, a squirrel is racing exuberantly from tree to tree, totally oblivious of my presence. As I walk along the fence, I notice that close to one end two bars are missing. The hole is just large enough for a dog or small child to squeeze through. Despite the flaw, the total impression is one of beauty, prosperity, safety. But when I turn back for one last look, I see a big flag fluttering in the breeze. No, I don't want to know who lives here—I have heard too many flags flap about my ears.

The lawn across the street is strewn with a pile of newly cut boards. I dismiss the thought of coffins. It is far more likely that somebody is getting ready to redo steps or a porch.

The sky is almost entirely covered by a dark gray cloud bank, but just above me there is an open area and the sun is burning down through it. I am hot, sticky and tense. Even if I manage to stay dry, it probably was not a good idea to walk to town today.

On that Sunday, too, the sun was hot. I was one of the first to arrive on the cemetery. Having changed into a bathing suit, I spread out my blanket. One by one, the others trickled in, among them Lea and Trude with whom Lea had become friendly after our breakup. A few more young people whom I don't remember, then Kurt and Ilse, Frieda and Heinzi, finally Harry and Renate. They arrived together but didn't separate themselves from the main group. A small contingent decided to play ball despite the heat. We others were lounging around, talking, napping or day-dreaming.

Around four, when it began to cool off, Ilse reminded us that life was not all play and no work. I got up to wash my feet under the hydrant before putting on shoes and heading toward the veg-etable patch. But a pool of mud had formed around the hydrant, and there were no stepping stones to rescue clean feet from new mud. I was still investigating the situation, when Harry appeared next to me. He had his shoes on. "Put your arm around my neck and I'll carry you out of here!"

He lowered me very slowly onto my blanket. For a few moments I lay still and overwhelmed. Then I began to kick my legs up in the air to dry them.

"What's going on here?" Dr. F. stood next to me with a suspi-cious look on his face.

"I have wet feet and forgot to bring a towel. Can you help me out?" I was not going to be intimidated by him.

"I see. No, I am afraid I don't have a towel either." He sounded perplexed but walked away without further comment. That was all I needed, his getting into the act.

"Come on, everybody! Time to work," Kurt shouted.

"I'll join you as soon as my feet are dry." I turned on my stomach, feet in the air.

"May I join you for a few minutes?" a husky voice asked softly right next to me.

"Why not, there is plenty of grass all around!" I didn't look up but my heart began to pump.

"Oh, but the grass is hard and you have a nice soft blanket, and even a pillow. Couldn't I have at least a corner of the pillow?"

I moved over but turned my head away from him. For the longest time we lay next to each other without speaking. He played with the fingers of my left hand, and his touch was soothing and cool. I knew well what he was doing and that I should put a stop to it, but I was as if in a trance, hypnotized, seduced, conquered.

A ball landed near us, with Renate in hot pursuit. "Come and join us," she called out as she ran off again with the ball.

"How about joining the ballgame?" I made a feeble effort at breaking the spell.

Although I was still looking the other way, I could tell that he was smiling. His head was right beside mine.

"Do you want to get rid of me?"

"Not necessarily, but what will Renate say?"

"She is busy. Don't worry about her." Then, after a pause: "If I only knew whether Eva is coming next Sunday!"

"Why shouldn't she?" I turned toward him, puzzled at the association.

"She has stood me up twice now, and if the weather is as beautiful as it is today, I would much rather be out here than wait for her at home."

"I am sure she will reward you for your faithful watch!" I tried to smile ironically.

"Tell me, Liesl, why are you so nasty to me? We merely play the piano together. She is the only partner I have and I assure you, there is nothing between us."

I shrugged. "It's none of my business anyway, so why talk about it?"

"Because I want you to know and believe me!"

"Do l have to?"

"Yes, it's important to me. Besides, my parents are always at home, and usually we have visitors as well. That should convince you if my words don't."

"Never mind, your Eva doesn't really interest me. But it's not very nice of her to keep you waiting."

Liesl, what are you doing? Remember your promise?

"You're right. I'll give her one more chance and that will be it."

I jumped up as I saw Renate approach again, scanning the landscape. "What are you looking for?"

She gave a half-amused, half-embarrassed smile. "Someone has hidden one of my shoes and I can't find it. That's not funny!"

We helped her look for the shoe. It was wedged in the fork of a tree limb, five feet above ground, close to the first row of graves.

By the time I reached the garden plot, the workers had finished. They were in the process of returning the tools to the shed. I hadn't realized that it was so late. Harry helped me pick a few wild roses to take home, and I helped him gather grass for his rabbits. Neither of us said much but I was sure he felt as good as I did.

While I was shaking Trude's hand in parting, she whispered to me:

"You are mean, Liesl. First Renate loses the ball, then her shoe, and then you take Harry away from her."

I laughed. What was there to say? I was gloriously happy.

15.

On Wednesday I stopped by the telephone exchange. I had to cope with a barrage of insinuations but was in too good a mood to mind. Ilse immediately started talking about Harry. With her most innocent expression she enumerated all his bad qualities, how conceited he was, what a skirt chaser, how unreliable, and on and on. I kept nodding. I knew all that and wasn't going to deny it, but who cared? I liked him the way he was, and the whole thing was not serious anyway. Had he been an angel I might have fallen in love with him, so it was just as well that I knew what was what. In the words of the popular song, *"Liebe war es nicht, nur eine kleine Liebelei,"* it wasn't real love, only a little game we played.

On Sunday I was on the streetcar with Ilse and Kurt.

"Who else is coming?" I asked.

Kurt's response could be relied on. "Harry won't be there—that's what you really want to know, isn't it? You needn't count on him."

"Don't be silly," I warded off. "I know very well that he isn't coming. I was talking about the others."

"Renate may not show up either. Without Harry, there is nothing to draw her, is there? It's bound to be dull, Liesl. With whom will you console yourself?"

I didn't answer but agreed tacitly that it was going to be a boring afternoon, with nothing to look forward to.

When we walked through the gate, we were welcomed by a hail of small stones whose originators remained invisible. It seemed that everyone had arrived before us. Kurt and Ilse dropped their bags and ran off to get even with the perpetrators of the assault. I looked around and noticed a small group in the distance, too far away to be recognized. One figure rose and came running toward me. It was Harry.

My heart began to hammer and, as we shook hands, I couldn't help smiling at him, against my better judgment.

"What are you doing here?" I asked. "I thought this was your Eva Sunday?"

Even before he answered, his eyes told me everything.

"I wanted to see you."

My heart lept but I took hold of myself.

"Really?" I said as ironically as I could, turned and ran after Ilse and Kurt. I felt like shouting or singing, but instead I changed into my shorts and sat down demurely next to Ilse. The three attackers were likewise there—Franz, Heinzi and Trude. A general amnesty must have been declared, unless Ilse and Kurt had already meted out justice.

Everybody was preoccupied with eating sunflower seeds in such a way that, as your teeth split the shell, the seed drops into your mouth. It took me a while to master the art. I knew that Harry was lying on a blanket nearby, but I didn't look in his direction.

When Ilse and Kurt took off to start weeding, Trude joined me. As we chatted, a shadow fell on us, and Mr. B. lay down between us. All of us called him Mr. B. and so I don't recall his name.

"That's nice, here I've found a cozy spot, and with two pretty girls on top!"

"Has it occurred to you to ask whether you are welcome?" I asked both amused and annoyed. Ilse didn't like Mr. B. She claimed that he had a lascivious look. I had not made up my mind about him.

"A man is always welcome among ladies!" he quipped with a grin, and I couldn't think of a fitting response. Trude didn't seem to mind. She exchanged a few words with him, then turned back to me. I noticed that Harry, his head resting on his hands, was watching us.

"Trude, I need your advice. What shall I do?"

"In the matter we were just discussing?" she asked.

"No, in last Sunday's matter," I rejoined.

"I see. Let me think about it." She winked at me. "Harry," she then called in his direction, "why are you lying there all by yourself? Don't you want to join us?"

"I was just getting ready," he called back. Moments later he was lying next to me on the blanket, covering himself with his own blanket. "Aren't you chilly, Liesl?" he asked and spread part of his blanket over me.

That must look impossible, it flashed through my mind, and I pushed the blanket off. "No, thanks."

But when his hand groped toward mine, I didn't withdraw. We spoke little, and yet it seemed to me that we were holding long, complicated conversations. Mr. B. had turned his back on us and was chatting with Trude.

"Where is Renate?" I suddenly remembered.

"How should I know? Not here, at any rate."

I felt sorry for her. She had undoubtedly stayed at home not expecting Harry to come. I was almost painfully exhilarated. Never before had I felt anything remotely similar. I lay there with my eyes closed, my hand in his, listening to his husky voice. It was uttering trifles to which anyone could have listened, and yet it seemed to be saying the nicest, sweetest things, things meant only for me. I wanted to believe every word of what that voice was implying, whether true or not. No one had ever talked to me like that. Only today would I let myself believe it, only today.

Trude got up and excused herself. She had to fetch something, she said. She asked Mr. B. to accompany her, and we were alone.

Harry pulled the blanket over me once more.

"Please don't! Someone might see us. In fact, I'd like to take a walk."

I jumped up. I was still in shorts, so I picked up my jacket and skirt and threw them over my arm. He took my beach bag and his blanket. Silently we walked toward the trees and into their shade, and were soon alone among the graves, around us moss, pine needles, trees and sky. We lay down on his blanket and he put his arm around me.

"Harry, I feel guilty because of Renate."

"Forget about Renate," he whispered. "She's a sweet kid but that has nothing to do with the two of us. And is it my fault that she isn't here today?"

"Oh, so it's only because she isn't here and you are bored—"

He put his hand over my mouth. "Hush! Haven't I told you that I came because of you? Come on, what do I have to do for you to believe me?"

"I would like to, but you have warned me yourself not to take you seriously!"

"I am not lying," he said firmly. "Believe me! I am not that bad, really."

I remained silent, both afraid and tempted to believe him, not knowing what to think or say. He kept his eyes on me for what seemed a long time, then he asked:

"Liesl, will you also send your father to talk to my mother?"

What in the world was I supposed to answer?

"Luckily, there's no need for that, is there?" But apparently my eyes gave him the answer he was waiting for and he kissed me, gently but firmly. That kiss was so different from the two kisses I had received before that I had to say or do something to regain my composure. And to make up for having let him kiss me. And for having responded. I slapped Harry.

"Thank you! Will I now get slapped after every kiss?" His expression was so comical that I could not help laughing.

"No, that was only in case you should decide to brag."

"Do you really think I will talk to anyone about something which concerns only the two of us?" I knew that he meant it but couldn't capitulate so quickly.

"What about Renate?"

His mouth closed mine, and although I made an effort at resistance, I acknowledged without regret that he was stronger.

It was August and the evening breeze had turned cool.

"Harry, we must get back. I bet they are wondering what has happened to us, and I don't want them to talk about me for weeks, as they have about Renate."

"Too bad, but tell me when I can see you again?"

"How about next Sunday?"

"But then Renate will be here!" He seemed genuinely distressed.

"So what?" I laughed. "I have to watch my reputation."

"But I want to see you!" Did he really mean it? Who cared.

"Would you like to come to my place on Wednesday evening, around six-thirty? If you are free."

"Why not before Wednesday? Won't you at least visit Ilse before then?"

"On Mondays and Thursdays I have English class, and on Tuesday I promised to visit Ditha. And now let me have my bag. We should go back separately to keep them from talking."

While walking back, I tried to compose myself. Had I transcended the bounds I had drawn for myself? Perhaps not. If he was playing Don Juan, I could play Doña Juana just as well. No hearts would get broken and eventually I would have pleasant memories. He seemed to understand perfectly that this was going to be just an episode, that it had to remain harmless and noncommital. But I had to calm down before my face would reveal our secret to everybody.

"There you are, Liesl! Considering Harry's habits, that went surprisingly fast!" I hadn't expected better of Kurt.

"Is there any work left for me or have you taken care of everything without me?"

"Now she comes," Ilse's voice was reproachful.

"Too bad! If I had known that you'll miss me, I would have come even later!"

"What?" An indignant chorus.

"It's such a pleasure to be missed! Kurt, don't make a sour face, that hasn't even grown in my own backyard. Free after Oscar Wilde. Let me have a rake and I'll get to work."

That should do it, I thought. But I had underestimated Kurt.

"Where did you leave Harry?"

"I haven't got him on a leash, have I? He walked with me for a while, then we separated."

That finally stopped him. Later I asked Trude if there had been much talk.

"One of them said that Harry was right to claim that all girls were running after him, but I pointed out that this time it was he who started it. That was all."

This didn't sound exactly reassuring, but I couldn't care less. Let them talk as long as they don't know anything. However, I decided to leave without saying goodbye to Harry, and that was duly noted by Ilse and Kurt.

On the streetcar, I thought how awful it would be should the exit permits arrive now.

16.

Despite my self-absolution, I felt guilty toward Renate. To be sure, she was only fourteen, but that didn't mean that she had no feelings—that soul which my father had denied me. And yet I was totally unable to tell what those feelings were. Our relationship was pleasant and relaxed but very superficial, quite unlike that with Lotte which had quickly become intimate, and perhaps for that reason so susceptible to tensions and hurts. Renate was always friendly, accommodating—and slightly spaced out. Any kidding she would brush off with a shrug or a smile, and I could not tell if they masked indifference, self-defense, or pleasure at the attention she was getting.

I began to wonder whether the fact that I was unable to figure her out, to know the "real" Renate, reflected the impossibility of knowing anyone. After all, one could only see people's surfaces, everything else was supposition or invention. Even Kurt and Ilse, in whose company I felt so much at ease, I knew only through their responses to me and to others, and I defined them by the qualities that seemed most constant and could therefore be presumed basic: their modesty and evenly meted out friendliness, their punctilious adherence to prescribed religious precepts, and their seemingly endless capacity for kidding.

And what about the insuperable gap between myself and everybody else? If it was impossible to know other people's selves because all one could see was their surfaces, the reverse was true with regard to one's own self. How was I to incorporate my surfaces into an entity that would be me, when I couldn't see any of these surfaces properly? Mirror images are not true since they are two-dimensional and reversed, and the reflections of me in my friends' eyes were even less precise, sometimes outright inaccurate—inconsistent eye-witness accounts. For all I could gather, my friends didn't know me any better than I knew them, and yet I was afraid of dispensing with their impressions of me because I didn't know whether, should I do so, I would be getting closer to my true self or reaching into emptiness.

It also occurred to me that it might be presumptuous to expect to truly "know" another human being. Wouldn't reducing others to constructs of my own mind be a violation of their autonomy and a dismissal of their uniqueness? By attempting to re-create them I would actually be inventing them, almost the way a writer invents characters. And isn't an invented character in some ways a travesty, a reduction to neat dimensionality of something that is in flux, multilayered and not entirely definable? And once I start inventing those around me, won't there also be the temptation to invent myself into a coherent, cleaned up self? It was dishonest to invent a self and live with invented people in an invented reality, even if that were the only way to make sense of the world and of myself.

Back in Ostrau, life had been so simple—why was everything now so confused and confusing? Perhaps there really was something wrong with me, and my father was right in claiming that I was not yet a person. I seemed to consist of nothing but separate and disparate impulses, some good, some bad, many of them contradictory and unpredictable. Brash and timid, sentimental and cynical, solicitous and mean, cowardly and foolhardy, selfish and ready to give all I had. I was either impossibly complex or totally fractured, and in either case further away from reaching my ideal than ever. And the worst was that there was no one to whom I could turn for guidance or reassurance. I had taken Ilse and Kurt for models except that their good-natured kidding turned flippant and harsh in my throat, and didn't begin to express what I would have liked to express.

I filled many diary pages with these speculations before finally resolving that there were no answers, that there could be no answers, and that I had better rely only on facts, on what I could see, hear and touch, and stop trying to analyse or synthesize.

During my recent visit with Frieda and Theo, I learned that Ilse's father, a well-known Hungarian journalist, had fled to Italy at the beginning of the war. He was interned there. The family lost contact with him and feared the worst—with good reason, it turned out. I could tell that both twins adored their father, but neither ever spoke of their anxiety. Perhaps all of us were playing the same game—for each other and for ourselves—in order to survive.

17.

On Tuesday afternoon I went to the movies with Kuno whom I had run into after a long hiatus. When I returned home, the door was double-locked and a message stuck in it, telling me to head for the consulate. My father was already there. A transport was being assembled, he told me, and since we couldn't be sure who would be targeted, he thought it wiser for us to sleep out.

However, this time we couldn't stay at the consulate. After some phoning around father had located a place for us. I didn't know the elderly couple who took us in. The evening was long and uncomfortable. I ate very little, which may have been just as well because at least I didn't deplete their supplies, and I didn't get much sleep on their hard, bumpy couch. We left right after breakfast so as to put them in as little danger as possible. I walked all over town with my shopping bag since father had given me orders not to show my face at home before the afternoon.

Father was already there when I arrived. He had learned that a transport of about fifty people had been assembled. Now we began to worry about our friends. He spent the next hour in the phone booth, trying to find out from his contact at the Community, who had been taken. I went to see Ditha whom I had stood up the evening before. She was always well-informed despite the fact that they didn't have a phone.

To our relief, no one we knew had been apprehended. But around six-thirty that evening the doorbell rang, with one very long ring. Since most of our friends were in the habit of sounding two or three short rings, this could mean trouble. Was this an *Aushebung*, a razzia? I was home alone. As, somewhat uneasy, I rose to open, there was such an insistent knocking on the door that my heart began to pound. They were coming for us, no question about it. The knocking, now also with a sharp instrument, possibly a key, continued.

I took off my shoes, tiptoed for my coat, filled the small bag which I had emptied only hours before and waited, barely daring to breathe. If the knocking stopped, and if there was no *Ordner* left behind to catch us, I would try to get to the Klügers and alert father.

After an eternity all grew quiet. I gave myself an additional five minutes, then I opened the door. No one was in sight but a used streetcar ticket was wedged in the keyhole. With some effort, I made out two penciled words: "Greetings—St."

I drew a deep breath, both relieved and concerned. Could it be Dr. Storfer? He had gone into hiding just before he was to be arrested. Since he was an important person, the Gestapo was especially angry that he had slipped through their fingers. He must need father's help badly to dare come to us. What a fright he had given me.

When I showed the note to my father, his face darkened. It was very risky to get involved in that affair. But then an alternative occurred to him. It might have been Frau Stiasny with whom he had assorted "business" dealings.

The following evening I was doing my homework for English class, at the last moment as always, when the doorbell rang. Preoccupied as I was, I went to the door without much thought and opened it. Outside the door stood Harry.

"Well, hi! What brought you here?" His existence had completely slipped my mind.

"But you told me to come and see you! Am I disturbing?"

"No, not at all. Come in. But I don't have much time, my class meets at seven. You know, we had so many worries the last few days that I forgot about you."

His eyes were laughing toward me. "That's all right. The main thing is that I've found you. I was just ready to put a note in your door—"

"Wait a minute," I interrupted, a light begining to dawn. "Were you here last night?"

"Yes, didn't you say to come on Wednesday night? But you weren't at home. Didn't you see my message?"

"So it was you! I read the *H* for an *ST* and thought that it was Dr. Storfer looking for my father. How could you be so thoughtless? To ring up a storm and knock like mad—nobody would open to that."

"You were in? Had I only realized! So close and yet unreachable. If you knew how difficult it was to find your apartment in the first place. I didn't have your address and couldn't remember the house. I went from door to door in the next house."

"Good god," I laughed, "that has three staircases!"

"Unfortunately not. It has four. Four floors to each, each floor four doors, that makes—"

"All right, all right," I covered my ears. "I won't say another word. But next time, please give two, or better three short rings, then I will know it's you."

"Fine, but don't I deserve a reward for my trouble?" He pulled me on his lap.

Just before he could kiss me, I drew back.

"Your eyes!"

"What about my eyes?"

"They aren't black! They are brown, solid brown! And I had liked your black eyes so much."

"There are no black eyes, didn't you know that? Only dark brown. It's the dark eyebows that make them appear black. But you like me with brown eyes too, don't you?"

When I was able to speak, I protested. "What a disappointment! And your black eyes were the only thing that attracted me to you. Now there's nothing to like."

He laughed at the gleam in my eyes and I blushed. And suddenly a strange thing happened. I seemed to have left my body, was watching myself from somewhere above and was shocked by what I saw. Was that me who was flirting so shamelessly, who allowed her body to yield without protest, who had thrown all caution to the wind and, worse, wasn't even trying to conceal her pleasure? What would grandma have said!

The split lasted for just a few seconds, then my eyes fell on the clock and I was myself again.

"A quarter to seven! Harry, I must leave this minute. Don't be angry that I am throwing you out but I'll be late."

"That's fine. I am ready to go. When do I see you again, Liesl?"

No, he probably said "Lieserl," a name I had never liked until he used it and made it sound melodious and affectionate. Only when it was all over except for his voice resounding in my mind's ear, did I realize that he had called me by that name.

"I can meet you at Ilse's later—if you want me to."

"Of course I want you to!"

"You can escort me home from her place. But please be careful that you don't give us away."

"That goes without saying. I'll see you in two hours."

"In two hours!" I shouted and flew to my class.

18.

"Good evening, Ilse! What's wrong?"

"Nothing. Come on in. I am glad to see you. I began to worry that you might have been nabbed too."

"No, we are all right. Did they take anyone we know?"

"It just goes on and on," Ilse said sadly. "When will God finally put an end to it?"

Had even she, with her bedrock faith, begun to waver? I had no answer, but our silence strengthened the bond between us.

Then the doorbell rang and Ilse put her face back on.

"Kurt, would you get the door?"

"Hello, Ilse! Greetings, Liesl—where have you been hiding out?"

Quite an actor, wasn't he. Perhaps he was also putting on an act when we were alone? How little I knew him.

"Hello, Harry. I was just about to tell Ilse how I'd spent the week and what a scare we'd had. I hope it won't bore you."

"Of course not." He bowed with studied politeness. I avoided his eyes and began to tell my story. When I mentioned the note which read *ST*, Kurt interrupted:

"Not Dr. Storfer! Do you know him?"

"Yes, and I also thought of him right away."

"And was it him?" Ilse asked. "How careless of him to come to this neighborhood. What a risk to take!"

"It wasn't him." I could feel Harry's eyes on me. "It was an acquaintance of my father's, Frau Stiasny. But I hope I never have to go through that fright again."

Harry and I left just before nine so that Kurt would not have to unlock the downstairs door for us. There was no moon, and when Harry put his arm around my shoulders, I didn't protest. I couldn't remember ever having been so happy.

We walked in silence. When it was time to part, he asked:

"What do we do about Sunday? You know, Renate will be at the cemetery."

"So what? You'll go for your usual walk with her or stay with the group, and I'll put in my time in the garden so that Kurt does not fire me."

"Joking aside, it's going to be awful. How about not going at all?"

"Come on, that would immediately attract attention. Besides, what about Eva? Isn't that her Sunday?"

"Well, she came last Sunday and left in a huff when she didn't find me at home. She didn't leave a message."

"I am sorry."

"I am not." His eyes, black or brown, were shining even in the deep darkness around us.

"Can I see you tomorrow?"

"Tomorrow I promised to drop in on Kuno."

"Kuno? Who is Kuno?"

"Someone I worked for long ago."

"Oh? And you are still seeing him? May I know more?"

"Of course. His name is Rolf Kunowski. He is German but not a Nazi. Perhaps he is red. Maybe even a Jew with false papers. For a few months I worked for him, painting St. Christopher figures on wooden pins and earrings. In a tiny studio, right by the Anker clock. It was my first job, actually my only paid job. Kuno has—" I almost confessed to his blond and very Germanic girl friend, but then only mentioned the dog and the tiny turtle which kept getting lost. "Once it was lost for two weeks."

"How old is he?"

"In his late twenties, I would guess. Come to think of it, I wonder how he has managed to stay out of the army. He is extremely well-read and well-informed, and fun to debate with."

"That doesn't do me any good!"

I couldn't help laughing. "And on Saturday I am going to the *Staatsoper* to hear *The Bartered Bride*. I can hardly wait."

"With whom are you going?"

"Alone. I stood in line for three hours on Bräunerstraße to get a ticket."

"You are brave. I wouldn't go near Bräunerstraße if you paid me!"

"I know. But the box office is not at all close to the Gestapo building."

"So where does all that leave me?" His expression of despair was very comical.

I relented. "If you think it worth your while, you can come up between five-thirty and six for a quick chat."

"Of course it is worth my while!" The flatterer. "And I won't forget to ring three times, right? Good night."

It was a long and wonderful goodnight kiss, even under the black, starless sky.

19.

Where am I? The house before which I have stopped looks familiar, but it isn't Untere Augartenstraße 25. And I am alone.

It takes me a few seconds to realize that I am on my way to town, today, forty-seven years later. I register almost with a shock that I am standing in front of the house from which I got married thirty-three years ago. How did I get here? I must have crossed several streets without noticing.

The house looks terrible. Has it always been this rundown? I wonder who lives in the second floor apartment now. Actually, it seems empty. There are no curtains on either of the two windows which face the almost flat roof where Wilbur, the kitten we had given each other as an engagement present, romped around until the day he disappeared. The neighbor was very rude when I asked whether he had seen Wilbur. "Don't bother me with your cat! Good riddance if it's gone, at least it will leave my antenna alone." A few days later Florence, the sweet old lady downstairs, took me aside to tell me that she was sure he had killed the cat and thrown the paper bag into the trash can. I couldn't get out of her how much she knew. Though I called the police and the SPCA, neither could do much since there was no proof, and Florence lived very much in a world of her own. Even so, I am convinced she had grasped the truth.

How dingy Main Street is! Shabby houses, peeling paint, sagging porches, weedy front yards. How come I haven't noticed it before? And above it all what a dismal sky.

On Saturday, September fourth, 1943, the sky was breathtakingly beautiful. Even without a moon and of course without streetlights, or perhaps just because of that, it was deeply, mysteriously luminous when, around ten, I set out for home from the opera. I stopped on the Augarten bridge and hugged the railing, my arms spread wide. All the stars of the universe seemed on display above a city which was totally quiet, for once totally peaceful. A gossamer-thin silvery blanket was floating above its sleep, and the shimmering outlines were like my happiness—unreal and overwhelming.

It was one of those enchanted moments that stay with you a lifetime, even though words can only approximate them. Like that time when Harry played the Moonlight Sonata for me during my visit to his aunt's, years later. He played from memory, his eyes on mine, and for a short time past and present fused and we were again nineteen.

Augarten Bridge was enveloped in stars but none came down. I made my wish to the stillness around me:

"Dear God, thank you for this moment. Please let me have many others like it!" I wasn't even ashamed of my effusiveness. Nor did it occur to me that I didn't believe in a personal god. Had anyone approached, I might have embraced them. Luckily, nobody came into sight. As I walked on I began to skip, like a child, humming *"Ich bin ja heut so glücklich, so glücklich"*—today I am so happy. Probably in the wrong key but who cared.

By a stroke of luck, my father wasn't in, and after having a bite—I was not even hungry—I could go to bed, turn off the light and relive the past two days once more: the good visit with Kuno and Wolf who had given me an enthusiastic wet welcome, the brief moments with Harry, the festively lit grand staircase at the opera, the sumptuous gold and crimson proscenium where the violins were tuning, the hum of voices, the moment of anticipation as the lights were dimming. But when I saw the colorful Czech folk costumes before me once more and heard the familiar tunes of the overture, my childhood rushed back at me. I envisaged grandma, aunts Erna and Paula, and cousin Walter, sitting on their packed suitcases and waiting for the van to take them away, and I cried myself to sleep.

20.

I have reached the railroad tracks. Though there is no sight or sound of a train, I cross as fast as I can. I don't want to see the tracks, I don't want to think about them, I don't want to know that they exist.

21.

The following Sunday the weather was perfect and I left for the cemetery quite early. By one o'clock I was stretched out in the sun, with closed eyes, again thinking of the previous night. Then Kurt dragged me to the fields, claiming that there was much work to be done. I threw myself into it with enthusiasm.

When I looked up, Harry and Renate were approaching together. For a while the two watched us workers irresolutely, then they sat down on a nearby bench.

I only looked up when I gathered from Kurt's remarks that something was going on. Squinting into the sun, I had to shield my eyes with my hand to believe what I saw. Renate was sitting at one end of the bench. Harry lay stretched out across its entire length, his head in Renate's lap. She was looking down on him.

To my dismay I realized that in addition to indignation there was a stab of pain. That's it, I said to myself as I bent down to my peas, everything is over. I would lose all self-respect if I put up with this. If they had at least settled somewhere else and not right in front of me and everyone else. What does he think? That anything goes? Not with me, it doesn't. But he mustn't know that I am jealous.

I forced myself to calm down, despite my aching heart. *"Immer nur lächeln..."* I began to hum. There was a song for everything. But it was very hard to keep smiling.

I made a special effort to kid Kurt, talk to Ilse about the opera, and crack jokes about the two on the bench—just like the others were doing. Then I saw Dr. F. head for the bench, Harry rise, and the two men disappear together.

Everyone looked up when Renate approached a little later and, half laughing half scowling, mumbled something about this not being funny. Then she wandered off again. We were puzzled but the mystery was soon solved. Heinzi came running toward us with a huge grin on his face.

"Dr. F. saw them lying there and got angry because that isn't proper. He said he was going to teach Harry a lesson and asked whether I would help him. So we locked Harry inside the tool-shed. Renate is now looking everywhere for the key—isn't it hilarious?"

Heinzi was fourteen at the time, lanky, awkward and sweet, still a real innocent.

We all laughed though I thought the joke in pretty bad taste. Only Dr. F. would do a thing like that. I went back to harvesting peas. When, some time later, right next to me someone began to whistle "I know a bride..." from *The Bartered Bride*, I turned the other way and started talking to Ilse who was working alongside.

After we had carried buckets, rakes and hoes into the shed, we spread our blankets on the small meadow behind it. Ilse sat on my left, Heinzi on my right. Harry arrived among the last, stopped in front of me and Ilse, and said:

"Between the two of you there is just enough room for me."

For the first time I looked at him. "There is plenty of room all over. No need to crowd each other."

Without another word he settled next to Heinzi. We chatted, sang, then lay down to relax. A pebble hit my shoulder. When I turned my head, Harry was looking at me, just as Michael

Kornblüh had done, many years before, only that now I knew enough to turn away. Nor did I react to any of the following pebbles or to the blade of grass which kept tickling my neck. Kurt's comment, placed strategically in a lull in the general conversation, took me by surprise:

"Isn't Harry efficient? He sings to Liesl and looks at Renate."

I ignored the remark but Ilse later explained that I had been humming the beginning of Nelson Eddy's "Sweetheart, sweetheart..." and he had promptly started to whistle along. I had not noticed.

While we were waiting for the streetcar, Harry and Renate showed up at the stop. Usually, they refused to travel with the gang. I soon found out whose decision it had been to join us.

"Look how crowded the platform is," Renate said. "Why don't we wait for the next car?"

"Come on, two more won't make that much of a difference," Harry replied and helped her up the steps.

There was much talking and laughing during the long ride. Harry kept trying to address me but I looked past him as if he were air. Renate was obviously frustrated, but now this almost pleased me. My mean streak was in the ascendant again. That evening I hated myself, Harry and the whole world.

When Ilse declared that she still had to take care of an errand and would be changing from the *71* to the *O* line, the others offered to accompany her. So did I. I couldn't stand the thought of riding alone with those two. I shook Renate's hand, sent a casual "so long" in Harry's direction and transferred. It had never been quite so difficult to look cheerful.

My pain lessened a little when—by then it was dark—I recognized the figure waiting near the entrance to our house.

"When will we see each other?" Harry asked as if nothing had happened.

"Who knows!" I tried to tear myself loose and move on, but he wouldn't let go of my arm.

"What's the matter? You are suddenly acting so strange!"

"You should be able to figure it out! I have learned an important lesson today."

"Look, Lieserl, you are usually so smart, but now you are silly. None of that meant anything, and am I to blame for Dr. F.'s dumb jokes?"

"No, but you are responsible for your own actions, and they were quite unambiguous."

"But you said yourself that I mustn't draw attention to you! And if you hadn't ignored me, I wouldn't have taken off with Renate."

"What do you mean—taken off? Why didn't you take off? To lie down right in front of us was in extremely poor taste."

"Don't you see? That shows you that the whole thing didn't amount to anything. I even fell asleep. Isn't that proof enough?"

I was not going to make it that easy for him. "Facts are facts, no matter how you interpret them. Please let go. It's too chilly out here for long discussions. Good night." He let go of my arm.

When I reached my apartment door, I saw a streetcar ticket wedged in the keyhole. On the back it said: "Please phone me!"

Suddenly the pain was gone and I could have danced with joy. What an obstinate and illogical thing the human heart is. Reason will preach and preach and the heart seems to be listening diligently, and yet all this time it is ready to capitulate at the first opportunity. But no, I wouldn't dream of calling him.

22.

On Monday, Renate came by. We went for a walk and she broached the subject by complaining about Dr. F.'s tactless joke. When I tried to tell her that it had been her own fault for sitting down in such a compromising position in front of us, she defended herself: "But there was nothing to it! At one point Harry even fell asleep and so I tried not to wake him." She sounded hurt and I was unable to tell whether it was because of Dr. F.'s insinuations or because Harry had fallen asleep in her lap.

On Tuesday I visited Ilse at the exchange to report that father had asked me to start packing. It looked as if this time we might really be leaving. Was I glad? Yes and no. Everything was so complicated, and I didn't know what I felt. But when Ilse had to phone the hospital, I made a mental note of the number. On Wednesday I still remembered it, but by then I had come to the conclusion that it was out of the question for me to phone him.

I avoided Ilse's home on Wednesday night for fear of meeting Harry there, and on Thursday I decided that I'd better omit my Friday night visit to her as well. However, by Friday morning I began to have second thoughts. Perhaps the episode with Renate had really been due to thoughtlessness on his part. And since I was likely to be gone for good in two weeks, why make myself miserable during those last few days? Where is your pride? my inner voice scoffed, but I countered: I have avoided him all week—isn't that enough?

By noon I was angry with myself for having even considered giving in. To have something similar happen again, perhaps the very next Sunday? If I let it pass once, how could I refuse to accept it a second time? No, it was out of the question.

But then it occurred to me that Ilse must be wondering why I had not come to see her all week. How selfish of me to think only of my own affairs! Lots of things might have happened in the meantime. In the evening I turned into Förstergasse.

My heart missed a beat when I saw Harry standing inside the downstairs entryway.

"What are you doing here?"

"I saw you come down the street so I thought I'd wait for you, in case you were on your way to Ilse."

"You didn't need to wait—I know the way!"

"But what if I wanted to see you?"

"You haven't tried very hard all week, have you? As if you did not know my address."

"I don't impose myself. If I am not welcome, I stay away."

"That's very sensible." We had arrived and I rang their door-bell.

"Here they are, Kurt, both of them together!" Ilse called out with that certain smile of hers. I ignored the remark.

"Please go into the living room and make yourselves comfortable. We are still eating, but it won't take long. Kurt, why don't you show them in."

Kurt who had stuck his head out the dining room door, grinned his big grin and lead the way into the living room. He pulled down the shades and turned on the light. I knew he would not leave without a comment, and he didn't.

"Be careful that Harry doesn't put his head in your lap while you are by yourselves. He's an old hand at it, you know."

For a while neither of us spoke. Harry sat in one armchair, I in the other, at considerable distance. He was looking at me, I was staring at the window shade.

"You are a silly girl, Lieserl," he began the conversation.

"The world is full of silly girls." I didn't turn to him. "I left the decision up to you, and you have decided. That takes care of it."

"Yes, I have decided."

"Then there's no need to talk about it, right?" Again I was suddenly outside my body, hovering somewhere in the air above us. Was this nasty, cold voice really mine? No, it wasn't, it couldn't be. The sentences had an impetus of their own, created their own theatrical tone of spite. But though ashamed, I was powerless to control that mean voice that was coming out of me.

And Harry? Why was he taking all this so patiently and good-naturedly instead of sending me to hell? Was he really so fond of me, or was my resistance a challenge to his vanity? I would never know.

"Yes, I have made my decision," he repeated with a chuckle which I ignored. "But I feel sorry for Renate."

"So do I. Who knows what's in store for the poor girl." With discomfort I heard my harsh, cheerless laugh. "Please, remain seated where you are. When Kurt comes in, he doesn't need a new conversation topic."

"Yes, I have made my decision," he repeated a third time, "and therefore I feel sorry for Renate. Don't you want to know what my decision is?"

"That's obvious, isn't it? So why don't you find something more interesting to talk about."

At that moment someone began to clear his throat outside the door so loudly and extensively that I was able to slip back into my body. Neither of us could help laughing.

Kurt came in and expressed his surprise at finding us in the same position in which he had left us. Soon Ilse appeared as well. As we talked, the sound of a loud, strident voice burst out from a loudspeaker somewhere outside. It was Hitler's voice. He had not spoken in a long time—something must have happened or be happening.

Harry's family had a clandestine short-wave radio and he was in a hurry to get home. I left as well. In the downstairs doorway he offered his hand in parting. I knew that his birthday was on the next day and, feeling very magnanimous, decided to wish him a happy birthday. He thanked me without saying a word but with a long handshake, and we parted.

The speech must have just ended as I was turning the corner, for Hitler's loudly barked "Sieg Heil!" came at me from all sides over the public address system. It was followed by the frenetic roar of a multitude of voices shouting "Heil!" And again, as if staged, his shrill "Sieg Heil!" and the mob's screamed response: "Heil!" And a third time, in a feverish crescendo "Sieg Heil!"— "Heil!" I had trouble unlocking the outer door because my hands were so unsteady.

Father was not at home but I waited up for him. "Did you hear Hitler's speech? Is it bad news?"

"No, I think the news is good. The Italians must have signed an armistice with the Allies because he called them traitors. The war in Italy might be over, and then Olga is safe."

My Czech cobbler friend thought otherwise. "The Allies have landed in Southern Italy," he told me the next day, "but they are dragging their feet and the German troops are rampaging all over Italy. Hitler is desperate and, madman that he is, he will have everybody killed rather than give up."

I couldn't handle this. Nor did the thought of Harry cheer me much. I spent a restless night, haunted by nightmares.

23.

The next morning, after much agonizing, I composed a short note to take to Ilse with the request that she hand it on to Harry. This is what I wrote:

"Dear Harry,
I need to contact someone and would appreciate your assistance. Perhaps you could drop in for a few minutes after lunch. Please tell Ilse the exact time. I will phone her at noon.
Greetings—Liesl."

I sat there looking at the note, well aware that I had no excuse whatsoever to send it. I tried to review every old argument against myself: Don't you see that he is not worth your heartache? He will hurt you again and again. Why don't you leave things as they are and be glad it's over. Remember, he behaves like that with every girl, looks at her seductively, presses her hand—wait a minute! He doesn't act that way with everybody, not really. Not with Ilse, nor Ditha or Trude, not to mention Lea. The mere thought made me laugh. But what about "his" Eva and who knows how many others? And Renate? But Renate is running after him rather than the other way round. And who cares about any others as long as I don't know about them!

I tried to think of someone I would want him to help me reach. If at least I had not wished him a happy birthday the evening before! That would have provided an excuse for wanting to see him. But I had. Let's face it, the letter meant that I was capitulating and, what was worse, doing so with a light heart.

Yet another betrayal—this time of myself? Come on, don't get melodramatic. At worst, I am betraying one single aspect of myself, and who knows how trustworthy or important that aspect is.

A few weeks earlier, just as I was opening the door to Ilse's exchange, I overheard Kurt saying: "Sometimes I can't figure her out at all."

When he saw me, his wide mouth spread into a cheerful grin, and he said: "Speak of the devil..."

Ilse was assiduously looking down at her notepad. She seemed to be blushing.

"So what is the devil like?" I asked with the laugh I considered worthy of the association. "A real monster?"

"Of course," Kurt said matter-of-factly and added with a twinkle: "But you are lucky—I have always liked monsters!"

There was nowhere to go from there. I couldn't rearrange myself, only play the part he had assigned to me. But I resolved to have a good talk with myself some time soon and reexamine my code of ethics.

Ilse assumed that the letter I handed her was a birthday note and acted neither surprised nor curious. Just in case, I mentioned that I wanted some information from Harry. When I rang her shortly after twelve, the message was that I should phone him. I didn't like that response but there was nothing I could do about it. By 12:45 we had finished eating and, while I was waiting for the dish water to come to a boil, I ran out to the phone booth once more.

"Finally!" His voice was impatient. "I've been waiting for your call for an hour." "That's good," I almost said but then bit my tongue.

"Why didn't you give Ilse a specific time as I asked you to?"

"It wasn't possible. I—I could come to your place at about two-thirty if that's all right. But I can't stay, we are getting company."

Why had he checked himself? Was there something I wasn't supposed to know? I must not sound too pleased.

"That's fine. I won't keep you long. I have to leave too." It was true. I had promised Renate to drop in on her.

"Then I'll see you at two-thirty. So long."

"Bye now."

At home my anticipation returned. I quickly did the dishes, changed and reached for a mirror to see if lipstick was needed. My cheeks were flushed, my lips were red and my eyes sparkled. I am quite attractive after all, I thought with surprised satisfaction.

Just then—it was after two—father returned and settled in the rocking chair with a newspaper. I went back into the kitchen to wrap a package for Theresienstadt, wondering how I could arrange to talk to Harry alone. At that moment the doorbell rang.

I showed him into the living room, introduced him to my father and asked him to take a seat. He inquired what help I needed and I asked for someone's whereabouts. Then father's question "What's new?" initiated a conversation between them which soon drifted toward politics.

Time was passing and father gave no indication of leaving. In fact, he seemed to be enjoying the discussion. I barely participated, for all my thoughts circled around the question of how I could get to talk to Harry alone. I had to talk to him, and it must be today. I had reached the conclusion that breaking off was silly and unnecessary. We were just having a good time together, that was all, so why stop? But I would warn him not to try anything like that Sunday episode again.

I excused myself and went back into the kitchen to my package. When that didn't stop the two from continuing their conversation, I called:

"Harry, could you come here for a minute and help me?"

He came and put his finger on the string so that I could tie a knot. Then I took a deep breath, turned toward him and said with as casual a smile as I could muster:

"I still owe you a birthday kiss."

I took his head between my hands and kissed him lightly on the forehead. The next moment he was holding me tight, his lips on mine, and I went limp with relief. After a while I freed myself with a glance at the closed living room door and, almost mechanically, resumed wrapping. He helped. Neither of us spoke.

A few minutes later father suddenly got up and left, mumbling something about having just remembered an appointment. I could have hugged him. An hour later I literally threw Harry out, reminding him that they had guests at home and that I, too, was busy. He warned me that he would not be at the cemetery the next day since Eva was coming. I decided not to go either.

24.

By Sunday noon, I had changed my mind. Although it was already the twelfth of September, the weather was summery and I didn't feel like staying at home and visualizing Harry playing duets with "his" Eva. It was bound to be nice at the cemetery even without him. Moreover, if both of us stayed away, there would be a new wave of gossip.

Was I really that worried about gossip? Yes and no. To some extent it had become a game which added spice to our relationship. There was also a touch of superstition that that fragile intimacy might not survive public scrutiny. And finally, Renate was still on my mind. Perhaps she was satisfied to be friends with Harry because she thought that I too was only friends with him. How would she feel if she had an inkling that we were really serious or at least somewhat serious about each other? She was a generous person but how would she act if she knew? I did not want to jeopardise our friendship or hurt her. If that was deception, there were, I told myself, good reasons for it.

The afternoon was pleasant and relaxing. We played ball, then Renate and I practiced some of our acrobatic stunts which were duly admired, Franz played his guitar and we sang, and my secret sang along inside me. Whenever Kurt or Ilse kidded Renate about Harry I thought: "If you only knew!" and was elated.

When I reached for the apartment key, a used streetcar ticket was wedged in the door. Somewhat surprised, I unfolded it and read: "1:30 pm"—"6 pm". For a moment I regretted not having been at home, but then I told myself that it was better for him to be looking for me than the other way round.

On Monday, Renate and I went rowing on the Old Danube. It was an adventuresome afternoon. First we discovered that one oar was shorter than the other, which made our trip to the island where we wanted to camp much longer and more strenuous than it should have been. Then an oar floated away and we only managed to spot it after a long search. Finally, when Renate jumped back into the boat, she tipped the boat over. As a result of these mishaps it got quite late and, when she offered to escort me home as usual, I declined, somewhat to her surprise. I didn't want us to run into Harry near my house.

When I described the afternoon to him, he shook his head. "What is all this? The two of you seem inseparable!"

"Perhaps we want to keep an eye on each other," I winked at him.

"Yes, and where does that leave me?"

"You poor, neglected orphan!" I caressed his hair and all was well again.

"But tell me, where were you yesterday? I thought you were not going to go to the cemetery?"

"It was such a gorgeous day that I couldn't stay at home. But how come you were looking for me?"

"I wanted to invite you to come and listen to Eva and me play. And then she stood me up so I tried again, but you were still not at home."

"I am sorry." But I wasn't. Not at all.

25.

Nothing very memorable happened during the following four weeks, but I engraved every little detail in my memory to retain it forever.

On Tuesday, September 14, the news was bad. In Italy everything was in chaos, one half of the country occupied by the Germans, the other by the Allies, and everywhere Italians were being killed. As I was heading toward Ilse's office that morning, I thought of aunt Olga and that we had not heard from her in ages, but almost immediately my mind switched to the thought that it would be smart to leave Ilse's office before eleven and not run into Harry. It was like a spell. I was unable to concentrate on anything or anybody except Harry. I caught myself listening for his footsteps on the stairs, and when Ilse talked to him on the phone, I felt an almost irresistible urge to ask her to hand me the receiver. But as if to punish myself, I whispered instead:

"Don't tell him that I am here. We don't need visitors."

As I walked down the stairs, I caught myself walking unusually slowly and forced myself to speed up.

All the more wonderful were the evenings, when he came or left his messages in the door. Once I complained that he had not put in an appearance in three days. When he explained that he knew I would not be at home, I countered:

"You could at least have left a slip of paper in the door to let me know that you were thinking of me!"

After that I found his sign almost every evening if I came home too late for his visit. If it wasn't there, I worried and phoned him as soon as I could get to a phone at a reasonable hour.

I was becoming careless. One Sunday, after we had settled on our blankets, Harry and I tested each other at identifying recent hit tunes. At one point Kurt began to rave about Peter Kreuder's *"Man müsste Klavier spielen können."* Trude was the only one to know the entire text—"he who plays the piano, is favored by love," it continues. Kurt wanted her to sing it for him again and again. Suddenly Heinzi heaved a deep sigh:

"I definitely must learn to play the piano!"

"Why?" I inquired.

"Well, then I will be favored by love!" He was so cute that I couldn't help laughing.

"Do you really think piano playing does it?"

Fortunately only I heard his response:

"Of course! I have seen it with Harry! First Renate and now you..."

I quickly changed the subject.

26.

On Thursday I felt so ill that I reached for the thermometer. To be sure, I had a fever. So much for *Pagliacci* that evening, after Inge and I had spent hours in line to secure tickets. To my surprise father offered to take my ticket back to her so that she could ask someone else. He also went to get the doctor.

The doctor diagnosed a digestive disorder caused by poor nutrition—a common ailment in those days. I was to stay on a tea-and-dry-toast diet for a week. If the fever was not gone by then, we were to notify him again. There was always the possibility of jaundice.

I had my doubts about the diagnosis and decided to add my own treatment or rather grandma's—a couple of aspirins and a laxative. To be sure, by evening my temperature was down and I felt better. I managed to stick to tea and toast for three days but then I rebelled and started eating normally—whatever that meant. I was weak but began to improve almost immediately.

When it looked like I would be housebound for a while, I asked father to phone Harry and tell him that I was sick. All day Friday I waited anxiously for the bell, but it remained silent. When father came home in the evening, he confessed that he had forgotten to relay the message. The next day he did and Harry sent word that he would drop by around three. Father stayed at home to let him in.

"How long are you planning to be here?" I inquired.

"My dear child, all afternoon, of course, since you are ill!"

I sighed. "All right, if it can't be helped."

"That was honest," father laughed, sounding almost like a friend. "Don't worry, I'll leave when Harry arrives." At that moment, I forgave him for many things.

When we were alone, I made tea. Harry settled by my bedside and began to tell me about his day at the hospital. "I shouldn't stay long," he said, "you might get other visitors, and what do we say if they find me here?"

"Don't worry, if anybody should come we'll tell them that you ran into my father, learned that I was sick and dropped in."

"I am only worrying on your account! I couldn't care less about what the others might think. But of course I bow to your superior wisdom and will henceforth do anything you say."

"For starters, stop kissing me or you'll catch jaundice!"

"You have jaundice? That's wonderful—then they'll take you to the hospital and I can sit by your bedside all day!"

"Wouldn't you like that, you egotist! I wouldn't dream of getting jaundice just to please you. Stop it—is that the way you are obeying me?"

"I am only trying to prove to you that I am unselfish enough to risk catching jaundice!"

Just then the doorbell rang.

"I wonder who that could be? At any rate, you know what to say." I put on my house coat and went to the door. It was Ditha and Franz. Ditha had run into my father and learned that I was ill. He had not mentioned it to me.

"How nice of you to come! I have had two very boring days. Harry is here too, he just dropped in a few minutes ago."

But when we entered the bedroom, there was no trace of Harry. One lonely teacup was sitting on the tray by my bed. I was as puzzled as they were until I opened the door to the other room. There stood Harry, teacup in hand.

"What are you doing in there, Harry? Ditha and Franz are here, so come and join us."

"Don't say anything to Ilse or Kurt about my being here," Harry started with mock apprehension, but I interrupted him.

"Don't worry, Ditha and Franz are discreet and, after all, there is nothing wrong with visiting an invalid."

Franz nodded with a simple smile, but Ditha's face was all red from the effort to remain serious. A moment later she exploded into peals of laughter. For a long time she was unable to stop. She must have had a far more vivid imagination than I had given her credit for.

I lay back down, Ditha made more tea and, at their request, I began to narrate the plot of a film I had seen recently. It was called *Damals*, my diary tells me, but I don't remember anything about it except that it had Zarah Leander in it. At least I think it did.

Suddenly the door bell rang again. "I'll go," I said and got up. "It might be someone looking for my father."

I closed the door behind me. If it was Renate, I would tell her that the doctor was here and she should come back later. What a liar I had become. It was high time to have that conversation on ethics with myself.

To my surprise, it was Lea. Somewhat embarrassed she explained that she had run into Franz and Ditha who conveyed to her that I was sick and suggested she pay me a visit. I told her how glad I was to see her, and escorted her in.

In my bedroom sat Ditha and Franz, with very red faces, biting their lips and barely able to remain serious. When I looked around, Ditha burst out laughing. Lea must have thought us crazy. I excused myself, went out into the hall and from there into the other room. I told Harry that in a few minutes he should follow me casually, as if he had been in the bathroom.

Lea didn't stay long, though I tried hard to act as if we were still the good friends we had been. It must have been difficult for her to take that first step. When she left, I urged her to come again, since I would have to stay put for a few days.

"If I won't disturb..." she said but then she didn't come.

Harry took his leave around seven, Ditha and Franz shortly thereafter. As they were walking out, Franz said: "Harry is o.k." From him, that meant a lot.

On Monday, Renate showed up and we spent the entire afternoon together, playing cards and chess, or just talking.

"By the way, I am supposed to convey greetings from Harry and to wish you a speedy recovery," she remembered suddenly.

"Oh?" Was that a trap?

"Yes, yesterday on the cemetery he gathered from my conversation with Ilse that you were sick. He asked me whether I thought it would be proper for him to visit you."

I had a laughing fit but managed to inquire:

"And what did you say?"

"I didn't know either. I said I would check with my mother. She knows these things."

"Never mind. It isn't that important."

We continued our chess game. Around six Renate left. At six-thirty Harry arrived.

"You've just missed Renate," I announced. "We played chess for most of the afternoon."

"Listen, you ought to be a bit more careful if you don't want to give us away! Fortunately I indicated to her that I might pay you a bedside visit so I would have had an excuse if worst came to worst."

"Yes, so Renate informed me. The two of us even considered if your visit would be proper."

"And what was your conclusion?"

"We didn't arrive at a conclusion. Renate offered to consult her mother."

"And you?"

"I am convinced that it would be totally improper for you to come. Mind you, how can a young girl who is all alone in an apartment receive male visitors? Unthinkable!"

"Especially when the defenseless child is ill on top of it, right? How are you, incidentally?"

"As you can see, still alive. And I don't seem to have jaundice either."

27.

By Wednesday I was back to normal. I didn't see Harry all week, but every evening a slip of paper was in the keyhole.

Friday noon we had an air raid alert just as I was on my way home from Ilse's office. As I was hurrying past the hospital, I saw Harry, in his white coat, escorting patients to the shelter. I whistled in his direction but then decided that it was smarter to run home and not wait for a policeman to stop me and direct me to an unfamiliar shelter.

I had intended to visit a patient that afternoon, but because of the air raid it was almost four by the time I arrived at the hospital. Fortunately, visiting hours had been extended and I obtained the necessary pass. While I was standing in the door to the ward, Harry walked by.

"You are here and I don't know about it?"

"Should I have had the public address system announce that I had arrived? I came to visit Frau Klein—do you know her?"

"How about coming up to my lab afterward so that I can show you where I work?"

"Fine."

He stayed close by until I said my goodbyes.

"And henceforth I expect you to inform me any time you plan to come to the hospital!"

"Yes, sir!"

Just then we ran into Heinz. He gaped at us with his mouth open.

"Hello, Heinzi," I said as nonchalantly as I could. "Nice to see you!"

"What are you doing here?" he asked. "Are you visiting Harry?"

"Of course. How did you guess?" I laughed in high spirits.

"Stop kidding," he said, scowling. "I know that isn't the reason. Is your father ill?"

"No, I came to see Frau Klein." He seemed satisfied and we parted.

Harry took me upstairs to the lab and showed me his telephone. "In the morning my father works here, but in the afternoon I have the lab to myself. And here is my own little room where I can read and study, or rest. The couch is for night service. Do you like it? Come and try it out."

I didn't stay long. "Will you escort me down?"

"That goes without saying. How about tomorrow?"

"I can't. I promised to see Ditha, and it will get late. What about Sunday? Actually, I don't feel much like the cemetery."

"Then we won't go. I can always say that I am expecting Eva. Come to my place and I will play for you."

"I'll phone you on Sunday morning."

On Sunday we decided to spend the afternoon at my place instead. We had a small radio, without short waves, of course, but we would be able to listen to music together.

When I dropped in on Ilse later that morning—on Sundays she worked till noon— Ditha and Kurt were there. Soon after I arrived, Renate walked in.

"What, you are alone?" Kurt asked promptly when she appeared in the doorway.

"Harry will be here shortly, he is still busy in the comptroller's office."

"How did you know whom I meant?" Kurt sounded surprised while the rest of us laughed. It was an old joke.

"Children," said Ilse, "you are all coming out this afternoon, aren't you?"

"I can't." I said. "Sorry."

"But Liesl, today Harry will be there!" Renate, of all people.

"That's too bad," I shrugged with a laugh but became tense. Was he playing another one of his tricks on me? But there he was himself.

"Harry, Renate has just alerted me to the fact that I will be missing your valuable company by not going to the cemetery today. What do you say?"

"You are not going?"

"No, I arranged to meet a friend." I looked at him searchingly. "But you are going, aren't you?"

"Yes—no, that is, I would like to but we are expecting company and I really ought to stay home."

"Come on," Renate urged. "We won't have many more fine days! Your parents will manage without you."

"I think so too," I agreed with perverse insistence. "Unless my absence would keep you from enjoying this beautiful Sunday."

Everybody laughed and he replied:

"You never know!"

"So?" Ilse asked. "Make up your mind. Should we wait for you at the streetcar stop or not?"

"No, you better not. Try to have fun without me if you can."

"I am sure they will," my demon made me confirm, and I left.

28.

The time we spent together at my place that Sunday afternoon was uneventful yet very special. We kissed, held hands and hugged, but Harry didn't try to go beyond that, and I was grateful. To this day I don't know if his relations with anyone else had been or were then any closer. Maybe not because that was how we'd been brought up.

We sat on the couch and listened to the radio. I remember that they played *Eine kleine Nachtmusik* and the piece has remained one of my favorites. We barely talked. When the news came on at five, Harry switched it off and pulled me down on the couch. There we lay side by side, without speaking, his arm around my shoulders. We didn't even kiss. After a long pause, I continued my thoughts aloud.

"You know, Harry, if I think that we might never have got together if Renate had been at the cemetery that first Sunday! It all came about by chance."

"Then let's be grateful to chance."

"Are you really glad that it happened that way? Now you can list another conquest." Oh *vanitas vanitatis*...

"You silly girl! It's wonderful to be in love."

"Tell me—what are you like when you are in love?"

"Just the way I am now."

"I don't believe it. Oh, I do, I do, please let go, I can't breathe. Do you want to suffocate me?"

"Murder is preferable to distrust!" He glared at me fiercely and both of us burst out laughing. For a while we again lay there without speaking, then another thought struck me:

"You know, if on that first Sunday I had not said that I wanted to take a walk, nothing would have happened. And now you are trying to convince me that you are in love with me."

He stroked my hair. "You are brooding too much. Stop dissecting everything. Why don't you simply accept what fate or chance or whatever it is gives us, and stop asking questions. Things are simple if you don't complicate them."

"Perhaps you are right," I sighed. I didn't know myself why I couldn't let go completely and just enjoy my happiness.

After the news there was more music and we listened until Harry had to leave.

29.

Friday, October 8, was Rosh Hashanah. The Klügers suggested that father and I accompany them to the evening service. As we were walking, slowly on account of old Mrs. Klüger, Grete put her arm around me. I would have loved to tell her about Harry, but even so it felt wonderful to be hugged by her. I saw Ilse and Kurt arrive and waved to them.

"Wait for us after the service!" Ilse called out to me as we were entering the synagogue. I nodded happily. After the service, while I was waiting for the twins, Harry suddenly appeared next to me.

"You are here? I didn't know you were religious!"

"I could ask you the same question. But I took a chance." He winked at me.

The four of us set out for home together. Kurt began walking so fast that we were barely able to keep up with him. He was pulling Ilse along. Harry shouted at them to stop running. We were breathless but stayed right next to them. Then Kurt changed tactics.

"We can't take up the whole width of the sidewalk, you know. Ilse and I will go on ahead."

"Come on, stop it, Kurt," I said, and for a while we walked peacefully four abreast. As we were approaching an intersection, Kurt suddenly declared:

"I am sorry to have to leave you but I must turn off here. Ilse, I hope you will come with me?"

"Quit this nonsense, Kurt, can't you ever be serious?" I was both annoyed and amused. "I know very well that you are going home and that means going straight."

He looked at me with the vague look of an infant. "No, unfortunately not. I must go that way. Would you like to join us?" turning to Harry.

"That's too much of a detour for me," Harry declared. "I still have to stop at the hospital."

"Well then, good night, you clowns!" I laughed and held out my hand to both of them. As Kurt shook it, he whispered with a mischievous wink:

"Aren't we tactful? Now it even looks as if you didn't want to stay behind with Harry. You owe it all to me!"

I didn't manage to scowl. Renate wasn't with us after all, and Kurt was really a sweetheart.

I learned only much later that two days before, on Wednesday, Harry's grandmother had been taken away. He had not said a word about it. The transport left for Theresienstadt that Saturday.

30.

Tuesday evening I was doing some last minute cramming for my English lesson when the doorbell rang three times.

"You? Have you forgotten that I have a class in fifteen minutes?"

"That gives us at least a little time, and then I can accompany you. Why haven't you told me that you leave for your class from home? I could have escorted you every time!"

"I don't always, so don't look at me that way." How good it felt that he wanted to be with me.

"What made you drop in?"

"I ran into your father at the entrance and asked him to say hello to you. That's when he told me that you were at home."

"We better go now."

"May I take your arm?"

"No, you may not," I protested knowing that he would ignore my words. I marveled at how perfectly each understood the other's thoughts despite our words. And it occurred to me that that was because the game had changed. We were no longer playing against one another but together, sending the ball back and forth for the joy of the volley.

"Tomorrow night I am going to the *Burgtheater* so we can't meet."

"When does it start?"

"At seven, but I need to change and get ready."

"That's fine, I'll come at six and escort you. I won't interfere."

He was not asking, he was telling me, and I didn't mind. Not one bit.

31.

That Wednesday evening, October 13, Harry arrived punctually at six. I had already put on the burgundy two-piece dress which was my favorite, and was doing my hair. Harry told me that he had been called to the hospital the night before, although it was to have been his night off. He had to escort a patient to the train station, for deportation. At the station, one police van after another emerged from the darkness to disgorge its contingent of terror-stricken victims. The meager bundles they carried contained all they had or were allowed to take with them. It was cold and dark. They were shoved into the cattle cars accompanied by the SS-men's curses—I put my hand over his mouth.

"If you go on, I won't be able to enjoy the play."

He stopped talking, and hugged and kissed me. For a moment we clung to each other as if we were the last people on earth and would be lost if we let go. But the moment passed and we returned to normal.

"I like your dress, but isn't it a bit somber?"

"Remember the proverb 'Never show unfinished work to children and fools?' Do I have so young or so foolish a sweetheart?" I handed him my turquoise necklace and turned around. "Make yourself useful."

It took him a while to secure the clasp and I almost made a crack about this surprising lack of skill. Then I thought better of it. "Well, do I meet your expectations now, your lordship?" It was quite obvious that I did.

We separated with a handshake at the corner where I had to turn off. How I wish we had kissed, right on the street, in plain view of everyone! What would it have mattered?

"Will you think of me in the theater?" He was still holding my hand.

"I hope *Das Fräulein von Scuderi* will be too good to let my mind wander. But I promise to think of you both before and after the play."

"If I don't get hiccoughs I'll know that you have broken your promise, so be careful! I'll be at your house tomorrow evening at six. Good night for now!"

"Good night! See you tomorrow."

Yes, tomorrow! How often we say that, and then there is no tomorrow, only yesterday's memories. But for those I thank you, my love, and will be thankful as long as I live.

1938

father
and
daughter

1942–43

acrobatics by the Old Danube

Thea and I at the Danube Canal

Sunday at
the cemetery

Clockwise from top left: Renate, Trude, Ilse, Franz, Anita, Ditha, Kurt, Heinzi, Lea. *Below:* the same group after chores.

In Memoriam

above: with Pulli and Lilli, 1940.
right: Ilse Markstein in Aschersleben,
1941

Grete Klüger in 1944

Frau Doktor back from
Auschwitz, 1946

New Beginnings

teaching English for the AJDC, 1946-47

departure for the United States, 1947

PART THREE:

The Deluge

1.

The first drops are falling, but I can already make out the traffic light at the main intersection. I walk past a tiny park, really just a narrow irregular triangle with a few trees and a fountain. The fountain is still hidden behind the strange beehive structure which has covered it all winter. In fact, it hasn't been uncovered since I have come to town, and that's been several years. Perhaps it's broken.

The park ends in a blunt point, with two delicate plumtrees stretching toward the sky. Their bases are carpeted with purple snow. Should the rain turn heavy, the last sprinkling of blossoms will be swept down, and then spring is over, from one moment to the next.

The town seems unusually deserted. All this available parking would be a treat except that today I don't need a parking space. You can't win, can you?

Across the street, the half-finished police station looms huge under scaffolding and sheets of plastic. I note uneasily how large it is. To protect our finest, I suppose, so that they can protect us. A policeman crosses the street toward me, and my heart contracts. I gaze past him, doing my best to look unconcerned and innocent. After all, I *am* innocent—at least I think I am. But innocence is such an unreliable concept. One phrase, one stroke of a pen can convey guilt, guilt by birth, guilt by association, guilt by surmised intention. Never mind, these are different times and a different place, remember? Sure, but even if we can now reject guilt, have we really escaped untainted? I take pride in being truthful, painfully truthful, and feel awkward about even a white lie. Yet I am instinctively ready to hold back, deny everything the moment I am confronted by a uniform. I did stop at the stop sign, officer, perhaps just not long enough.—No, I did not drive that fast, I am sure I didn't, unless there's something wrong with my speedometer.—Oh, but I mailed the bill before the deadline, note the date on the check. It must have been the post office.

My American friend whose husband is Czech claims that fudging is a typical East European trait. Though I protest that Moravia is not in Eastern Europe, I laugh in tacit agreement. But actually it isn't that at all, at least not with me. This immediate wariness, an automatic defensiveness when faced by a uniform, by anyone looking remotely "official"—the military, the police, even a train conductor— must be a hangup bequeathed by wartime Vienna. Uniforms connote authority, and authority is by definition hostile and dangerous. It has power over you, it can from one minute to the next switch from right to might. How can I, unbadged, ununiformed, unconnected, prevail—even if the truth is on my side? The truth? Forget about the truth. That's almost as ambiguous a concept as justice or love or friendship. Most animals don't trust, they watch and weigh. A different road to safety, perhaps a better one.

Out of the corner of my eye I notice that the policeman is waving at me. The sudden relief of recognition: he is a neighbor and passes the time of day whenever we run into each other on the parking lot. Being friends with a policeman—it is almost unthinkable. I wonder what he is after right now.

And what am I after? As I'm opening my umbrella, my mind is still blank, even though I know where I am. But why am I in town? Oh yes, the bank—I need cash. I may just make it before it closes. And the drugstore. I'm almost out of toothpaste and soap. After that, I could perhaps cross over to Bart's for an ice cream cone and a cup of coffee, and wait out the rain there. But as if to remind me of life's uncertainties, the skies suddenly split wide open to an enormous cloudburst. The rain comes down in torrents, changing from drops to a downpour from one minute to the next. My skirt is soaked in no time and the umbrella sends streams of water down my legs, while my feet slide in and out of my squeaky pumps as if I were fording a creek in clogs. I will be drenched long before I get to the intersection and the bank.

I look for shelter. Luckily, there are several small eating places nearby, two on my side, one across the street. Although that's the only one I have been in before and therefore know that it serves a good cup of coffee, at this point I head for the one closest by. Under cover, I shake my umbrella and myself like a wet dog. Outside the deluge seems in progress.

The café is an odd place, long and narrow, with a counter extending back along most of the left wall. Between the counter and the two rows of tables on the right runs a low partition, as long as the counter and parallel to it. It's not just a handrail but a solid, well-constructed wooden barrier, some four feet high, the kind you find in courtrooms. The walls are partly white, partly panelled in dark wood, which gives the entire place a formal and austere look. The coffee shop is totally empty except for the girl behind the counter. No music either. Good. And there's an inviting smell of fresh toast.

I must look like a drowned rat, even though the girl has not commented. She gives me that meaningless, wonderful American "have a nice day" smile. Perhaps the rain will have let up by the time I finish my coffee, although I may not get to the bank in time. It was a mistake to walk, a mistake from start to finish. Never mind. I have enough money to last until tomorrow. I might as well relax.

On Thursday, October 14, 1943, the day after I'd seen *Das Fräulein von Scuderi*, I went to the public baths, the *Dianabad*. The place was unusually crowded and I left later than usual. As I was rushing home, not wanting to miss Harry, I couldn't help thinking about how beautiful life was, despite the war and everything else. No, I wasn't sorry that I had allowed myself to get involved. He was not nearly as bad as they had made him out to be. In fact, he had been totally dependable so far. Not once had I caught him in a lie. Nor was he putting the faintest pressure on me to go beyond necking. The subject never came up, much to my relief. I wouldn't have known how to handle it, not having grandma there to advise me. (I remember distinctly that that was what I was thinking, though now the thought makes me smile.) As it was, I could allow myself to feel completely relaxed with Harry and enjoy his affection without any apprehension. Renate? My withdrawing would not have changed anything in his relationship with her, of that I was sure, so why should I deprive myself of these wonderful hours?

There was no tram ticket in the door. I had not missed him. But time was passing excruciatingly slowly. Why was he so late?

Finally the door bell—four times rather than three. Had he made a mistake? No, it was Ditha.

"Hello, Ditha, is anything wrong?"

"Yes. I wanted to tell you that they will be collecting people for a transport tonight."

"Thanks for letting me know. I'll inform father right away."

"Everything else you know by now, I suppose?"

"No, I don't. Is there something else?"

"They caught two U-boats yesterday, and they had addresses on them. As a result, several families were arrested, Harry and his parents among them. It happened last night—hadn't you heard?"

"No, I haven't seen anybody today." My voice was flat and I was unable to think. Finally I asked:

"Do you know any details?"

"No, not really, but it looks pretty bad for them. Harry's father was sheltering someone and they caught him there. They will be lucky if they are sent to Theresienstadt and not Auschwitz. I think they also helped several people with money and clothing, so they are in real trouble."

"I see. Thanks for letting me know. I'll go find father."

I put on my coat and went to the Klügers to inform father that we ought to spend the night away from home. Now there was no longer any need to wait for Harry or to notify him.

Strange, I felt nothing but emptiness. And I knew that I must not think. Nor did I have much time for thinking during the following hours. Overnight bags were readied, the apartment put in order. Then a long walk to someone's place, small talk, gin rummy, my refusal to play, the hostess's urging not to be a spoilsport, my father's angry look—until I played. Playing meant laughing at their jokes and witticisms, and looking cheerful to keep them from thinking that I minded losing a few pennies.

Soon, like after a tooth extraction when the anæsthetic wears off, the pain began to gnaw, then to surge in wave after wave. So it was all over, finished. But you didn't expect it to last, did you? No, I didn't, but not this way, not this way. At twelve-thirty we went to bed, and I could finally cry myself to sleep.

The next morning I wrote a poem. It began "You gave me your hand and said 'till tomorrow'..." It had four stanzas and a two-line modulated refrain. It took a lot of time and effort, but working at it made me feel better.

What else is there to say? The first days I missed Harry terribly. Whenever I came home at night and saw the empty keyhole, it hit me again. I repeated to myself over and over that I had known it wouldn't last, that it had only been a little flirtation, that I was not in love with him, that, luckily, nothing had happened between us, that I really didn't know him well at all nor he me since we never had any serious conversations, and that there were now other things to worry about.

They arrested quite a few people that night, including some forty foreigners, three Romanians among them. Another narrow escape.

Harry and his parents were interrogated and then taken to the "Liesl." The irony was lost on me then: That's what everybody called the huge police prison on Elisabeth Promenade.

Intermittently we were allowed to send food parcels or at least bread to them, via the Community. But the rules kept changing and we had no idea if any of our packages were reaching their destination.

Harry's father, I learned much later, had a long roster of "crimes" to his credit, for any one of which he could have been shot on the spot. As a physician he had been able—and was always willing—to give injections to hospital patients who had received a summons, thereby inducing a fever. Since sick people were not taken into transports, this enabled them to remain in Vienna at least a little longer. He likewise supplied several reluctant soldiers with a kidney poison which kept them from the front. By bying Aryan ration cards on the black market, he supplied several U-boats with food. Under an assumed name and of course without wearing the star, he registered in grocery stores in outlying districts to be able to redeem the coupons. He raised the necessary funds by installing a still in his kitchen. Through the hospital lab he had easy access to alcohol with 3% hydrochloric acid, which was used to identify TB bacilli. He distilled it at home and sold the liquor to tavern owners. In addition to the still, the

Gestapo also found the short-wave radio as well as a batch of erot-
ic photographs—Harry's???—which they admired before tearing
them up and tossing them into the toilet.

What had brought all this on? One evening there had been a
knock on the door. Three shabbily dressed men were asking for
help. They had escaped from a Polish labor camp and the underground network had given them the address of Harry's family.
The Gestapo trailed them to the apartment. Two had moved on by
the time the police arrived. The third was not in, but the police
was naturally ready to wait as long as it took.

At one point the phone rang. One of the policemen answered,
identifying himself as Harry's father. The caller explained that he
needed to sell some gold and had been given the doctor's name.
The Gestapoman encouraged him to come to the apartment,
where he arrested him. The man had an Aryan wife and would
have been protected.

At ten p.m. the U-boat returned and the two men were
marched off to Gestapo headquarters, the former Hotel Metropol
on Morzin Square. Harry and his mother were told to say goodbye: "You will never see your husband again!" Harry later told me
that he was calm and ready for death. Two policemen remained
behind to wait for the other two U-boats. When they didn't arrive
within an hour, Harry and his mother were likewise taken to
Gestapo headquarters.

During the interrogation, the Gestapoman kept threatening
Harry's father with his revolver. When, at one point, he left it on
the table and rose, the doctor picked it up and handed it to him:
"You forgot to take your gun, *Herr Obersturmführer*." Thereafter
the policeman didn't remove it from the holster.

When he was accused of having sheltered U-boats, Harry's
father answered with great dignity:

"I did only what you would also have done to protect your comrades during your illegal period before 1938!"

"If you weren't a Jew I would shake hands with you!" the officer supposedly said. He also seemed to know all about the episode
with the phony gasman, and these two factors may have saved
the family's lives. They were neither shot nor sent to one of the
death camps but, after a month in the *Liesl*, to Theresienstadt. Of
course, I knew none of that at the time.

2.

In mid-1944 father asked me to brush up on my minimal Hungarian. Though we had passports by then, it was impossible to get exit permits and father was certain that, were we to remain in Vienna, we would sooner or later be caught and deported. Someone recommended a good guide who had already escorted several groups across the Hungarian border, and whose fees were reasonable. Once in Hungary, we should be able to make our way across the next border into Romania. Since the woman didn't speak any German, I was to interpret the negotiations.

I was sorry to leave the twins and Ditha behind, but also more than ready to get out of Vienna. Anything would be better than the endless hours in line for the little food there was, the daily air raid alerts, and life with father unmitigated by Harry or communication from him.

The Klügers planned to come with us. I was glad because that meant that Grete would be along, and she had become my lifeline. Whenever I saw her, she had a smile for me and inquired how I was. During her visits with us she might pull me down next to her on the sofa and put her arm around me. As if she knew that her caress revived me no matter how blue I was. Sometimes she pressed into my hand a piece of fruit, a triangle of cheese, even candy. Then she would put her finger to her lips to indicate that that was our secret, and I thanked her with my eyes. She always took my side if father found fault with me in her presence, and I was torn between wanting her badly for a stepmother and fearing that, should she marry father, she was bound to be unhappy.

By then, the five of us may have been the only Jewish Romanians left in Vienna. Grete's mother was over eighty, and though she was quite strong and very determined, it was questionable if she could handle a long night march across rough terrain. I was to ascertain from the guide how difficult the crossing would be, how much of it would have to be on foot or whether a vehicle could be secured, at least for old Mrs. Klüger.

When the woman came, my Hungarian was just adequate for understanding that she had only one opening for the next crossing but could take us along the second time round, three weeks later. She would try to arrange it so that Frau Klüger wouldn't

have to walk much. It was agreed that Sylvia should go with her
this time, and we would follow on the later trip.

There was no later trip. The woman didn't show up when she
was supposed to, though our bags were packed and we were sitting on pins and needles. Nor was there any news from Sylvia. A
month later our original contact informed us that the entire group
had been caught at the border.

3.

I notice a cup of coffee on the table in front of me and realize that
I am still disoriented, no longer in Vienna and not entirely here.
Suspended in a no man's land without contours or time frame. It
is the same scary feeling that has often come over me, though not
lately: As if the earth were pulling away from under my feet and
I on the point of floating off into nothingness, like a balloon when
its string has slipped out of your hand. The only way to prevent
being blown away, sucked up into the void, was to tie as many
knots as I could between myself and time, myself and places,
myself and the people I felt close to, and hope that these bonds
would hold fast, would keep me secured to the earth and convince
me that that was where I belonged, despite everything.

"Dogs that bark don't bite," my father said when I threatened
suicide, which of course merely increased the temptation to prove
him wrong. Why didn't I do it? I don't think it was cowardice. I
could have turned on the gas and held my head into the oven, the
way the girl in that play had done, the last play I saw before the
Burgtheater burned out. It could have been achieved quite easily,
at least before the bombs cut off the gas. When it came back on
after that, it was so anæmic that it might not have accomplished
the job. But that wasn't the reason. I just didn't have the energy.
I was simply too worn out from spending endless hours in the cellar, from hauling buckets of water from the third house down the
street which, luckily, had a well in the courtyard. I was drained
from worrying that my father might have been hit by a bomb, but
most of all I was hurting from his unremitting criticism of everything I did and said, from his cutting me down again and again.

"Where are my slippers?"

"In your nightstand, of course."

"What do you mean by 'of course'? Nothing is of course, only your arrogance! And 'my' nightstand? Are you trying to imply that the other nightstand is yours? Nothing here is yours. Everything belongs to me, remember that! You had better try to earn the privilege of living here."

"Here are three eggs. Make me an omelette!"

"Could I have one of them?"

"Why should you? Did you pay for them, or did I? And may I remind you that when Grete gave you an egg the other day, you didn't offer it to me either!"

"What happened to the half pound of butter I brought home last night?"

"It's here. I divided it into equal halves—here is yours."

"Who asked you to do any dividing? I know your way of dividing. I hand out things around here if anyone does, not you!"

He locked both halves in his wardrobe and when I asked for my share, I was told that I wasn't entitled to anything he bought on the black market, and if he gave me some it was more than I deserved, miserable creature that I was. I responded that if I was a miserable creature it was due to having such a father, whereupon I was told that I was not normal but an imbecile who in outrageous impudence dared criticize others. I stopped answering, remembering that I had sworn to myself to remain calm, not to contradict him, not try to get back at him, not let any of it hurt me. The only way I could achieve this was by becoming numb, stop myself from thinking and feeling. The more drained I was, the easier it became to do just that.

This lethargy was sapping my strength but that was all to the good. I didn't really want to have to make an end of it all. Somewhere deep down I was still hoping that it would soon be over, that there would again be enough to eat and I would find someone who cared, and then I could begin to live again.

I remember a conversation with Ditha which took place on New Year's Day 1945, at her house.

"Isn't it odd," she said, "that one no longer clings to life? All I wish is that my whole family should either live or die together."

I nodded a shamefaced lie. How could I have told her that I hated my father and envied her wish? And what was most depressing was the knowledge that I had failed in my attempts at striving toward my ideal of becoming good and kind. Instead, I felt at times suffocatingly vengeful and bitter, at others overwhelmed by self-pity. And then there were those strange moments when I seemed to be stepping outside my body and was observing myself from somewhere above. But even dematerialized I was ashamed, and also afraid that I might not find my way back into my body.

As I look back at those dismal days, I wonder what made my father talk and act the way he did. To be sure, he was selfish and exasperatingly sure of himself, but he was also intelligent and levelheaded, definitely not a monster. In company he could be charming and witty. Everyone respected his opinion and sought his advice. In the presence of others he treated me with benevolent condescension, though I rarely dared say anything because he claimed that "children should be seen but not heard" and because I really had nothing much to contribute.

At home he seemed almost irrational in his hostility toward me. Was I really that stupid and awful? If so, how come grandma in Ostrau had loved and spoiled me— only now did I realize how much she had spoiled me—and even my Viennese friends seemed genuinely fond of me. And how come Harry had been so gentle and appreciative? Or had I only succeeded in concealing my inferiority, glossed over it, fooled everybody except my father? It was true, I seemed to consist of so many contradictory impulses that there was no telling what the real *me* was, or if there was a real *me*. The same nagging question surfaced again and again: Were others like that too or did I have a basic defect, some abnormality? Whenever I reached that point, I made myself stop reflecting, because such thoughts were pulling me toward suicide.

I don't think my father was aware of the effect his behavior had on me. When I eventually visited him in Vienna—it took me thirteen years to be able to do that—he acted like any normal father might, and his letters to me, although always full of advice on what I should and shouldn't do, invariably ended with "your loving father Albert." Strange.

Two years after my arrival in the States—by then I was in college on a scholarship—he wrote to ask that I secure an affidavit for him so that he could emigrate to America. I did it with a heavy heart. Much to my relief, his request was denied—if for the absurd reason that anyone who is or was at any time friendly with any country which is or was hostile to the United States could be denied entry. The wording is approximate, but the meaning is accurate. Only upon writing to my senator did I elicit that peculiar bit of information.

I tried to figure out where father had gone wrong. Could it be because of the weekly he contributed to and co-edited right after the war? *Der neue Weg* it was called—the new path. Then there was also *Weltenwende* (meaning something like "worlds in transition") which he published and wrote almost single-handedly in 1948-49. To be sure, both advocated cooperation with our then allies but later enemies, the Russians, and some people called *Der neue Weg* "red." Was that it? But I too had contributed a few items to both papers and yet I had been allowed to enter the States. Perhaps because I had used a pen name—*Lisa Mondo*. Or was the reason his interpreting for that Russian captain immediately after the liberation? It appeared that father still knew quite a bit of Russian from his POW days during World War One, and he spent many hours at the *Komendatura*. Once he didn't come home until the next morning. I was already imagining the worst, but he and his captain friend had merely been drinking vodka together all night.

Undoubtedly father was better off in Vienna than he would have been in the States. He was in his mid-fifties then. I doubt that he would have accepted this country and that it would have accepted him.

I saw him for the last time when he was close to seventy. I was appalled to find him thin and tiny, a pitiful old man. The lower half of his face had shrunk and disappeared in wrinkles. His high forehead, however, was still imposing, and his eyes were as large and penetrating as ever except that his bushy eyebrows, now gray, arched over the deep-set eyes more prominently than before. Angela, his former black-market supplier and now his wife, did not show much patience or affection. I remembered his writing to me that he had married her—"because any woman who is as good to her mother as she is must be a kind person." I was glad to be able to tell him that I was expecting a child and to see his pleasure at the news. Neither of us mentioned the past. He died a year later.

However, my life wasn't all gloom even during that last year of the war. I revived whenever I saw Ilse or Ditha. Especially Ilse's warmth and steadfastness helped me erase my homelife at least temporarily, and the fact that I was still able to be cheerful made me think that, if I could only hang on long enough, I might again become a normal human being once all this was over. Ditha too turned out to be a good, solid friend, reassuring by her mere presence and bright smile. Even so, I never told either of them about the problems with my father. How could I? How could I talk to anyone about this? Not even Grete—especially not Grete since she was close to him. Ilse and I would reminisce about the good old days, read *Vom Winde verweht—Gone with the Wind*—together, exchange rumors, write postcards to Frieda, and interpret the terse messages we received from her and other friends in Theresienstadt.

Kurt usually stopped by the telephone exchange twice a day. It was always good to see him, although even he found little to kid about now. Ditha, who worked at the cemetery office, could only drop in when she was nearby, "on loan" to the children's center. Renate had turned fourteen and been inducted into the labor force. She had found a niche in an office and was usually too busy to show her face.

Cemetery outings had become rare even before the arrival of winter. August 1944 was a dismal, wet month, and September not much better. I recall only one outing, on a suddenly warm Sunday in October. We weren't able to feign cheerfulness. It was too depressing to be constantly reminded of how much our group had shrunk. Harry and Frieda were in Theresienstadt, Ischu deported to who knows where, Trude and Theo had disappeared from sight.

Now and then we would get together at Ditha's or my place. It might be just the two of us—three if Franz joined in—and sometimes Renate. Ilse tended to stay away. She preferred to spend her Sundays by herself or with Kurt. Saturdays both would be at the synagogue. On a postcard dated September 25, 1944, Ilse wrote to Frieda: "During the high holidays it hit me again that there is no one left now who thinks as we do. As usual, I spent most of the holidays at work but did have a few opportunities to attend services. They were, despite everything, very beautiful, though not as solemn as usual. The official boxes were almost empty."

Lea no longer showed her face either. Only during my recent visit with her did I learn that the four story house in which she had lived was bombed into rubble as early as September 10, 1944, the day of the first American air raid on Vienna. Luckily, the cellar ceiling held, and they crawled out the window. They ran from the house, still during the raid, while angry voices shouted after them: "Jewish pigs, it's all their fault, let them have it!"

The Jewish Community fed them for a few days and settled them in an apartment with four other families. But their female *Hauswart*, who had a husband on the front and a lover in the SS, was an ogre, and they were convinced she would sooner or later set the SS on them. They only breathed more easily when, toward the end, the woman's lover deserted. Then she turned humble, knowing that they could denounce her if she were to try any funny business.

4.

The rain is pelting the metal roof of the restaurant overhang with the same hysterical staccato sound with which the high-pitched crackling of the anti-aircraft guns rose above the deeper thuds of the bombs.

Through most of 1944, the American bomber squadrons had merely passed over Vienna on their way to Germany, daily at eleven, so punctual that if the sirens didn't go off we wondered what had happened. But when they began to drop their bombs on the city itself, the activities of daily living became all-encompassing and the last modicum of normalcy came to an end. Vienna was mobbed with evacuees, bomb fugitives and Party high brass. Food was scarce and the daily bombardments held us captive in the public shelters or our cellars for the larger part of the day. The rest of the time was spent foraging for food and water.

It was a cold and hungry time. Our neighborhood had no public air raid shelter so that every morning, often as early as nine o'clock, long processions started out toward the first district. Its bunkers were presumably safe. Even better were the catacombs, a network of deep subterranean passageways below the Inner City. The shelter in the Jewish Community building was likewise considered very safe and many Jews spent their days there.

Most of the tenants in our building, myself included, set up house in the cellar as best we could. It was almost impossible to obtain coal, and gas and electricity would come and go. Candles became a highly valued commodity. After a bomb hit the neighboring house and broke most of our windows, it was more comfortable to spend the day by one of the two small coal burning stoves in the cellar than in the apartment.

I remember vividly the evening when Grete arrived with a present for me—a big candle. She stayed for supper, which meant that father brought out the butter and couldn't well stop her from urging me to put some on my bread. This cheered me greatly.

But there were far more moments of the other kind, when I was afraid and felt abandoned. I was alone in our cellar cubicle on the day the bomb hit the house next door. The lights went out almost immediately after the siren. I lit a candle and tried to write by it, one ear cocked toward the distant thuds. Suddenly there was that ominous whistle which announced that a bomb was heading straight at us. I crouched down, hiding my head between my knees. A deafening boom made the building shake to its foundation. It was followed by the sound of shattering glass and dribbling plaster, and by a cloud of choking dust. When the noise subsided, I took a deep breath. The candle had gone out, but I seemed to be all right. Then it occurred to me that we might be buried alive. Only when the neighbors' voices rose in the common room and candles began to light up the darkness, did I dare leave the cubicle. We huddled together, anxiously waiting for the all-clear, in order to rush upstairs, assess the damage and then venture outdoors to see which buildings had been hit and how badly.

Perhaps it was all to the good that fear, tension and lack of food thwarted my thoughts of suicide or any other wasteful expenditure of energy. I was almost in a state of suspended animation. At one point it became a relief to be alone at home or in the shelter. In fact, I was almost happy when I could sit by a window upstairs or with a candle in our cellar cubicle, and write. No, it wasn't only lethargy that kept me alive during those days. It was Katharina Brienne, more than anything else. How could I have forgotten her! She was my mentor and model, my consolation and hope. She was my great secret.

I had asked father whether I could use his typewriter, though I should have known the answer. He wasn't going to have me ruin it, and what did I need a typewriter for anyway. After my request he locked it in his wardrobe before going out, together with the victuals, soap and toothpaste he had procured for himself from his black market contacts.

Thus *Katharina Brienne* came into existence in longhand. Her world became my refuge. She was a young physician, attractive and brilliant. Abused by a man, she vowed revenge on all men. A combination of Medea and Scarlett O'Hara. I no longer recall her various peregrinations, but I poured into her most of my own yearnings and hatred. I can't even recall if I had her die or gave her a happy end, but at any rate I did finish the book. I hoped that it would legitimize me as a writer and person after the war. Cinderella as God-substitute—one could surely do worse.

5.

"Would you like a refill?"

"What? Oh, a refill. Yes, thank you. I would love a refill."

"It's not letting up, is it?"

"No, I guess it will take a while. You don't mind if I sit it out here, do you?"

"Not at all, take your time. Care for anything else?"

I feel obliged to order an English muffin, with butter and jam.

Yes—jam: in little jars filled with jam I smuggled my communications to Harry into Theresienstadt. They didn't amount to much, but even so they were comforting.

By the end of 1943, there were very few Jews left in Vienna, and even most of these were ferreted out and shipped off before the end of the war. Small transports continued to leave at irregular intervals, sometimes with just a handful of people, not even enough to fill one freight car. The staff of the Community and the establishments under its jurisdiction continued to be decimated and replaced by half-Jews. Each loss was mourned greatly. One physician after another was taken. So were Frieda and her parents. They were deported at about the same time as Harry. I was sad to see Frieda leave but relieved, as all of us were, that they were being sent to Theresienstadt.

At that time, we were allowed to write three postcards a month to any one address in Theresienstadt, channelled through the Community. Since there was censorship, we had to limit ourselves to reporting trivia. Even so, not all cards arrived and replies were even less frequent. I believe, only one longer communication, in block letters, was permitted per month, and even that permission kept being abrogated. But packages could be acknowledged on preprinted postcards: Address, date and signature, nothing else. That was when I hit upon the idea of putting tiny rolled-up strips of paper, with questions on them, into the jam I included in my packages to Harry. I asked him to answer my questions on his acknowledgement card by beginning each word with an upstroke for a *yes* and without one for a *no*, address first, then date, then signature. I asked questions like "are you healthy?" "hungry?" "with your parents?" "are many people dying?" "are you working?" "do they mistreat you?" "do you need food?" "clothing?" and so on. For a few weeks his cards supplied the answers.

Though the questions were simple and the answers of limited usefulness, the fact that we were communicating and outwitting the system cheered me greatly, and him undoubtedly too. At the same time I had no illusions. I was sure he had consoled himself with someone else by now. From what people wrote, life in Theresienstadt was fairly "normal." It even included amateur concerts and plays, dances and discussion circles.

I was slowly getting used to the idea that our romance was over and finished. After all, I had never expected it to lead to anything. At least he was well, and I had many wonderful memories. I wrote them down, in as much detail as I could remember, under the title "An Episode."

Writing my account was both thrilling and frustrating. I was unable to set it down in all its glory, as the marvellous experience it had been. How do you make love last? Nothing is permanent in this world except the word, and even that is elusive. It needs to be coaxed and courted, and I was very awkward at courting.

Strange: To this day I don't have much trouble integrating into new cultures, perhaps because what little of my old culture there was had been contaminated almost beyond recognition, so that much could be discarded without regrets. Being at home everywhere and nowhere has always struck me as a boon. But I can't claim the same about language. Though I know five languages reasonably well, I somehow find myself standing in the spaces between them, master of none. Even English, with which I have by now been living for over forty years, has remained a step-language, a tool which I can sometimes use skillfully, even imaginatively, but which at other times fights me to the finish. I don't dare take risks with it, to bend it to my will and whimsy. Perhaps because it has never been an integral part of my sight and hearing, my breath and my dreams, the way my native language was before it abandoned me.

Or am I still too hard on myself? Only now I understand—and wish I could let Mauri know this—why he kept urging me to let my hair down. My hair was short, and I failed to comprehend. But I have come to realize that reality has many doors. Perhaps one shouldn't worry so much about how to access truth. Inventing truth may approach its essense as much or as little as re-creating or copying it. Who was it that said: "The lies of poets are lies in the service of truth?" Miriam, the lyer, may have come closer to being a real writer than I ever will.

Or is it that not language but voice is the key? Some voices sing, others shout, some whisper and stammer. Yet every voice forges a meaningful link between the self and the outside world if it tries in earnest, and then its existence can reaffirm that of the others.

The link between Harry and me remained intact for several weeks. Then the acknowledgements began to be signed by his mother. After weeks of agony, a note from her informed me that they were well, but that Harry was away on a work detail.

I did not hear from him again until the war was over. He returned to Vienna in the summer of 1945. At first he said little about his life during that last year and a half of the war. I asked no questions and he volunteered no information. It was wonderful to see him again. We would go to the theater together, also to the first Court Ball, for which I made a lovely princess-style dress for myself, from a yellow-gold satin curtain.

My relationship with my father had not improved significantly, and Harry's presence was reassuring and soothing. But the feeling that we didn't really know one another persisted. We seemed to have little in common other than a mutual physical attraction, and our conversations remained pleasant but superficial. Nor was he, for all I could tell, interested in a serious commitment, and since I too was not at all certain that I would want to spend the rest of my life with him, I did nothing to prevent our drifting apart.

By then I had a new circle of friends. They were *Mischlinge* of the Second Class who, though starless, had not been allowed to attend school during the war but been assigned to "war-essential" enterprises, mostly outside Vienna. I met them in the course I took during the summer of 1945. They too had experienced hardships and losses, but they were a different breed—tougher, more self-assured and resourceful. Four of them, Christl, Hans and the sisters Evi and Kitty, constituted my last group of friends before I left for America.

In Christl's case, it was the mother who was not Jewish. Her father had committed suicide in 1938 in the hope that he would thereby protect both his family and his business. Christl thinks that he might have survived, had he not given up. The business was expropriated anyway. Christl was sent to Hamburg to her father's sister who had an Aryan husband. There she was able to study metallography, not at the university but at a technical school. Subsequently, she was assigned to a research concern in Traismauer, Lower Austria, where she worked until the bombs began to fall. Then she rejoined her mother in Vienna. During one of the last raids a bomb took with it half her bedroom, just after she had walked out of it.

Hans had been a co-worker of Christl's in Traismauer. His mother was a baptized Jew, an attractive, gentle and dignified woman. His father was a "von", and though nobility had been abolished officially, he seemed the epitome of the old-time officer, upright, correct and affable. Once, when Hans took me along to a gathering of friends, I noticed that many of the young men's faces were disfigured by duelling scars. It seemed a doubly unreal world, now, in the Second Austrian republic.

Evi and Kitty were sisters, with a non-Jewish mother. Both were short and unusually attractive, each in a very different way. Kitty was dark-haired, elegant and mature looking. Evi was blond, blue-eyed, vivacious, and a real tomboy. Twice she crossed the border into Germany illegally during that year, and returned with a knapsack full of victuals. I much admired her for this—I would never have dared.

Christl and Evi soon emigrated to the States. Kitty, much to my surprise, decided almost overnight to marry a German-Jewish refugee living in a South American country. Apparently this is how it came about: a visitor to Vienna took back with him snapshots of the city, and some of them included Kitty. "That's the girl I want to marry!" his friend exclaimed, took a week off and flew to Vienna. He introduced himself to the family, proposed by the end of the week, and was accepted.

"Of course I'm not in love," she told me when I met her at the New York airport, "but he is nice and decent, and this was my best chance to get out of Vienna. Let's face it, we aren't getting younger."

I have often wondered how that marriage fared. I visited Evi and her husband once in Kansas City where they had established a flocked teashirt factory, something very new at the time. Then I lost touch with both sisters, as with everyone else from those years. After my walk I felt an urge to find out if anyone was still alive. I succeeded in reestablishing contact with Christl, in Wisconsin, and with Bibi, in New Jersey. It felt good. Not that they can help me retrieve my past—no one can do that for you. But their presence has somehow confirmed its validity.

This new circle of friends sustained me during the two years which I spent in Vienna after the war. I was also buoyed by my decision to emigrate, get as far away from my father and from Vienna as I could and then begin a new life. I was fortunate. My Berlin birth put me on the German quota, and since very few German Jews had survived, the quota was not as oversubscribed as the Polish, Hungarian and Romanian quotas which took years to open up. While waiting for the immigration papers, I studied French and worked at whatever job I could find to pay for the French course. I was also trying to save some money in case my father made me move out of the apartment.

6.

On April 26, 1945, Mussolini was shot, and on April 30, ten days after his 56th birthday, Hitler committed suicide. Goebbels had still given a rousing birthday speech on behalf of the Führer, hinting at a last minute secret weapon.

On May 8, the day the war in Europe ended, we moved back into our apartment on Strudlhofgasse, or rather, into the somewhat smaller apartment one floor below. Father had discovered it to be empty—the Nazi in it had fled. In a drawer I found a copy of *Mein Kampf*, personally inscribed by the Führer, and I quickly tossed it into the trash before the Russians could find it.

On a neighbor's handcart we hauled our suitcases across the patched up Augarten Bridge, along the Ring and down the long Liechtensteinstraße. Then father disappeared and left me to clean and refurbish the apartment. I did it with pleasure. It seemed like both a homecoming and a new start. Even when he began to talk about this being his apartment and not mine, and that he would one day turn me out and make me get my own furnished room, the venom didn't penetrate the skin, especially after I saved some money for that eventuality. I contemplated it quite dispassionately, almost with anticipation. It never came about because neither father nor I took the initiative once it became clear that I would be able to emigrate to the States.

Another puzzle: When I finally had my visa in hand, in May of 1947, father asked me to consider seriously whether I really wanted to leave Vienna. Now I could, after all, attend the university and lead a normal life, close to family and friends. I merely said that I preferred to start that new life in America, as Christl and Evi had done by then.

My first job was fascinating and instructive in more ways than one. Christl had told me that a distant relative of hers, Frau von Alth, who worked as a reader for the Burgtheater, was looking for secretarial help; since I knew shorthand and could type, I might be just the right person for her. Apparently I was, for soon she not only dictated to me her assessments of the plays she was reviewing, but entrusted plays written in Czech or English to my evaluation. I worked for her half days and the pay was minimal, but I was thrilled to work within the ambiance of the Burgtheater, to be almost a member of the team. Incidentally, though the theater itself was burned out, performances were staged in other theaters almost from the moment the war ended. Frau von Alth was intelligent, critical and demanding. The fact that she took my opinions and critiques seriously made me feel like an adult for the first time in my life, and provided me with a challenge which I relished and tried hard to live up to.

Minna von Alth was an unusual person. I assume she was Jewish or half-Jewish, though I have no idea how she survived the war in Vienna or wherever else she was, and whether there was a Herr von Alth. She was about 35 or 40, short, with average figure and looks but with long, platinum blond hair and a large, sensual mouth. She dressed so exotically that her presence was striking, if odd rather than elegant. She smoked like a chimney, at first those awful, smelly Russian and Bulgarian cigarettes, but fairly soon American brands.

Only once did I see her truly upset. She had managed to find a taxi after an evening performance, but was stopped by the police: a woman had been brutalized, probably raped, and they needed the taxi to get her to a hospital. There was much blood and Frau von Alth almost became sick. I had been walking all over the city at any time of day or evening—the streetcars weren't yet running—without encountering problems. Therefore I had shrugged off the rumors about women being raped. After that incident I stayed off the streets at night.

My psychology professor at the accelerated summer course read *Katharina Brienne* and liked it. That seemed almost too easy, so I also asked Frau von Alth to assess the manuscript. She read it very thoroughly and her verdict was fairly negative. Of course, I needn't take her word for it. She suggested that I submit the manuscript to Ullstein Publishers. She even offered to send them a letter of recommendation.

I didn't submit it. Now that I was typing and editing her evaluations and also assessing manuscripts myself, I considered her critique well-founded. No, I was not a writer. A writer wouldn't use clichés, an inauthentic, plagiarized language, as I was doing.

Nor did real writers write about their own longings and frustrations. They transcended them and created new, richer worlds. Mine had merely been a clumsy, possibly disingenuous attempt at inventing a self for me because I had been unable to discover one. I resolved to stop navel-gazing and look outward instead.

When I emigrated, I left *Katharina Brienne* behind, but I will always cherish her memory. *Requiescat in pace,* Katharina, and thank you!

I admired Frau von Alth's intellect and learned much from her, but before long our relationship developed serious strains. She was moody and had a tendency to reverse herself, to promise me a ticket for a performance and then deny having done so, or to ask me to return a ticket she had already given me and which she now wanted for someone else. And since theater tickets were at a premium, these were painful disappointments.

She also turned into a real exploiter and could be quite nasty about it. She might keep me waiting for hours, asking me to be at her place at one and show up at three herself, and then not let me leave on time. For my meager salary I was expected to put in more and more hours at almost any time of day or night, and I was accused of disloyalty if I protested. When her demands began to interfere with my French course, I quit. She gave me a good recommendation for those six months, though.

After that I taught English for the American Joint Distribution Committee, a Jewish-American service organization. My students were a pleasure to work with. They consisted of survivors from concentration camps, and of displaced persons—"DPs"—who had fled to Vienna from the Eastern war zone or Russia proper after the end of the war, and who were now hoping to emigrate to America. They were slow but earnest learners and touchingly grateful for any effort made on their behalf. When I was ready to become a DP myself and leave Vienna—as a final nightmare, by cattle car—they gave me a big farewell party.

I don't recall if it was through the AJDC or by chance that I began to receive CARE packages from a Miss Edna Evert, bless her soul, in Lincoln, Nebraska. The packages were a godsend. Eventually, I visited Miss Evert and her sister and thanked them in person. Two sweet, kind old ladies. The packages and the two-week stay in Gastein with Christl and Gerd during that awful first winter after the war saved my digestion and health. Gastein did even more for Christl. She decided to stay in the American zone, found work at American army headquarters in Salzburg, and soon became engaged to a young lawyer from Wisconsin in an American uniform but originally from Vienna. By now they have been living in Wisconsin for some forty-five years.

Gerd had likewise been in that accelerated summer course, and the trip to Gastein was his idea. He knew some black-marketeers who were going back and forth, and they told him that the American sector was the land of milk and honey. Not only did you not starve there but you could even find heated rooms. (In Vienna, we were freezing bitterly.) Someone recommended Hofgastein and a small inn there that might put us up in exchange for clothing, jewelry, almost anything. Hofgastein it was going to be. Christl had jaundice and was in desperate need of milk and other nourishing food, and I was not only hungry but so depressed that I would have gone anywhere with anybody.

It was not easy to obtain the necessary border permits. My passport was no longer recognized and the "press card" from father's newspaper was of no help at all. I stood in endless lines at the Russian *Komendatura* to get the required *Identitätskarte*, which was made out in the four languages of the occupying powers. But finally the day came when the three of us met at the train station with our backpacks, pushed our way onto the crowded train and set out in the direction of Salzburg.

The trip was rough. The packed train was moving at a snail's pace, with constant stops, many in the middle of nowhere and for no apparent reason, so that everyone grew more and more nervous and apprehensive. We were standing or, whenever we managed to find enough floorspace, sitting on our bundles. Luckily, Gerd had brought along a chunk of bread and some water. After endless hours, we pulled into the dreaded Soviet checkpoint at Enns, at the border between the Russian and American occupation zones.

The train ground to a noisy and ominously definitive-sounding halt. And there we stood, and stood, for hours. As if we had been forgotten or didn't exist. Luckily, so many bodies in close proximity spread warmth, and that was something to be thankful for in midwinter. Finally, three Russian soldiers with machine guns shoved their way into our overcrowded carriage and began to check our permits. They were only the first of several such patrols, each equally loud and rude. By the time we received the last of some ten validations, it was dark outside. There was much shouting and gesturing on the platform and soldiers with police dogs marched up and down. Several people were taken off the train. Eventually, things quieted down again, but even then the train did not leave. Everybody tried to get to a window to figure out what was happening. The longer the delay lasted, the more worried we became. No telling whether something was very wrong or whether all this was routine.

Finally, with a jolt we began to move but backwards, to everyone's dismay. I was too tired to care. If they are taking us back, let's just hope it will be all the way to Vienna. But then we screeched to another halt, and the train reversed direction. It rumbled across the bridge over the Enns—and we were in the American sector.

I don't recall much about the American inspection except that they sprayed DDT into our blouses and jackets. However, the ride went faster now, there were no unexplained stops, and before long we were in Hofgastein. Next to it lies the bigger and brassier Badgastein, formerly (and now again) a famous ski resort. At that time it housed the headquarters of an American division which ran a large DP-Camp.

As we were walking from the station toward the lights of the village, we gasped. Though it was a moonless night, everything was white, covered by snow, beautiful, clean snow. The snow made the hilly landscape with its church steeples, white roofs and lit windows look like a Christmas card scene, a world without war, fear, or privation. We found it difficult to believe that it was real.

At the inn, Gerd conducted some skillful negotiations and soon we had two rooms, spotless, with wonderful down comforters inside red and white ticking.

However, even here food was in short supply or would have been, had not Gerd turned out to be very adept at "organizing." He had brought watches, a few small etchings of the "Steffl"—St.

Stephan's cathedral—books and knickknacks, all of which could be traded for bread, butter and canned goods. Even Nazi mementos were in great demand—the Russians would have shot us on the spot had they found those relics on us. It was just as well that I had not known what Gerd was taking across the border.

Besides trading with the *Amis*, Gerd would now and then interpret for them, and most of the soldiers were very generous. They gave away chewing gum, cigarettes and chocolate—real chocolate. Now and then, they even treated us to a meal.

Gerd looked like the typical American college athlete, tall, broadly built without seeming heavy, blond and goodlooking, the very picture of health. Alas, that was misleading. He had had several spinal operations, and something was apparently still wrong. Though often in pain he never let on, and you could only tell by his restlessness. He seemed to like me and was protective and gentle with me, and I tried to be as considerate and upbeat as I could.

After I left Austria, we exchanged one or two letters, then I lost track of him. One day, about ten years later, the mailman brought one of those ominous black-bordered envelopes which are used in Europe to convey death notices. It came from his mother and announced that Gerd had died, suddenly, in Beirut, Lebanon. Beirut, Lebanon? My inquiry remained unanswered.

It was ironic that peace, too, should have its casualties. Gerd was not the only one. In my French class I met the third person in my life to become my "best friend," though the English term doesn't quite convey the closeness of the German. Trude Zechmeister was not Jewish, but her father had refused to join the party and as a result lost his teaching job. He was too old to be drafted, and both he and his much younger wife worked themselves to the bone—no office jobs for them—to survive. He died before the end of the war. Trude's mother was still alive during my last visit to my father. We took a long walk through the Wienerwald together and talked about Trude.

Trude was the very opposite of Ilse Markstein, very quiet but equally spontaneous and affectionate. Her great love had been killed in the war. Her other great love was music, especially Bruckner. For hours she would play his symphonies for me and, with shining eyes, alert my not very musical ear to the subtleties

and beauties of his majestic sound. To her I was able to talk about
Harry and also about my father, though I wonder whether she
ever fully believed me. How could she? Her mother was gentle
and sweet, and language and behavior such as I was describing
must have been unimaginable to her. Whenever she met my
father, he was his usual polite and charming public self.

Some years before, Trude had contracted a heart defect from a
neglected tonsilitis. Although she managed to study law, work for
the municipality's legal department and marry a colleague, also a
lawyer, her heart was causing more and more problems, with
episodes of dangerous fibrillations. When I visited her for the last
time, she showed me, with great pride, the house they were building. It was going to be ready in a few months. But she also told
me that she had decided to have open heart surgery because "life
like this is no longer fun." They gave her a fifty-fifty chance.

When Trude visited me at the Strudlhofgasse apartment, I
asked her to step into the other room and took a snapshot of her.
It was all I could think of doing to hold on to her. She wore the
dress I had brought her from the States, something very airy and
dainty which had pleased her greatly. I can still see it, almost
transparent, with beige, ochre and white polka dots between hor-
izontal stripes in the same colors. I tried not to cry when I hugged
her for the last time, and so did she. Both of us seemed to know
that she wouldn't make it. In the black-rimmed envelope her
mother enclosed a long personal letter, telling me that during the
final weeks, Trude had begun to read the Bible and derived great
solace from it. I was glad.

7.

When I returned from Gastein in early 1946, quite a bit healthier
in body and spirit, I signed up for the Kautezky Language
School's French program. Soon thereafter, I entered Frau von
Alth's service. Harry was in medical school and we rarely saw
each other. With Christl remaining in Salzburg, my circle now
consisted of Hans, Kitty and Evi who, however, soon left for the
States. Kitty had a boyfriend by name of Hannes, but he hardly
ever joined our group. I gathered that theirs was a "real" rela-

tionship, and that both impressed and intimidated me.

There was also a newcomer, another Walter. He was Viennese but now a member of the British occupation forces and in uniform. Older than the rest of us, he wore thick glasses and had a big scar across one cheek, which he claimed to have received in a duel. But since he was quite a joker, I am not sure it was true. Not in the least good-looking but pleasant and easygoing, he liked to refer to himself as a *Schlemihl,* the proverbial bumbler. With a gleeful grin he told us that he had made the Queen dance with *him,* the insignificant Austrian refugee in a private's uniform: when she put in an official appearance at an armed forces ball, he asked her to dance, knowing that she couldn't refuse. They had the entire dance floor to themselves for a while. Luckily, Walter was a good dancer.

He was also good company, and I liked him a lot. He introduced me to "heavy petting" which I found pleasant, though slightly scary and not very meaningful. Whenever I reminded him that he had a wife in London, he would say with his disarming smirk: "Don't worry! I wouldn't dream of seducing a virgin!" I wasn't sure if that was a compliment or not.

In contrast to him, Hans, with whom Christl had worked during the war, became a real friend. Polite and considerate, he also made a good hiking partner. Though he seemed more like an older brother than a suitor, I found it reassuring that there were again people who considered me "normal" and liked me. One evening, as we were spending the night side by side (but next to several others) in a mountain hut, he proposed to me. I declined but felt very honored.

In June 1947, I was finally able to turn my back on Europe. Four years later, Harry likewise emigrated to the States. After taking the necessary examinations, he began to practice medicine. As so happened, we married in the same year, 1957. His daughter—is there magic in numbers?—was born seven months later, mine seven years later. We write to each other once a year, and neither has ever missed the other's birthday. We also met again, once at his aunt's with whom he stayed during the first years after his arrival, after that at the airport whenever I had a few hours between flights. There I learned the rest of his wartime story.

I was wrong in assuming that the family had been able to remain in Theresienstadt because Harry's father was a physician and therefore indispensable. It was Harry who protected his parents by volunteering, in February 1944, for a work detail that was to be sent away on a construction job. They were told that their families would be protected for the duration of the assignment, and for once the SS kept its word. In Zossen near Wulkow, not far from Berlin, this Jewish crew of one hundred and fifty built barracks and bunkers, actually a whole subterranean town, for the top brass of the security services. Harry saw most of them during their periodic inspections of the premises—Himmler, General Müller, the Head of the SS Security Services and the Gestapo, and Eichmann.

The group was convinced that, once the project was completed, they would be liquidated. Therefore Harry, like everyone else, tried his best to be declared unfit and sent back to Theresienstadt. He almost succeeded. His name was placed on the "exchange list" and he was told to be ready the next morning. Much envied, he took leave from his comrades, pocketed their letters to their families in Theresienstadt, and lined up with his bundle for the roll call of those selected for departure. But instead of his name another name beginning with the same syllable was called. It turned out that the young man had a severe case of athlete's foot. To get him out of there before he infected everybody else, they had simply substituted his name for Harry's. Later Harry learned that the entire group of exchangees had been sent to Auschwitz.

In February 1945, when the Russians were approaching Berlin, the work detail was loaded into freight cars and sent back to Theresienstadt. The trip took ten days. They stood on a siding outside the Berlin railroad station during the big air raid on Berlin, sitting ducks in locked cars listening to the bombardment around them. By some miracle, they were not hit. In Würzburg they were ordered out of the cars and lined up against the station building, while their guards disappeared in the bunkers. They saw the low-flying planes above their heads, but the planes flew on. The big raid which destroyed much of Würzburg took place a few days later. When they arrived in Theresienstadt, in the middle of the night, the whole town was out to welcome them.

In March, fifty of the best workers were selected from that same group to go to Bavaria and build bunkers there. Harry was not among them and considered himself fortunate. To everybody's amazement that group returned as well—just a few days ahead of the Russian tanks.

What Harry didn't know was that as early as May 1944 the decision had been reached to eventually liquidate the ghetto in Theresienstadt, and that its fate had hung in the balance to the last moment. Eichmann wanted to hand the camp over to the Allies, SS-*Hauptsturmführer* Günther to kill all inmates. Karl Rahm, the camp's commandant and, incidentally, an Austrian, at the very last moment and probably in his own interest, refrained from ordering the blood bath (9/146).

Those last days in Theresienstadt were apparently rather chaotic. The International Red Cross arrived on May 1st or 2nd. Shortly thereafter the Czechs came, bringing with them physicians to combat a spotted typhus epidemic in the camp. On May 5, the Red Cross representative ordered Rahm to leave. (Rahm was tried in the Czechoslovak Republic in 1947, and executed.) The Russians arrived on May 8.

8.

I asked Harry if he remembered the story of the "phony gasman." Of course he did.

A man in an official-looking uniform had been going from door to door to read the meters, except that he would rob and rape single women. Although the newspapers reported these occurrences in detail, he had so far eluded the police. Then he tried something different. A "Gestapo official" appeared in Harry's house and announced that he would give the Jewish families there one last chance to hand over illegal possessions such as gold, jewelry, furs etc. with impunity. He would be back the following day to collect.

When the tenants notified the Gestapo through the officially designated Jewish contact person, he was laughed at and told to go to the precinct police in Leopoldgasse. There they didn't take the matter seriously either, and the detective accused the Jews of lacking "civil courage" for not having caught the man themselves. He did, however, ask to be notified should the impostor return. When they did so, he went with them, though alone, on foot and without a weapon.

In a grotesque tragicomedy, it was Harry's father who confronted the man on the stairs, while the detective barricaded himself in the apartment from which the criminal, after firing several shots, had fled. Harry's father wrestled the man to the ground, even though the other was much taller and heavier, and the two rolled down the three floors interlocked while Harry was shouting for the police from an open window. They arrived but were at first unable to enter the house because the detective had ordered the entry door locked.

After they had subdued the crook, it turned out that he was a notorious gangster—in fact, the "false gasman" whom the police had been seeking for weeks. Eight days later, on December 2, 1942, he was beheaded with an axe. When Harry and his family were held in the *Liesl,* the interrogating officer must either have recognized Harry's father as the man who had apprehended the phony meterman or read about it in the file.

They arrived at the *Liesl,* Harry remembered, on the night of a transport. Terror-struck shorn prisoners were staring at them. For a week the family was separated, and despaired of ever seeing one another again. During the second week, a guard came for Harry. He was sure that he was going to be shot. Instead, he was reunited with his parents. But when he laid eyes on his mother, he was aghast: the formerly plump woman looked haggard and old, and her black hair had turned white.

They were informed that they had been reclassified as "political." This entitled them to certain privileges such as a newspaper, and the guard threw a *Völkischer Beobachter* at them. Having something to read, even that abominable party rag, had saved their sanity, Harry said. A few days later they were moved to the holding camp at Malzgasse No. 7, and on November 11 they left for Theresienstadt, together with 88 others.

9.

Spring 1945. Almost a year and a half since Harry's arrest. I had not heard from him in over a year, and packages were no longer accepted. But although the situation at home was dismal, I drew comfort from the knowledge that somewhere out there someone was fond of me—provided he was still alive. And there was of course also Katharina, in whose life I could forget mine.

By mid-March, barely a day was raidless and we spent most of our time in the cellar. On the twelfth, the lights went out right after the alert, and the deafening roar and eerie whistling told us that the bombs were hitting close by. It was a long raid, and when we finally emerged after the all-clear, the rumor spread like wildfire that the opera house was burning. Everybody headed into the Inner City to see for themselves. There was wreckage everywhere, a strong gas smell, the air full of soot and dust, and the sky so red that it seemed painted with blood.

When I walked past the Hotel Bristol, I didn't believe my eyes. All windows were blown out so that the ground floor dining room had become an outdoor restaurant. But a restaurant it still was. Since there was no electricity, a candle lit every table, and the tables were set with the usual white damask table cloths. White-gloved and frockcoated waiters were serving dinner. Almost every table was taken.

Later that evening, Ditha's familiar four-ring bell sounded. But she looked like a ghost.

"For heaven's sake, Ditha, what has happened?"

For a long time she couldn't speak. Then, with tears streaming down her face, the news:

"Ilse is dead."

Ditha had been in the same shelter, the Community's two-tier cellar which was supposed to be bombproof, almost as safe as the catacombs. It was also accessible from the Gestapo headquarters nearby and so, in ironic togetherness, the Jews were relegated to the upper level while the non-star wearers assembled below. The shelter was crowded and Ilse and her mother had stood close to the door. The bomb hit on a slant and exploded at street level, right by the entrance. Ilse's mother was badly injured and in the hospital. They had not yet found Ilse's body.

"Could she still be alive?" The merest glimmer of hope but, as we were crying in each other's arms, Ditha shook her head. She had seen the devastation when she and the other survivors climbed out of the ruins. Anita, a bright, pretty six year old with enormous black eyes whom both of us knew, was also dead. "Mommy," she whimpered when they dug her out. An hour later, she was still. There might easily be fifty casualties, Ditha said. Lea and her parents had been there too, Lea told me much later, but they had hidden the star and gone down to the lower level. They were led out through the network of subterranean passages which crisscrosses the Inner City, and emerged near the Graben, still during the raid.

On the second day, Ilse's mother was allowed to have visitors and I went to see her. Never again. My presence only brought it all back to her. "You were fond of her too, weren't you?" she sobbed and pressed me tightly to her. "Go, go look for her and bring my child back to me!" I wept with her.

Two days later they identified the body. They had had it all along but had not recognized her. Ilse was buried on March 23, 1945, right after the all-clear. They even managed to secure a coffin. Her twenty-first birthday would have been on May 13.

In cruel irony, Ilse's grandmother returned from Theresienstadt at the end of the war. "The truth would kill her," Frau Mezei said and told her that the twins were in Argentina. For years she fabricated letters from them to read to her mother. Frau Mezei died only recently—at 93.

Ilse was the kind of person I would have liked to be. Friendly, concerned, thoughtful, even-tempered, with a humor that was never malicious, always helpful, doing things for others, worrying about them, consoling everyone. She was a genuinely religious person, both by adhering to all religious observances and by living a truly religious life. If God didn't protect someone like her, I was thinking during the funeral service, and the many others who had died equally innocently and senselessly, He quite obviously did not care about anybody. Whether this meant that He didn't exist or that He was an indifferent if not sadistic God made little difference. Ivan Karamazov had been right. Such a god was not wanted and you owed it to yourself to reject him. And so I did, this time definitively, on Tuesday, March 23, 1945, even though it made things even harder.

During those final weeks everything came to a halt. There was no longer any public transport, and the few private cars that managed to "organize" gasoline were barely able to navigate the glass- and debris-strewn streets which were pitted with bomb craters and blocked by cave-ins. Few telephone lines worked and if you wanted to know whether your friends had survived the most recent bomb attack, you had to make your way to them on foot. Even then you might find their building in ruins and would not know if they were underneath or safe. Water was hard to come by, we had no coal—and that April was especially cold—and for long intervals there was no gas and electricity.

After the almost daily air raids a quiet day felt uncanny. The long lines for the few groceries still on the shelves dispersed in a flash when the sirens began to howl. Did I say I survived without nightmares? The siren of a police car or ambulance and the droning of a low flying plane still send shivers down my spine.

The Russian bombs were small and didn't do much damage, unlike those of the Americans. The Americans arrived every morning at eleven—you could almost set your watch by them. Sometimes they overflew Vienna and everything remained quiet, but more and more frequently we could hear the low thuds of distant impacts or the eerie whistle and ear-splitting noise of a hit close by, with clouds of dust entering our cellars. The high-pitched crackling of the anti-aircraft guns of the *Fliegerabwehr-kanonen—FLAK* for short—reminded me of the yapping of aunt Olga's chihuahua. One such gun tower stood at the bottom of our street. It still stands there, in the midst of the lush vegetation of the Augarten Palace Park. A forgotten relic? Grim monument of the war? Avatar of the future? Possibly all of the above.

We were torn between wanting the Americans to destroy everything in sight and the hope that they would spare Vienna. Sometimes it was four or five hours between the shrill howling of the alarm and the even-pitched all-clear. More and more frequently the planes seemed to aim not so much at military targets as at entire sections of the city. It was called saturation bombing. The last raids were especially devastating. One in particular seemed aimed deliberately at the city's most famous historic buildings. We didn't know whether to cry or curse when in the same air raid the opera, the *Musikverein*, Vienna's most famous concert hall, and the Burgtheater were hit and in part reduced to rubble, in part fire-bombed into silent, mutilated shells. Shortly thereafter, either the withdrawing Germans or a gang of looters started a fire in St. Stephan's Cathedral. The roof burned, and the *Pummerin*, the second largest bell in Western Europe, came crashing down and shattered. It had been cast from the metal of captured Turkish canons after Vienna had been liberated from the second Turkish siege in 1683.

We were spending most of our days and nights in the cellars. Our cubicles were just big enough to hold one or two narrow folding cots, and the low wooden partitions barely provided privacy. During a lull in the shelling or after the all-clear we would rush upstairs to use bathrooms, wash, change clothes, and take a few more cans of food or another jug of drinking water down into the cellar.

When the Russians reached the bank of the Danube Canal, they began to shell the Leopoldstadt. Little did we know when we moved to Untere Augartenstraße how fortunate that location would be for us. Was there someone up there watching out over my father and me after all? But why should he? How did we deserve to be luckier than those others, Ilse, presumably safe in the Community shelter, or the neighbor who was killed by one tiny shrapnel? More likely, it was a mere fluke, another lucky coincidence without rhyme or reason, and also another debt to carry.

A few hours before the Russians marched down our street, the SS dragged all Jews they could lay their hands on out into the street and shot them, the sounds of their machine guns and hand grenades drowned out by the noise of the shelling. Since our street, as the access road to the bridge, was under heavy fire, they couldn't approach the front entrance. The back entrance was bricked up, and so no one heard their pounding. When I was in Vienna last year, I noticed with an eerie feeling that that entrance was open, the double doors covered with announcements and posters.

When they came for us we were in the cellar, all except Frau Pospíchal, a good Czech and Nazi hater. She lived in the flat above us and was upstairs when she heard the banging on the back door. From behind a curtain she saw the uniforms. No one responded, and after a while they moved on. But we learned all that only later.

10.

A diary page:

On February 7, a heavy raid. The main railroad station hit.

Feb. 8—four hour raid.

Feb. 9—five hours.

Feb. 10—four hours.

Feb. 11—NO RAID!

Feb. 17—NO RAID!

2/21: A bad one. An unexploded time bomb near the Burgtheater. The area cordoned off. A huge bomb crater on the Karlsplatz. No public transport. Pedestrians are stopped and asked to help clear debris.

3/3: NO RAID, but it is very cold and impossible to get coal.

3/12: A devastating raid—KG shelter hit, the Burgtheater, the Albertina, the Musikverein. The opera is burning.

3/16: Long raid. Huge processions heading for the catacombs early every morning.

3/17: A bad five hour raid.

3/19: Saturation raid.

3/20: A SHORT raid!

3/21: A five hour alert but no bombs on Vienna.

3/25: A bad one.

3/28: The Russians are rumored to have reached Wiener Neustadt. A lot of troop movement between raids. Are they fleeing or massing?

11.

On April 2, the Russians stood within forty kilometers of Vienna. Everybody was hoping that Vienna would be declared an open city, but then the radio announced that the city was to be defended: "Every house a fortress—we win or die!" We knew what that meant. In Budapest they had been fighting for weeks, street by street and door to door, with lots of casualties, no food, no water, and the threat of cholera. On Easter Sunday, big posters everywhere were urging people to defend Vienna "against the barbarians." They were signed by Baldur von Schirach, Vienna's *Gauleiter*. He was one of the few who at the Nuremberg trials admitted his guilt. Prison life seemed to agree with him—or was he rewarded for confessing? He lived until 1974.

My father was hardly ever at home now, not even for meals. Probably he was supplying the Klügers with black market goods and eating there. And Grete was undoubtedly a better cook than I. That meant that he no longer brought provisions home, and there was hardly anything to be had legally except potatoes and dry, crumbly cornmeal bread, at best also a little lard and salt.

The front was moving toward us rapidly. Within three days it had reached the city. The rumbling of the cannons sounded like continual distant thunder. Planes flew overhead almost without a letup. Most of them were Russian, which meant that they were not very large and did little damage. The anti-aircraft guns of the *FLAK* tower at the lower end of our street must by then have been low on ammunition. They only came to life if the planes flew low enough to make good targets. Even so, the air raid alerts lasted most of the day, and only early in the morning or toward evening did a semblance of life fill the streets.

Vienna was being readied for battle. The army had mined the bridges across the Danube Canal and posted sentries. I was told that convoys of horse-drawn carts crammed with refugees and their bundles were coming down Mariahilfer Straße—I wondered where on earth they thought they were heading. People tried to get out of town whichever way they could. There was a run on any train that might still be leaving, even if it was only the *Donauuferbahn* from Franz Josef Station. "*Schnackerlbahn*" everyone called it, because it chugged along at a snail's pace between the small towns and villages along the Danube. Those with connections, valuables or foreign currencies tried to buy gasoline coupons from the military. Many left on foot, pulling small carts behind them, some loaded with the weirdest possessions imaginable—a pair of antlers, a stuffed bird. One case fell off and spilled, strewing the street with cutlery and bringing the entire procession to a halt.

Inge and her father had left several weeks before for Bregenz, at the Western end of Austria. "I know what war is like," Inge's father said. "I've gone through it. Only a fool would stay in Vienna. I'm getting as far away from the front as I can." His wife remained behind to close the office and then follow. Since their maid and a tenant planned to remain in the house, she hoped it would be safe from looters.

Early on April 2, well before the eleven o'clock alert, I packed a small suitcase and carried it to Inge's mother. In the suitcase were my most treasured possessions—my collapsible umbrella, my burgundy dress, my best underwear, letters and a few photographs. I asked if I could leave it with her. Everyone was doing this—distributing at least some belongings among friends since it was not likely that all houses would be destroyed.

"Isn't it absurd," I said to her. "Here I am worrying about a dress and I may not even survive. Well, if I die, I die." But I did not really mean it. Deep down I still couldn't imagine that I might not make it. I didn't even consider that possibility until the moment when the SS aimed their guns at us, the day before the Russians marched down Augartenstraße. Even so, I was scared and wished fervently to have someone to be with, to talk to. If she had suggested it, I would have left for Bregenz with her then and there.

When I told father that afternoon, after the alert was over, that I was afraid of the impending fighting and wanted to get away, he said that I should either stop moaning or take off. He would even let me have some money, and I could start out on foot if there were no trains. When he left the house, I sat down by the window where the light was still good and escaped to *Katharina*.

Her mother, Inge told me much later, did manage to get out the following day—on the last train to leave Vienna. It reached Krems during the raid which battered the town to bits. They sat in a tunnel for six hours.

12.

April 5. It is unseasonally hot but the heat comes as a relief after the bone-chilling weather of the previous weeks. It took me more than two hours to secure our meat ration this morning, but I waited it out. Since the Russians are at the gate, you might not get anything edible unless you pick it up now. Almost everything is at a standstill.

In the middle of the wait the *FLAK* started up with such an earsplitting din that everybody dispersed in panic. At first we thought that the bridges were being blown up. Every time things calmed down some and the line reassembled, the hellish noise started up again.

By noon I had grown so accustomed to the racket that I didn't even wince when a low plane almost grazed us. You can get used to anything, no doubt about it.

As I was carrying drinking water into the cellar, I noticed that our neighbors were taking down bundles and blankets. Would we have to sleep in the cellars? There was only one narrow cot in our cubicle and father would probably claim it. Someone said that the Russians had already crossed the *Gürtel*, the outer of the two rings around the city. Once again we began to hope that the Germans might withdraw without a fight. But the cannons boomed all afternoon and the thuds came closer and closer. The Russians must be very near.

In the evening, father arrived with the news that the Russians were not all that close. It might take another two weeks or longer. A hundred thousand SS-men were to defend the city. I was glad that I would be able to spend another night in my own bed, but my fear of the impending fighting returned and I barely slept. An attempt at bravado: since I still stubbornly believed that I would survive, I resolved to keep as detailed a diary as possible. However, I was unable to get into the right mindset.

13.

A police car is howling past. Are they looking for me? No, I am sitting in a café, drinking coffee, unknown, undisturbed. But I was sitting as calmly in the common room of that inn in Hofgastein when two American military policemen entered and asked the innkeeper for my whereabouts. They wanted me to come to headquarters, right then and there, and wouldn't say why. They were polite but didn't crack a smile. To my relief, Christl offered to accompany me. As we drove through the village in the open MP jeep, we saw Gerd walk toward the inn and stare. I waved at him, trying to look unconcerned. I wonder what he thought. Perhaps that we had found an especially lucrative supply source.

We were made to wait a good half hour, then I was called in to the commanding officer. Christl had to stay outside. He too was anything but affable. He put me through a regular interrogation. Who I was, where I lived, how I had got out of the Russian zone, what I was doing in Gastein. My explanation that in Vienna there was practically nothing to eat, not even bread, and that I was hoping to spend a few weeks here and eat properly, didn't satisfy him. Why had I visited the DP camp, claiming to represent a newspaper? So that was it. Indeed, I had. I told him about *Der Neue Weg* which published local news as well as human interest stories—I had a few issues in my room if he would like to see them. I wanted to contribute an article about the camp, and the officer in charge had been most obliging and shown me around himself. I complimented my interrogator on how well-run the camp seemed.

That was exactly where the problem lay, he explained to me, a touch friendlier. He was sorry but I couldn't publish my story about the camp. He would have to ask me to give my word of honor that I would refrain from reporting anything. Why? The camp was already filled to capacity, and if word got out how well off these refugees were, he could expect an invasion of DPs and other fugitives from the Russian zone. Sorry, but it was out of the question. I gave my word. Christl was relieved when I reemerged. The fear of uniforms was still too potent in us to allow for a clear conscience.

I had one other encounter with American bureaucracy abroad, and it almost dissuaded me from emigrating to the States.

At the American embassy I met a Hungarian lady who was going to travel in the same DP-transport as I, and we quickly became friends. Kitty Farkas was in her fifties, blond, attractive in a mature sort of way, lively and for all I could tell very resourceful. She had been a U-boat in Hungary during the war and was now going to California, where she had a sister. A job was waiting for her there, as a housekeeper to a widower whose cotton plantations in the South paid for a luxurious home in Bel Air. On pictures it looked like an English manor house in an enormous garden, and it had a large outdoor swimming pool.

The first shock came when, at Vienna's northern railroad station where we had to assemble with two suitcases per person, we were directed toward cattle cars—just as the transports for the concentration camps had been! When the doors closed on us and left us sitting on our bags in the dark, our indignation exploded. How dare they treat us the way the Nazis had! But neither our loudly voiced protests nor our hammering on the doors elicited any response. We were locked in, trapped. Vainly did a few voices try to calm the uproar. It only subsided when the train began to move. Apprehensively, we tried to cheer each other. We were, after all, on our way now and would soon be in America, cattle cars or not.

Periodically, the doors would be opened and we were allowed out to relieve ourselves. However, since the train always stopped at outlying sidings, quite far from any passenger platforms, we were not able to ascertain the names of the stations. Nor did we dare move away from our carriage, for fear that we might be left behind.

On the second day, June 13, 1947, we had only got as far as Linz but on the 14th we did arrive in Munich. There we were unloaded and transported by truck to the *Funkkaserne*, the local military barracks. The rows of bunks looked uncomfortably similar to how we imagined—and some of us knew—those in detention camps. There were mattresses, sheets and blankets, but they were dirty and torn, and the food atrocious. Even so, as we kept reminding one another, Munich lay in the right direction for

Bremerhaven, where we were supposed to embark on an American troop ship.

Then came the second shock. Right next to the barracks was a DP-Camp, and it didn't take our group long to initiate conversations and black market negotiations with the camp's inmates. Since I didn't speak Yiddish, I had to rely on Frau Farkas to secure soap and toilet paper for me. When the camp's residents heard that we considered ourselves "in transit" and expected to leave soon for the States, they burst out laughing: that was what they had been told when they arrived, and months had gone by since then. I began to regret the day I decided to emigrate.

Worst of all was the treatment we received from the camp guards. Most of them were Ukrainians, and we began to suspect that they were the same Ukrainians who supported Hitler before it became obvious that he was going to lose the war. They treated us with derision, often outright hostility, and subjected us to an infinite number of minor chicaneries, from inspecting our bags to confiscating things they claimed were unsafe, to insisting that we be up for breakfast at the crack of dawn. They had a large assortment of tasks for us, cleaning toilets, sweeping stairs, peeling potatoes, and more. Nor were we allowed out of the building without a pass. But when they made us get out of bed in the middle of the night and assemble for a roll call, we had had it. A group of us held counsel and decided to dispatch a delegation to the American officer in charge and complain about the way we, with our legitimate American immigration papers, were being treated by those semiliterate antisemitic flunkies. Since I spoke the best English, I was the designated spokesperson.

The officer heard me out with interest, or so it seemed. His feet were on the desk and he was chewing gum. He paid special attention when I complained that we were being treated like inmates of a concentration camp. He wanted to know whether I had been in one. No, I had not, but some in our group had, and they had confirmed the impression.

Then he spoke, calmly, with the gum in one cheek and a cigarette dangling from the other corner of his mouth.

"Look here," he said. "I have been running this transit camp for months now, and I haven't had any trouble. I won't on your account fire my staff and start all over again. You can tell your friends that this is the way it is and is going to be, and if they don't like it, they can go right back to where they came from." With that, he motioned to us to leave the room.

Outside, there was a long, gloomy silence while his translated words sank in. Finally, an older man, a Pole, said:

"Look, there's not a thing we can do. We are trapped. But at least the Americans won't gas us, and eventually they will have to let us go. If we protest too much, they may take away our papers and then we are really sunk."

We who, because of our visas, had looked down on the DPs next door, now went to them humbly and apologetically to procure the basic necessities for a prolonged stay. It was humiliating and we felt almost more helpless than during the war, because then we had at least held the hope that things would improve eventually.

Two depressing days later the Ukrainian guard called another late night roll and announced in his crude and rude German that we were expected to be packed up and ready to leave early the following morning. Nobody rejoiced, for fear still lay heavily on us and visions of further deportation loomed large. They seemed confirmed when we were loaded back into the cattle cars. However, after endless hours of being shunted from station to station, prey to the suppressed suspicion that we were travelling in circles, we arrived in Bremen.

We revived when we saw that we were being put up in a real hotel. On the following morning normal buses transported us to Bremerhaven for embarcation. The SS Castel Felice, despite its large windowless double-decker dormitories, which recalled our accommodations at the *Funkkaserne*, regaled us with good food and enormous amounts of it, and now we really were on our way across the Atlantic.

14.

The rain is still coming down in sheets. It is drumming on the tin roof in a steady canonade, just like—no, enough of the past. It is, after all, over and done with. Why keep dredging it up? Let's see if I can find a newspaper to escape to.

Escape? Still trying to escape? You have escaped as far as you could go, all the way to the Pacific, and it was no use. At one point one must stop running and begin to return.—Oh, but I did return!—No, coming back East, even going back to Vienna won't do. For years you have been repressing your childhood, your youth, and now that they have caught up with you, you are trying to disown them once more. They are your past, the only past you have. It has shaped you, made you what you are, so stop resisting. Welcome it, make it your own, once and for all!—Come on, nothing is once and for all. We all know that.—All the more, accept what there is and cherish it.

I will try.

On April 8, the steady noise of the *FLAK* cannons was for the first time accompanied by the rattling of machine guns and the whistling of bullets. It was only bad during the first few hours, after that you had incorporated it into the sound pattern surrounding you. I was darning father's socks and thinking of Katharina. Not until I tried to hum a tune and couldn't hear my voice, did I again take in the decibels.

That night we slept on the cot in our cellar cubicle, just in case. It was tight and uncomfortable, but you sleep if you are tired enough. In fact, it felt good not to be alone. The night remained quiet. On the next day, though, just as we were having lunch upstairs, instead of the customary cannonade which no longer shook anyone's equanimity, a plane dropped a bomb on us. The air pressure broke the remaining window panes and almost pierced my ear drums. A cloud of dust rushed through the broken window, and the noise blocked my ears. After a few seconds, things calmed down again. Piles of dirt and bricks were littering the deck. The bomb must have hit our roof but been small enough not to do serious damage. Only the gas under the kitchen burners had expired.

Later it turned out that someone in the cellar had, belatedly, remembered the air raid regulations and turned off the main gas switch. So now we again have gas, but it is weak and water takes forever to boil. The electric light is gone, though. In the apartment we can manage, but the cellars are pitch black. I hope our candle supply lasts until the Russians get here.

Most water mains are broken and people are hauling water from the reservoir if they can get to it although it is probably pol-

luted. Fortunately for us, house No. 31 has a well in the courtyard. The last few days we were able to fill our bottles there during quieter moments, but now a neighbor reported that troops
have moved into the courtyard and don't allow civilians to draw
water. What is worse, an SS unit has stationed itself in front of
our house. It apparently intends to defend us with a machine gun
and grenades. The machine gun is aimed at the bridge and sits
in the middle of the street, in full view of any plane flying above.
By contrast, the houses around us are displaying big white sheets
of paper which say "civilians only." We are appalled. How can we
get rid of our protectors?

Much to our relief, they move on a few hours later. Apparently
No. 31 was cleared as well, but the courtyard remains inaccessible. The shelling is too heavy to venture out.

April 10. During the night they blew up the bridges and set
fire to the army barracks. The Russians must be very near. The
shooting is not really bad as long as you stay under cover. We
could have slept in the apartment. But you don't know that
beforehand.

When father went to get water, he returned with the news
that the warehouses were open and people were helping themselves to provisions. I ran over during the first quieter moment.
It was an incredible sight. Mobs surged back and forth, dragged
crates, bags and baskets, dropped one thing to pick up another,
climbed over boxes and people, elbowed their way up staircases,
cut or tore open sacks and boxes, waded in green peas and yellow
corn meal, then tumbled downstairs when someone announced
candy crates in the basement.

It was pitch black down there. You had to grope along the wall
and lift your feet carefully. Somebody lit a piece of paper, then
dropped it on the floor. During the flash I saw a stack of closed
boxes in a corner. Then another piece of paper on the floor caught
fire. A woman stepped on the paper and extinguished the fire.
Deep blackness once more. Hands touch me, I push them away,
shouts, curses. A speck of light from behind a corner. I head
toward it and find myself outside, to my immense relief.

People are passing me, carrying huge chunks of meat. Others
tear them out of their hands, then a whistling of bullets. "Away!"
someone shouts. "It's the Russians." People grab their boxes and

crates, drag them along, some drop everything, a few ignore the bullets and run back inside.

When I reach our house, empty-handed, a big chalk sign on the entrance says "Civilians only." I head straight into the cellar. The shelling is so intense that it is out of the question to venture out. I am lucky to have made it back. Now the gas is definitely gone. Fortunately we still have a few cans of food that can be eaten cold. Where are the Russians???

15.

April 11 arrives cold and clammy. I have earphones on and am waiting for the army report. Yesterday it announced skirmishes in the Inner City, and we expected to be liberated that night. Somebody brought the news that the *Volkssturm*, the militia, had switched sides and was fighting the SS. But aside from an increase in the intensity of the cannonade, nothing is happening. It's impossible to go for water and our supply is almost gone. The cellar is dark and uncomfortable, and so many people are crowding around the two small stoves that I go upstairs, burn the last coal and cook a meal. I call father when the food is ready.

Periodically, both of us rush into a corner, hoping for more protection there. Another load of bricks comes crashing down on the deck. At one point the noise is so fierce that father wants us to go back down, but I don't have the heart to waste the hot water. By the time we decide that we had better get back into the cellar, everything has again quieted down.

I have used the time well. I have given myself a sponge bath, feel clean from top to bottom—who knows when I'll again be able to wash—and the dishes are done. Luckily, I finished the second part of *Katharina Brienne* a week ago, on the last quiet day. Now she rests, carefully wrapped, in my air-raid bag.

Yesterday they almost got us. That was when we came up for air from the cellars. The Germans fired at us from a rooftop. (Or so I thought, but now Egon tells me that the roofs were all pitched. When I tried to check this out during my recent Vienna stay, I found new, modern buildings on either side of ours.)

We were standing under the arch which led into the courtyard, under cover, or so we thought. A red flash exterminated everything, and an unbearably penetrating hissing sound settled in my ears. Other than the hissing, there was no sound until my father shouted my name and it reached me, faintly, as if from a great distance. It was a relief to know I wasn't deaf. Only today my ears are clear.

Except for the man who was hit in the stomach, there were only minor injuries, miraculously. The tip of one man's shoe has a gaping hole but his toes are intact. The shoe, "organized" during the storage raid, had been too big. His wife's cheek was bleeding but unless a splinter has lodged inside she will be all right. The rest of us are unhurt.

This morning two men, father and son, tried to get water during a lull. The son dragged himself back in with four bullets. They were not able to retrieve the father's body. Higher justice? The caprice of chance? The two were the biggest Nazis in our building. Nobody was particularly sorry when the son died as well, two hours later. They had been the ones to call the SS unit in to protect us. Now their own SS has done them in. But still no trace of the Russians.

16.

Those final forty-eight hours seemed years.

Sometime during the night from Thursday to Friday our neighbor died, in great pain and conscious to the end. It had been impossible to get a doctor—the SS were shooting at anything that moved. I stayed as far away as possible from the cubicle of the dying man but could of course not help hearing. He kept asking whether his finger nails weren't blue yet, and was begging people to shoot him or hand him a gun. Then he apparently tried to bite open his veins. We were waiting for the Russians the way one waits for the Messiah. If they came soon, it might still be possible to get help for him. But nothing happened, and my prediction that this moonless night might be just right for the Russians to cross the Canal was received with skepticism. Toward evening we heard considerable commotion outside and began to wonder whether we could risk undressing for the night. It sounded as if tanks were rolling by, one after another, on and on. It had to be retreating German tanks.

At some point, it was already the Russians. Possibly a little like what Harry described to me later, when he talked about the liberation of Theresienstadt. Looking out of a window on the main road outside the fortified walls, he saw an endless convoy of German tanks lumbering by, one after another. Suddenly one tank stopped. The soldiers jumped out, lined up facing backward and raised their arms. The next tank pulled up behind them. It was a Russian tank. It had to stop because the road was blocked, but nobody climbed out. Instead, the Russians motioned to the German soldiers to get back into their tank and continue moving.

From February to May 5, 1945, the day Theresienstadt's commandant was turned out, Harry had to work for the SS, first carrying coal, then helping them pack and burn documents. In the process he managed to swipe a typewriter which he hid in the attic, and also a radio. The Russians took the radio but either did not notice or weren't interested in the typewriter. They gave Harry boots and a whip, and ordered him to watch over a work crew of Sudeten Germans. He was embarrassed but also amused at the irony of the situation. How long did it last? He couldn't remember. In July, his parents succeeded in buying space for him on a truck going to Vienna. They followed a few weeks later.

At five-thirty on Friday morning, April 13, I was awakened by loud knocks on the cellar entrance. Then excited voices. I quickly got dressed and was sitting on the bed—father had gone upstairs to use the bathroom—when a good-looking young man in a Russian uniform opened the door to our cubicle. Since Czech is fairly close to Russian, I understood his assurances that I need not be afraid, that all the horror stories disseminated by the Germans were only scare tactics. I assured him that I was not afraid. He was delighted that I understood him and we were able to communicate. He said that he wanted to look around, but when he raised the candle and realized that the room was too small to hide anybody, he thanked me, apologized for disturbing and withdrew. My bliss was overwhelming: at last it was over! Now all would be well.

Later that morning we lined the street to watch the long columns file by, on tanks and on foot. Women ran out to shake

hands with the grimy, tired soldiers, some embraced and kissed
them, others handed flowers to them. One or the other soldier
would not let go of the extended hand until he had stripped the
watch off the wrist. One soldier proudly displayed his arm, over
which he had strung several wrist watches, and grinned at us.
Another was showing off a captured alarm clock, but he dropped
it. When it started to ring, he emptied his gun at it. By a pile of
bricks in front of the house across the street lay a dead man.
Perhaps he had been shot the evening before, or run over during
the night. I was glad to be nearsighted so that I couldn't make out
details. The vehicles carefully went around him.

At that point, an acquaintance who lived next door came over
and asked me if it was true that on Förstergasse several Jews had
been shot. My father and I were standing in the entrance deliberating whether it was safe to go and investigate when Martin
Scheier arrived. He and his wife lived in the apartment below the
Klügers.

His face told us everything. He could barely speak. They were
dead, all of them. His wife Jenny, the pediatrician next door and
her sister, the three Jewish men who had Christian wives, Grete,
her mother, and Kurt, Ilse's brother Kurt.

Martin had been in the hallway to have a cigarette when he
overheard a voice saying: "We still have time to get us the Jews!"
Martin rushed back into the cellar to urge everyone to get out and
hide, either in a neighboring cellar—they were all connected—or
in their apartments. After some deliberating they decided that the
women would be safe and so would the mixed marriages, but that
he and Kurt ought to disappear. Kurt refused. With Ilse gone, he
didn't care if he lived or died, he said. Martin squeezed into a narrow passageway that led to another cellar. From there he could
hear how they were ordered to line up, all of them, men and
women, told to hand over watches and rings, then marched out of
the cellar. There was a bomb crater in the middle of the street. The
SS pushed them into the crater and threw grenades and stones in
after them.

Father went with Martin to dig out the bodies. I withdrew into
our cellar cubicle to be alone with my anguish and fury. Those
beasts, those monsters—may they be cursed forever, they and the
Hauswart who had betrayed to them that there were still Jews in

the building! Grete must have tried to escape, father told me later, for one leg was dislocated.

Father helped Martin pull out seven of them, then he was unable to continue. When he returned, tears were running down his cheeks.

On the same day, April 12, 1945, President Roosevelt died, the man we considered our savior.

17.

While father was still gone and I stood in a corner crying, I heard commotion, then anxious voices and sobs. I walked into the common area and saw a Russian soldier holding Roger by the arm and motioning to him to follow. Roger was French, in his early twenties. Several months earlier, he, his parents and his sister Janine who was eighteen or nineteen, had moved into our building. They spoke little German and kept to themselves. None of us knew much about them. Now Roger's mother was crying and holding on to him while she tried to explain something to the Russian in her minimal German. The soldier was short, stocky, with a flat yellow face, prominent cheekbones and narrow slits for eyes. I had already noticed him before, out in the street, limping on a cane. He was apparently in charge of the small troop of dusty, weary men who had settled inside the entryway of our building.

I asked him in Czech what he wanted, and then explained that Roger was not a German soldier but a French refugee. Thereupon he motioned Roger away, then turned to me and inquired about my linguistic talents. He told me that he had been in the front line almost continually for four years. Before that he had studied to become a teacher. He came from Mongolia and spoke six languages, Japanese among them. His only European language other than Russian was Latin. During the crossing of the canal he had been wounded. He unbuttoned his tunic to show me his bandaged chest. One knee was also bound up.

At twenty-three he was already a captain. He seemed very intelligent and was very ugly. I was proud of my Czech-Russian and glad to be distracted from that awful thing around the corner which was crouching in my memory and with which I would have to come to terms later.

He asked me to escort him and interpret for him, and I complied gladly. But when I realized that he was not letting me out of his sight, I became uneasy. Those German horror stories were undoubtedly not true but even so. When he disappeared in somebody's bathroom I ran up to our apartment and locked myself in, hoping that father wouldn't show up just then. After a while I heard the familiar heavy tread and the sound of the cane. He knocked on every door but people were in their cellars, and I didn't move. After a while he wandered off. When father showed up, he for once approved of my action.

In the evening, father went down to reconnoiter, and when I heard our neighbors' voices I followed. To be sure, my captain had been looking for me all over the cellar, but by now he was gone. The entire detail had moved on.

While we were still talking, Janine rushed in in a panic. A Russian was asking for "two young women." We were petrified. Father calmed us down, saying that it must be a misunderstanding. He went to mediate, while Janine and I hid in the farthest, darkest corner of the apartment. Soon father was back and reassured us. Two young girls from the front building had accepted food from a soldier and flirted with him, then they disappeared and he was now looking for them. Great relief. Then another scary knock on the door.

This time it was Janine's father. All men should immediately go up on the roof and into the upper apartments. The house next door must be on fire—sparks were flying everywhere and they could ignite our roof. Indeed, the sky was crimson and glowing particles were flying through the air. Every now and then, one made it all the way down into the light shaft. Many buildings must be on fire to spread this much red across the sky. We looked at one another. We knew what that meant, with hardly any water available.

On the roof someone established that it was the supply building that was burning. While they were still collecting buckets, with people emptying their water bottles into them, the wind changed direction and we were out of danger. At least for the moment.

Everybody was deliberating whether it would be safe to sleep upstairs, but since the shooting wasn't letting up, we decided to head back into the cellars, stay dressed and keep a few candles burning all night.

I was lying next to father in my coat—I had already taken the bedding upstairs—and freezing miserably. Eventually, I fell asleep. In the middle of the night suddenly loud voices—Russian voices. Three men and their officer. They wanted to inspect all cubicles for hidden German soldiers. Before father opened the door, he whispered to me to tie a kerchief round my hair, look sleepy and not say a word. When he opened the door, the officer shone a flashlight around the cubicle, then focused it on me so that the light blinded me and I squinted.

"Who is this?" he wanted to know.

"My little girl," father answered in Russian. "She was asleep."

"That's all right, tell her to go back to sleep," the officer said and closed the door. For once, I was grateful for looking so young.

Both of us lay in the dark, listening to the agitated voices outside. The Frenchman was explaining something in his flawed German which the Russian officer didn't seem to understand. He, on the other hand, made himself well understood—too well: he wanted Janine. Negotiations, begging, futile efforts at communication, increasing agitation. My father lies stock still, even when Janine's father knocks on our door and pleads: "Please, help us!"

I whisper: "You can't just lie there, go and help them!"

He gets up, leaves, carefully closing the door behind him. I can hear his calm voice explaining something in Russian, then the officer's voice in turn explaining something. My father translates. They are threatening to shoot the entire family if the girl won't come. We have been risking our lives for months to save you, and you are making such a fuss about so small a thing. The officer is willing to give his word of honor that his men won't touch her, nor will anybody get hurt if they let him have the girl. A conversation in French, interrupted by the mother's sobs, then commotion. The parents are leaving the cubicle, the officer moves in. Darkness and silence except for the loud voices of the guards who are talking in the hallway. Subdued sounds, the mother's crying fit, the father's soothing words.

Then Janine's loud voice, in French: "Don't worry, mother, he has fallen asleep." Renewed commotion after that, and now sobs and moans. Then silence. Finally steps and voices, a triple "Good

night!" in Russian. Everything is totally quiet for a while, then the
mother groans—she has a heart condition—and one can make out
the father's and Janine's low voices.

After a while, I couldn't stand it any longer. I knew that father
was awake too. "I am going upstairs," I whispered. He followed me
to the apartment, and both of us fell asleep in our beds.

When we came down the next morning, Frau Pospíchal told us
that the French family was gone. They must have left during the
night. Nobody saw them leave and we never saw them again.

18.

Soon there was new excitement. The street was again filled with
Soviet tanks, but now all of them were heading back toward the
bridge. Somebody said that the Germans had received reinforce-
ments and the Russians were retreating. The troops that had
camped in our entryway and in those of the neighboring houses
were likewise gone. General dismay. We knew only too well what
reoccupation by the Germans would mean.

Endless tank columns were moving toward the bridge which, it
turned out, had not been blown up completely and was usable. A
stream of pedestrians, each with a small suitcase or bag, followed
the troops. We joined them. The Germans had yielded the inner
city without much resistance, but were entrenched on our island
between the canal and the river. We needed to get off the island.
The Russian guards at the bridge didn't stop us. They did not even
ask for our watches.

A half hour later we arrived at Frau Dina's apartment in
Währing. When she let us in, I didn't believe my eyes. She was in
the kitchen cooking, had gas, water, electricity, and window panes.
On the outer door was an announcement by the Russian command
to the effect that the apartment was under their protection.
Russian officers were coming and going, sipping tea, exchanging
information. If it had not been for the uniforms, one might have
thought she was having a party with a few old friends and no
worry in the world. It was unreal—like a stage set. Father tried to
talk about some of the things that had been happening across the
canal but soon gave up. How could they understand? We were

worlds apart.

They laughed at our anxiety. The Germans? They are miles away, no need to worry.

We stayed a while and then, reassured, started back. But when we came to the bridge, the tanks were still rolling toward us and a stream of people were leaving the Leopoldstadt. We turned around and went back to Frau Dina's. I was physically and emotionally exhausted, father probably too. Now we found several Bulgarian officers there whom Mitko, the Bulgarian student-tenant, must have brought. Notices were posted on all buildings to the effect that looting was punishable by death. Everything was quiet and looked incredibly normal. After a brief respite, we turned back once more. By now, it was dark.

Our building seemed deserted. Only one apartment had lit candles, two women. They told us that there had been a rumor that the Russians were rounding up all men and shooting them, so everybody had taken off. We decided to go back to the city and this time stay there, but not before we had rested our weary feet and eaten something. When father returned with drinking water, he reported running into an Austrian communist he knew. He was told that during the night a large convoy of tanks had come down the street to relieve the vanguard, which was now withdrawing. Again we deliberated, tempted to stay put, but when the shooting increased, we grabbed our bags and headed for the door.

Downstairs we ran into our next door neighbors. They were just returning from a visit to the man's parents, who lived in the twentieth district, by the Big Danube. When they had heard that the men were going to be shot, they wanted to see his parents one last time. It was a long walk and the area was full of Russian tanks and troops. The artillery fire was faint though. The Germans must be far beyond the river, no doubt about it.

While we were still rejoicing, someone brought the news that in a neighboring house the cellars had been plundered, and we rushed downstairs to carry everything back into the apartment. A torch almost caused a fire in the cellar but was extinguished in the nick of time. Someone wedged a red flag into the front entrance of the building. This, we hoped, would be understood to mean that looting was punishable by death. Then we locked all gates and doors, and went to bed. The night remained quiet.

"Well hello, Elizabeth! Fancy running into you here. May I join you? I am soaked, so I thought I'd get myself a cup of tea. I am not disturbing, am I?"

"Not at all. I came in when the downpour started. I guess, it's beginning to clear. I was so deep in thought I did not even notice."

"So what's been on your mind, or shouldn't I ask?"

"Why not? I was thinking about my childhood, trying to recall it."

"Wait, you grew up in Europe, didn't you? In Austria, was it? I love Austria—such a beautiful country!"

"It wasn't very beautiful then. I grew up during the war, and that was pretty rough."

"Really? I would never have guessed—I don't mean about the war, but that you had a rough time of it. You seem so much at home everywhere. But your real home is California, isn't it?"

"No, not any more. I spent eighteen years there but then I decided to move back East."

"You know, most of the people who come from *over there* and were there during *that* time have real problems. They aren't quite right, if you know what I mean. But you are such a cheerful and level-headed person that it never occurred to me. I guess you must have been lucky!"

"Yes," I said. "I have been lucky."

**Vienna
1945**

center: The Phillipshof, home of
the Jockey Club

The burning opera—March 12, 1945

The "Steffl," roofless, at war's end.

Works Cited

1. "Bericht über die Tätigkeit der IKG Wien und des Ältestenrats der Juden Wiens im Jahre 1942" (Jerusalem: Yad Vashem Archives, original document, n.d.)

2. Bor, Josef: *The Terezín Requiem*. Transl. from the Czech by Edith Pargeter (New York: Knopf 1963)

3. *Der Wiener Stadttempel. Die Wiener Juden.* J&V Edition (Wien: IKG 1988)

4. Fraenkel, Josef, ed.: *The Jews of Austria. Essays on their Life. History and Destruction* (London: Vallentine, Mitchell & Co. 1967)

5. Gold, Hugo: *Geschichte der Juden in Wien. Ein Gedenkbuch* (Tel Aviv: Olamenu 1966)

6. Israelitische Kultusgemeinde Wien Annual Report: *Activity during twelve Months of War. Sept. 1, 1939—August 31, 1940* (Wien: IKG 1941)

7. *Jüdisches Nachrichtenblatt* (Wien: IKG & Ältestenrat der Juden Wiens 1940-1943)

8. Klüger, Ruth & Mann, Peggy: *The Last Escape. The Launching of the Largest Secret Rescue Movement of All Time* (New York: Doubleday 1973)

9. Lederer, Zdeněk: *Ghetto Theresienstadt* (London: Edward Goldstein and Sons, Ltd. 1953)

10. Moser, Jonny: *Die Judenverfolgung in Österreich 1938-1945* (Wien-München: Europa Verlag 1966)

11. ——: "Die Katastrophe der Juden in Österreich 1938-1945— ihre Voraussetzungen und ihre Überwindung," in *Der gelbe Stern in Österreich. Katalog und Einführung zur Dokumentation*. Studia Judaica Austriaca. Bd. V (Eisenstadt 1977) 67-131.

12. ——: *Nisko. The First Experiment in Deportation*. Simon Wiesenthal Center Annual, vol. 2 (New York 1985)

13. Rosenkranz, Herbert: *Verfolgung und Selbstbehauptung. Die Juden in Österreich 1938-1945* (Wien: Herold Verlag 1978)

14. Stern, Willy: "Israelitische Kultusgemeinde—Ältestenrat der Juden in Wien 1939-1945" in Kurt Schmid & Robert Streibel: *Der Pogrom 1938. Judenverfolgung in Österreich und Deutschland* (Wien: Picus Verlag 1990) 93-96.

15. Steinhauser, Mary, ed.: *Totenbuch Theresienstadt. Damit sie nicht vergessen werden*. DAÖW (Wien: Junius Verlag 1987)

16. Mendelsohn, John, ed.: *The Wannsee Protocol & A 1944 Report on Auschwitz* (bilingual document). Office of Strategic Services: *The Holocaust Series*, vol. 11. (New York: Garland Pub. 1982)

17. Weinzierl, Erika: *Zu wenig Gerechte. Österreicher und Judenverfolgung 1938-1945* (Graz-Wien-Köln: Styria Verlag 1969)

18. Wyman, David S.: *The Abandonment of the Jews* (New York: Pantheon Bks. 1981)

Literature and the Sciences of Man

This interdisciplinary series is predicated on the conviction that the inevitable development toward increasing specialization requires as its correlative a movement toward integration between the humanities, social sciences, and natural sciences. Titles in the series will deal with "multidisciplinary" figures, as well as with movements affecting a variety of disciplines. The series editor will also consider manuscripts dealing with methods and strategies in the domains of aesthetic creation, the arts of criticism, and scientific exploration.

Please direct all inquiries to the series editor.

Peter Heller
Dept. of Modern Languages &
        Literatures
SUNY-Buffalo
Buffalo, NY 14260